THE HOUSE OF THE MESSIAH ·

Ahmed Osman was born in Cairo and read Law at Cairo University. He has lived in Britain since 1965, teaching Arabic and studying Ancient Egyptian history and language as well as Hebrew. His own researches (in biblical, archaeological and other sources) led him – in his book *Stranger in the Valley of Kings* – to make the first link between a major biblical figure and a leading figure in Egyptian history.

His second book, *Moses: Pharaoh of Egypt*, provides dramatic evidence that the prophet Moses and the revolutionary monotheistic Pharaoh Akhenaten were one and the same person.

The House of the Messiah, with its revelations concerning the identity of the historical Jesus, is the third of Ahmed Osman's biblical investigations.

D1081794

AHMED OSMAN

The House of the Messiah

Controversial Revelations
on the Historical Jesus

HarperCollins*Publishers*

To Nagla, my wife

HarperCollins*Publishers*
77–85 Fulham Palace Road,
Hammersmith, London W6 8JB

This paperback edition 1994
1 3 5 7 9 8 6 4 2

First published in paperback by Grafton 1993

First published in Great Britain by
HarperCollins*Publishers* 1992

Copyright © Ahmed Osman 1992

The Author asserts the moral right to
be identified as the author of this work

ISBN 0 586 21685 5

Set in Bembo

Printed in Great Britain by
HarperCollinsManufacturing Glasgow

CONTENTS

BOOK 2: THE HOUSE OF THE MESSIAH

BOOK 3: CHRIST THE KING

APPENDICES

ACKNOWLEDGEMENTS

I should like to thank Harry Weaver who, despite some initial doubts because of his personal beliefs, was persuaded by the evidence to give his valuable help in preparing the manuscript for this book. Also thanks to Richard Johnson, my editor at HarperCollins, for his understanding, support and advice.

PHOTO CREDITS

Modern Jerusalem *Author's collection*
The 6th-century statue of Isis and her son *Turin Museum*
'The Virgin and Child' by Masaccio *The National Gallery, London*
The monastery of St Catherine *Author's collection*
'The Beheading of John the Baptist' by Puvis de Chavannes
The National Gallery, London

All other photographs reproduced by courtesy
of the *Cairo Museum*

WHAT IS TRUTH?

THEN Pilate entered into the judgment hall again, and called Jesus, and said unto him, Art thou the King of the Jews?

Jesus answered him, Sayest thou this thing of thyself, or did others tell it thee of me?

Pilate answered, Am I a Jew? Thine own nation and the chief priests have delivered thee unto me: what hast thou done?

Jesus answered, My kingdom is not of this world: if my kingdom were of this world, then would my servants fight, that I should not be delivered to the Jews: but now is my kingdom not from hence.

Pilate therefore said unto him, Art thou a king then? Jesus answered, thou sayest that I am a king. To this end was I born, and for this cause came I into the world, that I should bear witness unto the truth. Every one that is of the truth heareth my voice.

Pilate saith unto him, What is truth? And when he had said this, he went out again unto the Jews, and saith unto them, I find in him no fault at all.

(JOHN, 18:33–38)

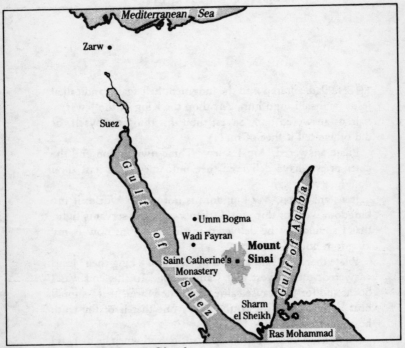

The location of Mount Sinai

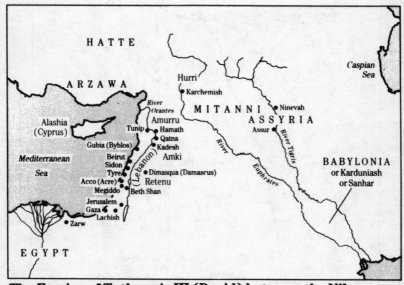

The Empire of Tuthmosis III (David) between the Nile and the Euphrates during the fifteenth century BC

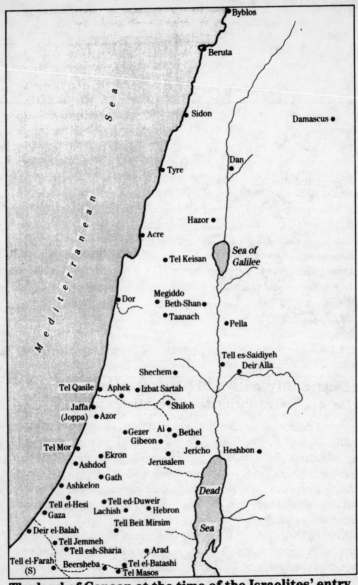

The land of Canaan at the time of the Israelites' entry into the Holyland, c.1200–1000 BC

INTRODUCTION

VIEWS about the Bible fall into three basic categories – that, despite its many contradictions, every word it contains is to be taken literally; that it is basically a historical work which became distorted as a result of its initial long oral tradition and also to some extent at the hands of the biblical editors who eventually set it down in writing; and that it is simply a collection of fanciful fairy tales couched in extravagant language.

My own view – that it is fundamentally a historical work – brought me to London from my native Egypt more than a quarter of a century ago. The choice of London was dictated by the superior research facilities to be found there. These would, I hoped, enable me to succeed in a task that had baffled scholars since the eighteenth century – that of identifying a major figure in Egyptian history as a major figure in the Bible.

These efforts, it became clear, had failed for two reasons. In the first place, the main thrust of research had been to try to fit Egyptian history into the Bible rather than, as common sense would suggest, fit the Bible into Egyptian history; secondly, of the two dates given in the Old Testament for the length of the Israelite Sojourn in Egypt – four generations or four hundred years – acceptance of the incorrect figure of four centuries meant that scholars had been seeking their evidence at the wrong time and in the wrong place.

After twenty-five years of study and research, I cannot claim to have made a great deal of progress myself until what, in retrospect, seems like a moment of inspiration. It came one night when, unable to sleep, I made a pot of tea and sat down to read again in the Book of Genesis the story of Joseph the Patriarch, the favourite son of Jacob, who was sold into slavery in Egypt by his jealous half-brothers and was appointed the virtual ruler of the country under the unnamed Pharaoh after, according to the Bible, foretelling the seven lean years that would follow seven good years. I was suddenly struck by a phrase in the account of how Joseph revealed his identity to his half-brothers when they made the second of two visits to Egypt from Canaan at a time of famine. He told them that they should not reproach themselves for what they had done for 'it was not you that sent me hither, but God: and he hath made me a father to Pharaoh, and lord of all his house, and a ruler throughout all the land of Egypt' – and he obtained Pharaoh's permission for his father, half-brothers and the tribe of Israel to join him in Egypt.

A father to Pharaoh. I thought at once – and could not fathom why I had not made the connection before – of Yuya, a minister of the Pharaohs Tuthmosis IV (c.1413–1405 B.C.) and his son Amenhotep III (c.1405–1367 B.C.). Although he was not apparently of royal blood, the tomb of Yuya was found in the Valley of the Kings in 1905 and, more significantly, he is the only person we know of in Egyptian history to have the title *it ntr n nb tawi*, holy father of the Lord of the Two Lands (Pharaoh's formal title). It occurs once on one of his *ushabti* (royal funeral statuette No. 51028 in the Cairo Museum catalogue) and more than twenty times on his funerary papyrus. Could Joseph and Yuya be the same person?

The case for this is argued in my first book, *Stranger in the Valley of the Kings*. This argument received support with the discovery late in 1989 of the tomb, almost intact, of Aper-el, the hitherto unknown vizier of the Pharaoh Akhenaten, the son of Amenhotep III. The name 'Aper-el' provides a semantic link between the Israelites and the Amarna regime, of which Akhenaten was the first of four rulers. Similar names are known to have existed in Egypt at this time, but never in the case of high officials. The name 'Aper' corresponds to the Egyptian word for 'Hebrew', which meant to ancient Egyptians a nomad, and the final 'el' is the short form of 'Elohim', one of the words used in the Bible as the name of 'the Lord'.

The fact that Akhenaten's vizier was a Hebrew worshipper of El confirms the link between the king and Israelites living in Egypt at the time. Furthermore, the fact that Queen Tiye, the mother of Akhenaten, was associated with her husband, Amenhotep III, in donating a box to the funerary furniture of Aper-el indicates the possibility that the vizier was a relation of the queen's, most probably through her Israelite father, Yuya (Joseph).

Once Yuya was identified as Joseph, a number of other aspects of the Israelite story fell into place – that the arrival of the Israelites in Egypt occurred more than two centuries later than had been thought; that their Sojourn lasted for four generations, not four centuries, and that the four Amarna kings – Akhenaten, Semenkhkàre, Tutankhamun and Aye – who ruled during the tumultuous period in Egyptian history when an attempt was made to replace the country's multitude of ancient gods with a monotheistic God, were all descendants of Joseph the Patriarch.

The prime mover in this religious upheaval was Akhenaten in the years (c. 1367–1361 B.C.) when, following a period as co-regent, he became sole ruler upon the death of his father, Amenhotep III. In a second book, *Moses: Pharaoh of Egypt*, I argued that Akhenaten was to be identified as the biblical Moses. The purpose of this present volume is to identify David, from whose House the promised Messiah would come, and to establish the historical figure of Jesus, who lived, suffered and died many centuries earlier than is conventionally thought.

Book One

THE SCARLET THREAD

1

SCANDAL OF THE DEAD
SEA SCROLLS

JESUS is a mysterious figure in a historical sense. All that we know about him comes mainly from the Gospels and the Koran. Two thousand years ago, at the time he is said to have lived, Palestine was part of the Roman Empire. Yet no Roman record exists that can bear witness, directly or indirectly, to the Gospel story of Jesus. Even more surprising is the absence of any reference to Jesus in the writings of Jewish authors living at that period in Jerusalem or Alexandria, although we know from Talmudic writings that the Jews did know of Jesus, even if they refused to accept that he was either the Messiah (Christ) or descended from the House of David.

As a result, some authors have concluded that Jesus never lived, but was an ancient mythological figure, adapted later as a historical figure. On the other hand, thousands of authors have written books about Jesus as a real person. Some claim to be giving an account of the historical Christ. Not one of them, however, has produced a shred of *historical* evidence in support of this claim. Such works are to be looked upon as pure speculation – editings of the stories and teachings we find in the New Testament with some additional information interpolated about life in Palestine and the Roman Empire at what is accepted as the start of the Christian era.

The earliest Gospel account of the life of Jesus did not appear until the last quarter of the first century A.D., at least fifty years after the supposed date of his death. Great excitement was therefore generated by the discovery of the Dead Sea Scrolls in a series of caves at Qumran, to the west of the north end of the Dead Sea in what is now the Israeli-occupied West Bank, beginning in the summer of 1947. The Scrolls proved to be the remains of the library of the Essenes, a secret Jewish sect that separated itself from the Jewish community at large and from the Jerusalem priesthood, whose beliefs and teachings they regarded as false.

The manuscripts, in Hebrew and Aramaic, were dated between 200 B.C. and 50 A.D. and include biblical and sectarian texts, Jewish literature and other documents. Scientific verification of the age of the Scrolls was announced as recently as Easter 1991, after they had been subjected to carbon-dating tests. Dr Magen Broshi, curator of the Rockefeller Museum's Shrine of the Book in Jerusalem, where some of the Scrolls are displayed, said: 'Until now we have been able to establish the age of the Scrolls by paleography (the study of ancient writing). From time to time people have challenged this method as not being sufficiently accurate, but now what we have always believed has been confirmed scientifically.'

As they came from the Holy Land and covered the period before and after the years when Jesus is generally accepted to have lived, it was widely hoped that the Scrolls would provide first-hand evidence to support the Gospel stories and shed new light on Jewish and Christian history. By the late 1950s, practically all the documents found in Cave One had been published as well as a good deal of the material that had come to light in other caves. Far from confirming accepted ideas about the origins of Christianity, however, these texts contradicted them. On the one hand they provided negative information about Jesus of Nazareth; on the other they provided positive information of a Christ and a Christian Church that pre-dated the supposed start of the Christian era by at least two centuries.

The Essenes believed themselves to be the people of the New Covenant (believe in me and you shall have eternal life), which they regarded as both the renewed Old Covenant (keep my Commandments) that the Lord had made with Moses and the Eternal Covenant to be established, precisely in the New Testament sense, when their Teacher returned at the end of the world. The Messianic leader of the Essenes was named simply as the Teacher of Righteousness, who, like Jesus, had met a violent end at an unspecified time in the past, in his case at the hands of someone referred to as 'the Wicked Priest', but according to the *Commentary on Habakkuk*, a manuscript found at Qumran: 'God made known to him all the Mysteries of the words of his servants the Prophets.'

As texts of the Scrolls were published, scholars became divided about their significance. One school tried to ignore their effects on understanding of the Gospels and early Christian history, disclaiming any serious relations between the Essene community and the early Christian Church; the other saw the Essenes as the early Christians. For instance, W. F. Albright, one of the most highly qualified American Orientalists, who had himself carried out a great deal of archaeological work in the Holy Land, has been quoted as saying: 'The new evidence . . . bids fair to revolutionize our approach to the beginnings of Christianity.'[1]

Dr J. L. Teicher, himself a Jew and a distinguished Cambridge scholar, went as far as arguing that the Dead Sea manuscripts 'are quite simply Christian documents'.[2] Although the manuscripts come from as early as 200 B.C., he also maintained that the leader of the Essenes, the Teacher of Righteousness, was none other than Jesus Christ himself.

The French scholar André Dupont-Sommer, after reading the *Commentary on Habakkuk*, came to the conclusion that Jesus now seemed an 'astonishing reincarnation of the Teacher of Righteousness'. Like Jesus, he said, the Teacher was believed by his disciples to be God's Elect, the Messiah, the Redeemer of the world. Both characters were opposed by the priesthood; both were condemned and put to death; both proclaimed judgment on Jerusalem; both established communities whose members expected them to return to judge the world.[3]

One of the original team of eight who performed editorial work on the Scrolls was the British Semitic scholar John Marco Allegro, a lecturer on the Old Testament at the University of Manchester. He, too, set out initially to identify Jesus as the Teacher of Righteousness. However, in a book published in 1970[4] he put forward the bizarre-sounding theory that 'Jesus' was the name of a sacred drug mushroom that had been transformed into a historical character by the authors of the Gospels.

Edmund Wilson, the distinguished American critic and author who wrote a treatise about the Scrolls, pitched at a popular level, concluded that the cradle of Christianity is not Bethlehem, but the monastic settlement of the men who produced the Scrolls. Wilson also advanced the view that Christian scholars were afraid to work on the Scrolls because 'the uniqueness of Christ is at stake' and he had encountered resistance to admitting 'that the morality and mysticism of the Gospels may perfectly well be explained as the creation of several generations of Jews working by and for themselves, in their own religious tradition . . .'[5]

Although the majority of scholars did not follow such extreme views, preferring to try to defend the orthodox version of the origins of Christianity, the whole question of the true significance of the Scrolls has been clouded by the fact that, despite the passage of the better part of half a century, a large amount of their contents – some scholars put it as high as eighty per cent – remains unpublished and there are indications that some of the published material has been subjected to discreet censorship.

Only a handful of new texts have, in fact, been released since the early 1960s. Fresh attention was focused on the mantle of secrecy that has descended on the hidden manuscripts of the Scrolls when the biblical scholar Hershel Shanks published a fragment in his Washington-based magazines *Biblical Archaeological Review* and *Bible Review* in 1990. It read: 'He shall be great upon the earth . . . he shall be called the Son of God and they shall call him the Son of the Most High.' The intriguing aspect of this fragment is the uncanny resemblance to the account of the Annunciation to the Virgin Mary that we find in the first chapter of St Luke's Gospel: 'He shall be great and shall be called the Son of the Highest . . . that holy thing which shall be born of thee shall be called the Son of God.'

In an article published shortly afterwards by the London newspaper *The Mail on Sunday*, under the headline SCANDAL OF THE SCROLLS, the writer Angus Macpherson made the point that the fragment was 'challenging more than 2,000 years of Christian belief and one of the Bible's most accepted teachings . . . (The text) was set down long before the earliest copies of the New Testament, probably even before the birth of Christ and his disciples. Alarmingly, it undermines the theory held by many that St Luke was reporting a miraculous event in his own time, probably as an eye-witness, but at least from first-hand information.'

Macpherson interviewed Shanks at a seminar in Jerusalem – the Scrolls have been under the control of the Israeli Antiquity Department since the fall of East Jerusalem in the Six Day War of 1967 – where he complained: 'We are talking about one of the great historical treasures of humanity that has been quite unjustifiably withheld from view year after year.' Shanks refused to say how he had managed to obtain the heavily-guarded fragment, but it is thought to have formed part of the *Damascus Document*, a huge cache of the Scrolls entrusted in the 1950s to Joseph Milik, a Polish Roman Catholic priest. Milik, another of the original eight scholars given the task of publishing the manuscripts, has since left the priesthood and married. The Son of God text, however, had not appeared in the translation of the *Damascus Document* published by Milik. Milik admitted when interviewed that he himself had not published any of the Essene manuscripts for thirteen years, putting forward the seemingly lame excuse in view of the Scrolls' historical importance: 'I have many other interests.'

Dr Geza Vermes, reader in Jewish studies at Oxford University, takes the view that the only way to end 'the academic scandal of the century' is for photographs of the whole of the Scroll material to be made available for any qualified scholar to study. The Israeli government is reported to have set up a committee to examine the matter. What the outcome will be is debatable. Robert Eisenman, a Californian professor of religious studies who says he wasted a whole year in Jerusalem trying to obtain a sight of the remaining Scrolls, believes that the shroud of secrecy surrounding them lies in the fact that the material they contain would give religious offence to Jews as well as Christians.

Work on the Scrolls has been largely dominated by Roman Catholic priests based at the Ecole Biblique et Archéologique in Jerusalem. The Ecole has close links with the Pontifical Biblical Commission, founded by the Vatican at the turn of the century to protect 'God's words' from 'every rash opinion' and to endeavour to 'safeguard the authority of the scriptures and to promote their right interpretation'. Since 1956, every director of the Ecole has been a member of the Commission. One of them, the late Father Roland de Vaux, told Edmund Wilson: 'My faith has nothing to fear from my scholarship.' The statement prompted the authors of a more recent book on the Scrolls to ask: 'The real question was whether his scholarship, and its reliability, had anything to fear from his faith.'[6]

That the secrecy surrounding the unpublished Scrolls lies in the sensitive religious nature of their contents is suggested by the sacking of Professor John Strugnell, a British-born Roman Catholic, as chief editor of the Scrolls, on which he had worked since 1952. Failing health and emotional distress were cited as the reason for his dismissal in December 1990 by his own research team. A few weeks later, Dr Strugnell, who was also divinity professor at Harvard University, was reported to be incommunicado in a Massachusetts hospital where he was being treated for a leg ailment, alcoholism and psychological problems. There has been speculation, however, that the real reason for his dismissal was an interview he gave to an Israeli newspaper in which he said that Judaism was a 'horrible religion', 'based on folklore', and was 'a Christian heresy' which 'has survived when it should have disappeared'. The only solution for Judaism, he added, 'is mass conversion'.

These are intemperate, and to Jews highly offensive, opinions. Yet they come from a man who has spent virtually his entire working life absorbed with the Dead Sea Scrolls. Do his views suggest that these ancient documents, now hidden from the world and so jealously guarded, point to origins of Christianity different from those generally accepted, origins that also make it possible to describe Judaism as a Christian heresy?

2

A FALSE DAWN?

THE orthodox Christian view, based on the Gospels of Matthew, Mark, Luke and John, written several decades after the events they describe, is that Jesus was born in Judaea during the time of Herod the Great (37–4 B.C.), that his ministry began when he was thirty years of age, and that his condemnation to death, suffering and crucifixion took place three years later when Judaea had become a Roman province and Pontius Pilate was its procurator (26–36 A.D.). Subsequently, during the fourth century A.D., when Christianity had become the official religion of the Roman Empire, a date was fixed for his birth, which became accepted as the dawn of the Christian era.

Judaea – in modern Israel – lies between the Mediterranean and the Jordan–Dead Sea–Araba depression. It is *the* Holy Land for Jews and Christians, *a* Holy Land for Muslims. The geographical position of Judaea on the main route connecting Egypt with the Euphrates valley and Asia Minor resulted, in the course of the centuries, in its coming under the domination of Egypt, Assyria, Babylonia, Persia, Macedonia, the Ptolemies (a dynasty of Macedonian kings who seized Egypt), the Seleucids (Greek kings controlling Babylon and Syria) and eventually Rome.

Pompey, the Roman general, defeated the Greek rulers of Asia Minor and Syria in 64 B.C. and made them into new Roman provinces. At this time Judaea was allowed to remain as an independent client state under local rulers. However, in 40 B.C., the Roman Senate granted Herod the Great control over Judaea, plus Idumaea to the south, Samaria and Galilee to the north, and Peraea to the east of the Jordan. Herod was the son of Antipater, adviser to the last of the Jewish Hasmonaean princes who ruled Judaea. Mark Antony appointed Herod as governor after Antipater's death, and three years later he became *de facto* king. His position was confirmed in 31 B.C. by Octavian after the latter's defeat of Mark Antony and Cleopatra, the last of the Ptolemies, at the naval battle of Actium. Four years later, the Senate gave the victorious Octavian the title Augustus Caesar. This was the point at which the Roman Republic came to an end and the Roman Empire, encircling the Mediterranean and stretching as far north as Britain and Germany, began.

When Herod the Great died in 4 B.C., his dominions were divided between his three sons. However, Archelaus, the son who ruled over Judaea, was deposed by the Romans in 6 A.D. and the territory came under direct Roman rule. From this time onward, Judaea was ruled by a Roman procurator, who seems to have had his residence at Caesarea on the Mediterranean coast, north-west of Jerusalem. The first of these procurators was appointed in 6 A.D. under the supervision of Quirinius, governor of Syria. Pontius Pilate was the fifth, appointed during the reign of Tiberius Caesar (14–37 A.D.), Augustus's stepson, who had succeeded him.

The Gospels themselves suggest in accounts of the birth and death of Jesus that, in the accepted date for the start of the Christian era, we may be dealing with a false dawn. Only two of them refer to the birth of Jesus: yet they differ in their details.

Matthew places his birth firmly in the time of Herod the Great: 'Jesus was born in Bethlehem of Judaea in the days of Herod the King' (Matthew, 2:1). Then we are told that Herod the Great, learning that a King of the Jews had been born, was troubled and 'exceeding wroth, and sent forth, and slew all the children that were in Bethlehem, and in all the coasts thereof, from two years old and under' (Matthew, 2:16). In the meantime, Joseph, the husband of Mary, had been warned by an angel: 'Arise, and take the young child and his mother, and flee into Egypt, and be thou there until I bring thee word' (Matthew, 2:13). Joseph did as he had been told and remained in Egypt 'until the death of Herod: that it might be fulfilled which was spoken of the Lord by the prophet, saying, "Out of Egypt have I called my son"' (Matthew, 2:15). After the death of Herod the Great, the angel appeared to Joseph again and said: 'Arise, and take the young child and his mother, and go into the land of Israel: for they are dead which sought the young child's life. And he arose, and took the young child and his mother, and came into the land of Israel' (Matthew, 2:20–1). The implication of this account is that we are dealing with quite a short span of time as Jesus, a baby when Joseph and Mary, his mother, fled with him into Egypt, was still a 'young child' when they returned to Israel on learning of the death of Herod the Great (4 B.C.).

Luke is the other Gospel author who deals with the birth of Jesus, which he relates to that of John the Baptist, who was also born 'in the days of Herod, the king of Judaea' (Luke, 1:5) after Zacharias had been informed by an angel: 'Fear not, Zacharias . . . thy wife Elisabeth shall bear thee a son, and thou shalt call his name John' (Luke, 1:13). The story goes on to relate that in the sixth month of Elisabeth's pregnancy 'the angel Gabriel was sent from God unto a city of Galilee, named Nazareth, To a virgin espoused of a man whose name was Joseph, of the house of David; and the virgin's name was Mary . . . And the angel said unto her, Fear not, Mary: for thou hast found favour with God. And, behold, thou shalt conceive in thy womb, and bring forth a son, and shalt call his name Jesus. He shall be great, and shall be called the Son of the Highest: and the Lord God shall give unto him the throne of his father David' (Luke 1:26–7, 30–2).

Up to this point, both authors agree in placing the birth of Jesus in the time of Herod the Great. Here, however, Luke introduces a contradiction in recounting the familiar Christian story of the birth of Jesus: 'And it came to pass in those days, that there went out a decree from Caesar Augustus, that all the world should be taxed. (And this taxing was first made when Cyrenius [Quirinius] was governor of Syria.) And all went to be taxed, every one into his own city. And Joseph also went up from Galilee, out of the city of Nazareth, into Judaea, unto the city of David, which is called Bethlehem; (because he was of the house and lineage of David)' (Luke, 2:1–4).

We know from Roman sources that this event could not have taken place before 6 A.D., the year in which Quirinius was appointed governor of Syria and Judaea became a Roman province. The purpose of the census in 6 A.D., attested from other non-biblical sources, was to assess the amount of tribute which the new province of Judaea would have to pay.

In the next chapter of Luke's narrative, however, we are offered yet a third possible date for the birth of Jesus when he describes John's baptism of Christ, which all four Gospels agree preceded immediately the start of his mission: 'In the fifteenth year of the reign of Tiberius Caesar, Pontius Pilate being governor of Judaea . . . Annas and Caiaphas being the high priests, the word of God came unto John the son of Zacharias in the wilderness. And he came into all the country about Jordan, preaching the baptism of repentance for the remission of sins' (Luke, 3:1–3) . . . 'Now when all the people were baptized, it came to pass, that Jesus also being baptized, and praying, the heaven was opened, And the Holy Ghost descended in a bodily shape like a dove upon him, and a voice came from heaven, which said, Thou art my beloved son; in thee I am well pleased' (Luke, 3:21–2).

As Tiberius became emperor in 14 A.D., this would place the baptism of Jesus in 29 A.D. Luke then goes on to say: 'And Jesus began to be about thirty years of age' (3:23) when he started his ministry. If he was about thirty in 29 A.D., he cannot have been born before the end of Herod the Great's reign in 4 B.C. or at the time of the census in 6 A.D., but during the last year before the end of the pre-Christian era. No doubt it was this account that persuaded the Roman Catholic Church to fix this year as the turning point in world history.

Similar difficulties arise when it comes to trying to arrive at a precise conclusion about the date of the Crucifixion. All four Gospels agree that it took place when Pontius Pilate was the governor of Judaea (26–36 A.D.) and that the high priest of Jewish Jerusalem at the time was named Caiaphas, known from other sources as Josephus Caiaphas, who held the office from 18 A.D. until 37 A.D. The situation is further complicated by the fact that the Gospels disagree about how long the ministry of Jesus lasted: Matthew, Mark and Luke favour one year, John indicates two or three years.

The majority of New Testament scholars agree that Jesus met his death around 30 A.D. If this is the case, his age at the time would have been thirty-six or more if he was born towards the end of Herod the Great's rule and we allow at least two years for Herod to have all children up to the age of two slain; twenty-five if he was born at the time of the 6 A.D. census, or thirty-one if one accepts Luke's account of his baptism and his age at the start of his ministry.

To summarize the argument so far, on the basis of known historical facts all we can be certain about concerning the figure presented to us in the Gospels as Jesus is that he lived and died between 27 B.C., when the Roman Senate appointed Octavian as the Emperor Augustus, and 37 A.D., the year of the death of Augustus's successor, Tiberius.

3

SILENT WITNESS

IF Jesus lived, suffered and died in the period of Roman rule over Palestine, it is curious that his name does not appear in the writings of three distinguished contemporary authors – Philo Judaeus, Justus of Tiberias and Flavius Josephus.

This absence is particularly striking in the case of the thirty-eight works left behind by Philo Judaeus, who was born c. 15 B.C. and died some two decades after the supposed date of the Crucifixion. Philo was a man of eminence and importance. His brother was the head of the Jewish community living in Alexandria, his son was married to a granddaughter of King Herod and Philo himself was chosen to head a mission to Rome to plead with Caligula, the third Roman emperor (37–41 A.D.), who believed he was divine, to withdraw an edict ordering the Jews to place the imperial image in their Temple at Alexandria and worship it.

Although a Jew, Philo was also a follower of the Greek philosopher Plato, and is known as the first of the neo-Platonists who tried to reconcile Greek doctrines with the revelations of the Old Testament. His works were recognized as having a close affinity with Christian ideas and many scholars have seen in him the connecting link between Greek thought and the New Testament. Some have even gone as far as to suggest that Philo's philosophy influenced the thinking of St Paul. It has also been asserted by Eusebius (c. 260–342 A.D.), one of the early Church Fathers who wrote an ecclesiastical history down to his own time, that Philo formed an acquaintanceship with St Peter in Rome, but this particular statement lacks confirmation.

Although Philo wrote admiringly about the monastic Essene sect of his time, and despite his close links with Christian thought, we find only one New Testament figure mentioned in his works, Pontius Pilate.

It is a similar story with Justus of Tiberias, a place on the west shore of the Sea of Galilee, which is mentioned frequently in the Gospels. Justus wrote a history of Herod the Great. Nowhere does he refer to Jesus or Herod's order to slaughter all children under the age of two. Although his work is now lost, it was known to Photius, Bishop of Constantinople in the ninth century A.D., who confirmed the absence in it of any mention of Jesus.[1]

In the circumstances it was a consolation to Christians to learn, once the work of Flavius Josephus, the first century A.D. Jewish historian, had been translated into Latin, that the text included references not only to Pontius Pilate but to John the Baptist, Jesus and his brother James.

Josephus, who was a Palestinian Jew of priestly family, was born in 37 A.D., shortly after the Crucifixion is said to have taken place. In the latter years of his life, he settled in Rome during the reign of Domitian (81–96 A.D.), the eleventh emperor. There he wrote *Antiquities of the Jews*, a long historical work of twenty books that, in surviving copies, are in some cases the only source we have for details of events in Syria/Palestine during the first century of the Christian era.

In Book 18 we find an account of a war between Aretas, Arab king of Nabatea, to the south and east of the Dead Sea, and Herod Antipas, the Tetrarch of Galilee and the son of Herod the Great. The cause of the quarrel lay in the fact that Herod Antipas, who had been married to the daughter of Aretas, sent her back to her father and took a new wife – his sister-in-law, Herodias. In the subsequent hostilities, Herod's army was destroyed. The Jews took the view that this defeat was a punishment from God for what Herod had done 'against John, that was called the Baptist; for Herod slew him, who was a good man, and commanded the Jews to exercise virtue, both as to righteousness towards one another, and piety towards God, and so to come to baptism; . . . not . . . for the putting away . . . of some sins . . . but for the purification of the body; supposing still that the soul was thoroughly purified beforehand by righteousness.'

This is not a strictly accurate account of the nature of John's baptism. The word 'baptism' comes from the Greek *bapteim*, which means to plunge, to immerse or to wash. It is the symbolic value of baptism and the psychological intent underlying it that provide the true definition of the rite, which is usually associated with a religious initiation. John the Baptist linked immersion in a flowing river to erasing sin. His baptism was a sign of divine pardon, and seems to have been a substitute for the practice of offering a sacrifice in atonement for sin. However, it differed fundamentally, as we shall see, from both the Baptism of the Essenes and that of the Christian Church.

Not surprisingly, John's offer of forgiveness of sin made him extremely popular with the Israelites, and Herod became disturbed by the enthusiastic crowds that gathered to hear him preach: 'Herod, who feared lest the great influence John had over the people might put it into his power and inclination to raise a rebellion (for they seemed ready to do anything he should advise), thought it best, by putting him to death, to prevent any mischief he might cause . . . Accordingly he was sent a prisoner, out of Herod's suspicious temper, to Macherus, the castle (on Herod's border with Nabatea to the east of the Dead Sea) . . . and was there put to death.'[2]

This account by Josephus, while establishing John the Baptist as a historical figure, also differs in some respects from the Gospels. There is, for example, no reference to Jesus, no support for the Gospel statement that John was 'preparing the way' for him. Nor, unlike the Gospel, does Josephus suggest that it was his denunciation of Herod's new marriage that led to John's execution: 'Herod (Antipas) had sent forth and laid hold upon John, and bound him in prison for Herodias' sake, his brother Philip's wife: for he had married her' (Mark, 6:17). Josephus also describes Herodias not as the wife of Philip, but of another brother called Herod, 'who was his brother indeed, but by another mother'.[3]

In the fourth chapter of Book 18 we also find a mention of Jesus: 'Now, there was about this time Jesus, a wise man, if it be lawful to call him a man, for he was a doer of wonderful works − a teacher of such men as receive the truth with pleasure. He drew over to him both many of the Jews, and many of the Gentiles. He was (the) Christ; and when Pilate, at the suggestion of the principal men amongst us, had condemned him to the cross, those that loved him at the first did not forsake him, for he appeared to them alive again the third day, as the divine prophets had foretold these and ten thousand other wonderful things concerning him;

and the tribe of Christians, so named from him, are not extinct to this day.'⁴

This passage was greatly valued during the Middle Ages as the only external testimony from the first century A.D. pointing to Jesus having lived at that time. Unfortunately, it has since become an embarrassment, having been exposed as a forgery, an interpolation placed in the work of Josephus by a Christian copyist or editor frustrated by the historian's silence over the birth, suffering and death of Jesus. It first came under suspicion when *Antiquities of the Jews* was translated into English and French in the sixteenth century and has since occupied the attention of some distinguished critics. The genuineness of the passage was called into question on two grounds – the silence of early authors and the nature of the words used.

Until 320 A.D., two and a quarter centuries after publication of Josephus's work, no mention was made of this passage. Origen (c. 185–254 A.D.), a Father of the early Christian Church, whose writings covered every aspect of Christianity, was familiar with the writings of Josephus. In his own writings, he referred to the account of John the Baptist's life and death to be found in Book 18 of *Antiquities of the Jews*, but made no reference whatever to Jesus, a curious omission by someone who believed in him. The first person to mention this testimony was, in fact, Eusebius in his *Demonstration of the Gospel*, written around 320 A.D.

Literary criticism of the passage falls into three categories. In the first place, the clause 'if it be lawful to call him a man' looks like an attempt by an orthodox Christian to remind readers that Jesus was also divine; secondly, the sentence 'He was (the) Christ' is a straightforward confession of faith in Jesus as being the Jewish Messiah, but this could not be possible in the case of Josephus as Origen himself in one of his works, *Against Celsius*, describes the Jewish historian as 'not receiving our Jesus as Christ'; and, thirdly, the reference to the resurrection of Jesus would suggest that the author believed in it. For these reasons, scholars have come to the conclusion that the passage must have been interpolated by some Christian copyist or editor between the time of Origen in the third century and the time of Eusebius a century later.

Howell Smith, the British biblical critic, summarized the situation by saying that the passage in question 'obviously fits badly the matter preceding and following it, and appears moreover to have had a shifting place in the text . . . its authenticity seems to be rationally indefensible. Only a Christian hand could have penned a panegyric of Jesus as the Christ, who had actually worked miracles in fulfilment of the predictions of the Hebrew Prophets, and had risen from the dead after having been condemned to the cross by Pontius Pilate.'[5]

There was great excitement in 1906 when a long-forgotten medi-aeval Slavonic (Old Russian) version of *The Jewish War*, another of Josephus's works, was found. *The Jewish War* not only pre-dated *Antiquities of the Jews* by twenty years, but included another reference to Jesus. He was described as the 'wonder worker' and portrayed as being pressed by his followers to lead a rebellion against Rome. It was thought at first that this Russian translation must have been made from the now-lost original Aramaic text of Josephus. However, after careful examination it became clear that it derived from the Greek text and had been made around the twelfth century A.D. No traces of Semitic Aramaic idiom have been found in it, and the opening of the section about Jesus is clearly an expanded version of the interpolated testimony quoted earlier in this chapter: 'In fact, it is as certain as anything can be in the realm of literary criticism that they were not part of what Josephus wrote at all, but had been interpolated into the Greek manuscripts from which the Old Russian translation was made.'[6]

Another mention of Jesus occurs in Book 20 of *Antiquities of the Jews* where Josephus relates how the Roman procurator Festus died suddenly in office around 62 A.D. and an interval of three months elapsed before the arrival in Judaea of his successor, Albinus. Then the high priest, Ananus, 'assembled the sanhedrin (highest court of justice) of judges, and brought before them the brother of Jesus, who was called Christ, whose name was James, and some others; and when he had formed an accusation against them as breakers of the law, he delivered them to be stoned.'[7]

The description of James as the brother of Jesus agrees with the words in St Paul's letter to the Galatians: 'But other of the apostles saw I none, save James the Lord's brother' (Galatians, 1:19). This reference, too, has been shown by scholars to be an interpolation into the work of Josephus although, as was noted by Origen in the third century, it must have pre-dated the one analysed earlier.

We therefore have the situation that, while the account of the life and execution of John the Baptist in Josephus is accepted by scholars as a description of actual historical events, there is nothing to link him with 'preparing the way' for Jesus in the accepted sense, and once we remove the insertions made to the Jewish historians' texts, we have no contemporary evidence about his life, suffering and death.

4

A MISCHIEVOUS SUPERSTITION

No official report by Pontius Pilate about Jesus and his Crucifixion exists, although a few centuries later some forged writings called *Acts of Pilate* appeared. They included an account of Jesus of Nazareth. However, they were produced either by Christians who wished to confirm the historicity of their Lord, or enemies of Christianity who wished to attack the religion.

The first references to Christianity in Roman writings are found in the works of the historians Suetonius and Tacitus, and Pliny the Younger, who were friends and held posts under Roman emperors.

Suetonius, who was born around 69 A.D., served as a secretary to Hadrian, the fourteenth emperor (117–38 A.D.), and thus had access to the imperial archives. His major historical work, *The Lives of the Caesars*, published about 120 A.D., gave accounts of the reigns of Julius Caesar and the eleven emperors who followed him. The mention of Christ occurs in the twenty-fifth chapter where the author is discussing events in the reign of Claudius (41–54 A.D.), who had succeeded as the fourth emperor after the assassination of Caligula. Suetonius makes a brief mention of riots that took place in Rome in 49 A.D.: 'As the Jews, at the instigation of Chrestus, were constantly raising riots, he (Claudius) drove them out of Rome.'[1]

Chrestus, a common name in Rome, must have been substituted for the Greek Christus because the two names were pronounced alike and Suetonius thought – wrongly – that someone called Christ was in Rome at the time, instigating these riots. These troubles in Rome were not the result of Roman oppression but of internal conflicts within the Jewish community between Jews (Christians) who believed the Messiah (Christ) had already come and Jews who believed that he was still to appear. An echo of these troubles is found in the Acts of the Apostles (18:2–3) where we read of a Jew, Aquila, and his wife, Priscilla, who, having been driven from Rome by an edict of Claudius, went to start a building business in Corinth where they met Paul.

After these events, the attitude of Claudius towards the Jews softened under the persuasive influence of his close friend Agrippa, the grandson of Herod the Great. The emperor issued an edict granting the Jews who lived in Alexandria equal privileges to those of the Greeks of that city and allowing them to follow their own customs. A further edict was sent to Syria granting the same rights and privileges to Jews throughout the Roman Empire.

Although the work of Suetonius is the oldest written testimony about the followers of Christ in Rome, it does not refer to the historical Jesus, only to the fact that his followers thought he had already come and the rest of the Jews rejected this view. We find no date, place or even name for the Messiah (Christ), which is a title.

After ruling for thirteen years, Claudius met his death at the hands of his wife, Agrippina, who poisoned him in order to ensure the succession of Nero, her son by a previous marriage.

Nero (54–68 A.D.) was a sadist who, soon after coming to power, rewarded his mother by putting her to death in public. He also killed his wife. In 64 A.D. a disastrous fire swept Rome and it was suspected that Nero had been responsible for starting the fire in order to give himself the opportunity to rebuild the city. He responded to this charge by blaming the Christians. Suetonius mentions the Christians briefly again in the section of his work dealing with the life of Nero: 'Punishment was inflicted on the Christians, a body of people addicted to a novel and mischievous superstition.'

Here again Suetonius does not refer to Jesus of Nazareth, but simply to believers in Christianity who lived in Rome. The same is true of Tacitus, giving an account of these events in his *Annals*: 'Nero suspected certain persons to be the authors of the crime. Them he condemned to the most cruel torture. They were those who, hated for their infamy, were vulgarly called Christians. The originator of the name, the Christ, had been condemned to death in the reign of Tiberius by the procurator, Pontius Pilate.'

At the time Tacitus wrote his *Annals* (c. 115 A.D.), no historical source existed to justify the view that Pontius Pilate had condemned Jesus to death in the reign of Tiberius. On what evidence, therefore, did Tacitus base his statement? In the second century A.D., many Christians, believers in the fact that the Messiah had already come, had lived in Rome for a considerable time and the traditional Gospel legend was well established. P. L. Couchoud, the French scholar, took the view that Tacitus was simply quoting the existing tradition, still accepted today, that Jesus 'suffered under Pontius Pilate': '. . . it is probable that he (Tacitus) merely echoes the current belief of Christians when he explained their name . . . It would be rash to quote Tacitus as giving independent evidence as to the existence of Jesus.'[2]

Pliny the Younger, the third of these Roman authors, also refers to Christ. In 103 A.D., the thirteenth emperor, Trajan (97–117 A.D.), sent him to rule Bithynia and Pontus, a province in northern Asia Minor overlooking the Black Sea. Christians were brought to him for punishment and, unsure how to treat them, he wrote to Rome for advice: '. . . this is the course I have taken with those who were accused before me as Christians. I asked them whether they were Christians . . . with threats of punishment. If they kept to it, I ordered them taken off for execution . . . As for those who said they neither were nor ever had been Christians, I thought it right to let them go, when they recited a prayer to the gods at my dictation, and made supplication with incense and wine to your statue . . . and, moreover, cursed Christ, things which . . . those who are really Christians cannot be made to do.'

Pliny the Younger bears witness to the existence of Christian communities in Asia Minor and to the fact that Christ was worshipped as a god, but, as with the other two Roman authors, we find no reference to the historical figure of Jesus in his writings. This, in fact, is all that we can learn from Rome about Christ and Christianity until the later works of the Christian Fathers.

What did the Jews make of Jesus? The Gospel account describes how Caiaphas, the Jewish high priest, and other chief priests and elders of the time were deeply involved in the accusations against Jesus and his subsequent arrest, trial and condemnation. They are even said to have gone as far as to refuse Pilate's offer to release him for the occasion of the Passover feast, commemorating the liberation of the Israelites from Egyptian bondage, demanding instead the release of another prisoner, Barabbas. In the circumstances, we should expect to find that Jewish literature has kept some memory of him.

The intricate and incoherent mass of Rabbinical Scriptures, dating from the first five centuries A.D., make it clear that the Jews *did* know Jesus well, but did not wish to reveal *all* that they knew about him. His name, Yeshu, the Hebrew form of the Greek Jesus, is found at least twenty times in the Talmud, the Jewish commentaries and interpretative writings that were written during this time and are looked upon as only second in authority to the Old Testament, although there is a tendency to refer to him as 'a certain person' rather than use his name. In some passages he is also named as Balaam or Ben Pandira, 'the son of Pandira'. As the Jews disputed the claim that Jesus was the Son of God, they put forward the view that Pandira was a lover, not the husband, of Mary, but they confirm her name: 'Miriam (Hebrew for Mary) . . . the mother of "a certain person"' (b. Hag., 4b).

This is only one of many points of agreement between the four Gospels and both the Talmud and the *Midrash*, the ancient Jewish commentary on part of the Hebrew Scriptures. At the same time, there are important areas of contradiction, particularly those that can help to establish when Jesus actually lived. To deal first with the areas of agreement:

The Royal Descent of Jesus:

'Jesus Christ, the son of (king) David' (Matthew, 1:1).

Jesus's mother 'was the descendant of princes and rulers' (b. Sanh., 106a).

His Being in Egypt:

'Out of Egypt have I called my son' (Matthew, 2:15).

The Talmud says that Jesus was in Egypt during his early manhood and also places 'Jesus the Nazarene' who 'practised magic' in Egypt (b. Sanh., 107b).

Miracles and Wonders:

'Then was brought to him one possessed with a devil, blind, and dumb: and he healed him . . .' (Matthew, 12:22). 'From whence hath this man these things? and what wisdom is this . . . that even such mighty works are wrought by his hands?' (Mark, 6:2).

What the Bible calls signs and wonders, the rabbis called Egyptian magic, not miracles worked by the power of God: 'Jesus the Nazarene practised magic and led astray and deceived Israel' (b. Sanh., 107b).

The Conflict with Scribes and Pharisees:

When they described his miracles as the work of the devil, Jesus mocked the Pharisees: 'O generation of vipers, how can ye, being evil, speak good things? . . .' (Matthew, 12:34).

For their part the rabbis described Jesus as saying: 'Everyone who mocks at the words of the wise is punished by boiling filth' (b. Gitt., 56b, 57a).

The Son of Man

'And Jesus going up to Jerusalem, took the twelve disciples apart in the way, and said unto them . . . the Son of man shall be betrayed . . .' (Matthew, 20:17–18).

'(He says: "I am) the Son of man".' (j. Taanith, 65b).

Disciples

Jesus said to the fishermen Simon and his brother Andrew: 'Come ye after me, and I will make you to become fishers of men' (Mark, 1:17).

'Jesus (the Nazarene) had five disciples' (b. Sanh., 43a).

Jesus a Prophet

'And when he was come into Jerusalem . . . the multitude said, This is Jesus the prophet of Nazareth of Galilee' (Matthew, 21:10–11).

'In the beginning a prophet, in the end a deceiver' (b. Sanh., 106a).

Condemned to Death by the Priesthood

'. . . the Son of man shall be betrayed unto the chief priests . . . and they shall condemn him to death' (Matthew, 20:18).

Although no mention of a trial of Jesus is found in the Talmud, Jewish rabbis accepted full responsibility for his execution: '. . . they hanged Jesus (the Nazarene) . . . because he hath practised magic and deceived and led astray Israel' (b. Sanh., 43a).

Passover Execution

'And it was the preparation of the passover . . .' (John, 19:14).

'On the eve of the Passover they hanged Jesus (the Nazarene)' (b. Sanh., 43a).

Jesus Died Young

Jesus was 'about thirty years of age' (Luke, 3:23) when he began his ministry. He is known to have died one to three years later.

'He died young: "Men of blood and deceit shall not live out half their days"' (b. Sanh., 106b, quoting Psalm 55:23).

King of Israel

'And they clothed him with purple, and plaited a crown of thorns, and put it about his head, And began to salute him, Hail, King of the Jews' (Mark, 15:17–18).

When Jesus was executed, 'everyone who passed to and fro said: "It seems that the king is crucified"' (T. Sanh., 9.7).

Life After Death

'Likewise also the chief priests mocking said . . . Let Christ the King of Israel descend now from the cross, that we may see and believe . . .' (Mark, 15:31–2).
'. . . If he be the King of Israel, let him now come down from the cross . . .' (Matthew, 27:42).
'And they shall mock him, and shall scourge him, and shall spit upon him, and shall kill him: and the third day he shall rise again' (Mark, 10:34).

To this claim of rising from the dead, which has, of course, to be by the power of God, the rabbis say: 'Woe unto him who maketh himself live by the name of God' (b. Sanh., 106a).

Curing the Sick in His Name

'And when he had called unto him his twelve disciples, he gave them power against unclean spirits, to cast them out, and to heal all manner of sickness and all manner of disease' (Matthew, 10:1)

The disciples are said to have been curing the sick 'in the name of Jesus Ben Pandira' (T. Hull, 2, 22–3).

Here at last we find Jewish confirmation of many of the essential points in the life of Jesus that are related in the four Gospels. Yet the Talmudic rabbis, who compiled the interpretation of Jewish laws as well as legends and commentaries in the early centuries after the supposed date of the life and death of Jesus, would not have relied simply on the Christian traditions of the time, but would have referred to their previous Jewish authority, for both the details they did not dispute and those they disagreed with.

5

THE NAZARENE

THE authority on which the rabbis relied in compiling the Talmud was the Law of Moses as found in the Pentateuch, the first five books of the Old Testament, which the Jews call the Torah. Their laws did not allow them to make any changes, even of the smallest kind, in the account, although they were free to explain the significance of the older traditions, which had originally been transmitted orally from generation to generation, and to offer interpretations of obscurities and contradictions.

In terms of establishing when Jesus actually lived, one significant aspect of the Rabbinical writings is that at no point do they refer to his execution as having taken place during the rule of Herod or when Caiaphas was high priest, despite the fact that the Talmudic account includes many other chronological assumptions. This is particularly strange as the rabbis, busy compiling their own version of events, must have been aware of the account given in the four Gospels. Nor do we find any reference within the pages of the Talmud to personalities who lived in the era of Herod, such as John the Baptist. This gives additional significance to the fact that Jesus should, in one form or another, have so many Talmudic references devoted to him.

The Talmud also contradicts the Gospels in some essential points concerning Jesus. For instance, it never mentions that he was a Galilean or came from the city of Nazareth. Although it refers to him as being a Nazarene, this is a word (Greek, *Nazoraios*) used to indicate a religious sect, not a geographical location. This meaning is clear from Acts, 24:5 where the Jews address Felix, the Roman procurator, accusing Paul of stirring up trouble among Jews throughout the world and describing him as 'a ringleader of the sect of the Nazarenes'. In fact, Paul himself always referred to Jesus as 'the Nazarene' and never mentions that he came from Nazareth. Yet, elsewhere in Acts, Nazarene is always translated in the English version of the New Testament as 'of Nazareth', which is incorrect and has become a cause of misunderstanding among English readers.

The Nazarenes were one of a number of Gnostic sects (seekers of knowledge through spiritual experience) like the Essenes, and the term 'Nazarene' is still the designation given to Christians by Hebrew Jews to this day. Although Jesus was accepted by the Koran as the Messiah (Christ), his followers are referred to as Nasara – that is, Nazarenes: 'Among the terms by which the Qumran community referred to themselves was "Keepers of the Covenant", which appears in the original Hebrew as "Nazrie ha-Brit". From this term derives the word "Nazrim", one of the earliest Hebrew designations for the sect subsequently known as Christian.'[1]

The Semitic word is derived from the root *nsr*, which means to 'guard' or 'protect' and indicates 'devotee'. The existence of the Nazarene sect is confirmed by both classical and Christian authors. Pliny the Elder, the Roman geographer of the second half of the first century A.D., says that there was a tetrarchy (fourth part of a country or province) of Nazarini in Coele-Syria, the area of Damascus.[2]

The name Nazareth is not found in the Book of Acts, the letters of the Apostles, any books of the Old Testament, the Talmud or the works of Josephus, who was himself given command in Galilee at the time of the Jewish revolt against the Romans in 66 A.D. The first time we hear of this location is in the writings of Mark, the earliest of the Gospel authors. After the section dealing with John the Baptist, we find this verse: 'And it came to pass in those days, that Jesus came from Nazareth of Galilee, and was baptized of John in Jordan' (Mark, 1:9).

Mark's example was followed by Matthew and Luke. However, their accounts contradict one another. Matthew tells us how, fearing Herod's son, Archelaus, Joseph took Mary and the child Jesus and 'came and dwelt in a city called Nazareth: that it might be fulfilled which was spoken by the prophets, He shall be called a Nazarene' (Matthew, 2:23). For his part, Luke has Joseph and Mary already settled in Nazareth at the time of the Annunciation: 'And in the sixth month the angel Gabriel was sent from God unto a city of Galilee, named Nazareth, To a virgin espoused to a man whose name was Joseph . . . And the virgin's name was Mary' (Luke, 1:26–7).

We have no definite knowledge of when the Gospel of Mark was written, but it is believed by biblical critics to have been about 75 A.D. At this time, Nazareth was a small village in Lower Galilee, set in the hill area north of the great plain of Esdraelon, about fifteen miles west of the Sea of Galilee. The fact that Mark chose to relate the word 'Nazarene' to a geographical location rather than a sect was a consequence of his attempt to place the account of the life and death of Jesus in a Roman framework. It was later to have the effect of turning Nazareth into a place of pilgrimage – but not until the sixth century A.D.

The Cross is identified as the symbol of Christ. The four Gospels are consistent in saying that Jesus was crucified: 'And they crucified him . . .' (Matthew, 27:35); 'And when they had crucified him . . .' (Mark, 15:24); 'And when they were come to the place, which is called Calvary, there they crucified him . . .' (Luke, 23:33); 'Then the soldiers, when they had crucified Jesus . . .' (John, 19:23). Paul, too, describes this as the means by which Jesus met his death: '. . . Jesus, whom ye have crucified . . .' (Acts, 2:36).

This is what one would expect if Jesus had been tried and condemned to death in Roman times. Crucifixion – nailing someone to a cross – was a Roman, not an Israelite, form of execution. The Israelites (who became recognized as Jews only from the time of the Babylonian exile in the sixth century B.C.), according to ancient tradition, hanged the condemned person from a tree: 'And if a man have committed a sin worthy of death . . . thou hang him on a tree' (Deuteronomy, 21:22).

However, while the Talmud refers to Jesus as having been crucified ('It seems that the king [Jesus] is crucified', T. Sanh. 9.7), it also claims, as we saw in the previous chapter, that he was hanged: 'Jesus was hanged' (b. Sanh., 106b) and 'They hanged him on the eve of the Passover' (b. Sanh., 43a). This would appear to be a serious contradiction but for the fact that we find in the New Testament also references to Jesus having been hanged rather than crucified. The account of Jesus's death given by Peter, for instance, reads: '. . . whom they slew and hanged on a tree' (Acts, 10:39), and Paul, having in an earlier reference used the term 'crucified', is now found declaring: '. . . they took him down from the tree, and laid him in a sepulchre' (Acts, 13:29).

Thus, in terms of the words used, it is possible to suggest that there is not necessarily a contradiction between the Talmudic and Gospel versions of how Jesus met his death, and that 'crucifixion' and 'hanging' can be looked upon as synonyms. Later, however, a more positive attempt was made to adapt his story to the Roman era. John, the least historical of the evangelists, added more details that favoured the Roman practice of nailing to a cross rather than the Israelite punishment of hanging. These details are to be found in the story of doubting Thomas, who sought physical proof of Christ's resurrection: '. . . he (Thomas) said unto them, Except I shall see in his hands the print of the nails, and put my finger into the print of the nails, and thrust my hand into his side, I will not believe' (John, 20:25).

Adapting the story of Jesus to fit into the Roman period has resulted in conflicting accounts not only of how he met his death, but of who was responsible for condemning him – Israelite priests or the Roman authority. The New Testament is unanimous in blaming the Israelite priests: '. . . the Son of man shall be betrayed unto the chief priests and unto the scribes, and they shall condemn him to death' (Matthew, 20:18); Peter, addressing the Jerusalem priests, says: '. . . Jesus, whom ye slew and hanged on a tree' (Acts, 5:30); Paul refers to 'the Jews, who killed the Lord Jesus' (I Thessalonians, 2:14–15), and again, when addressing the 'house of Israel', he referred to '. . . Jesus, whom ye have crucified . . .' (Acts, 2:36).

However, while the rabbis accepted that the Israelite priests were responsible for the condemnation of Jesus as a punishment for his having led Israel astray, we find in Talmudic tradition no additional involvement of Pontius Pilate or Roman as opposed to Israelite authorities in the circumstances surrounding his death. Instead, they point the accusing finger at Pinhas – an Israelite priest who lived in the fourteenth century B.C. and was a contemporary of Moses.

6

ANOTHER TIME, ANOTHER PLACE

THE Talmud is quite specific: 'Pinhas . . . killed him [Jesus]' (b. Sanh., 106b). Pinhas, or Phinehas, to use the name we find in the Old Testament, was the priest, the son of Eleazar, the son of Aaron, who is identified in the Book of Numbers as a contemporary of Moses in a passage where the Lord reveals to the Jewish lawgiver that he has promised Pinhas and his descendants 'the covenant of an everlasting priesthood' (Numbers, 25:10–13). Support for the view that the death of Jesus took place fourteen centuries earlier than the Gospel account suggests is not to be found solely in the Talmud, but in the Bible and the Koran.

In order to explain the apparent contradiction of the Gospel accounts, some scholars have suggested that the name Pinhas could have been a corruption of the name Pilate. This might have been a possibility but for the consistency of Talmudic references that relate Jesus to the time of Pinhas and Moses. For example, we find in Deuteronomy an account of the fate that shall await a deceiver prophet: 'If there arise among you a prophet, or a dreamer of dreams, and giveth thee a sign or a wonder, And the sign or the wonder come to pass, whereof he spake unto thee, saying, Let us go after other gods, which thou hast not known, and let us serve them; Thou shalt not hearken unto the words of that prophet, or that dreamer of dreams . . . that prophet, or that dreamer of dreams, shall be put to death . . . Thou shalt not consent unto him, nor hearken unto him; neither shall thine eye pity him, neither shalt thou spare, neither shalt thou conceal him' (Deuteronomy, 13:1–3,5,8).

These verses are echoed in the Talmud where they are related to Jesus and Deuteronomy is actually quoted: 'It is tradition: On the eve of the Passover they hanged Jesus (the Nazarene) . . . because he hath practised magic and deceived and led astray Israel . . . He was a deceiver, and the Merciful hath said (Deuteronomy, 13:8), thou shalt not spare, neither shalt thou conceal him' (b. Sanh., 43a). As we shall see later, while the historical Jesus did not preach the worship of other gods, he contradicted the teaching of Moses on two points – he did not force the Israelite God on other people, but allowed them to worship their own gods, who came to be regarded as angels and saints, and he believed in resurrection and life after death.

Another verse from Deuteronomy is used in the Talmud (T. Sanh., 9.7) to relate to the death of Jesus: 'His body shall not remain all night upon the tree, but thou shalt in any wise bury him that day; (for he that is hanged is accursed of God) . . .' (Deuteronomy, 21:23). Again, in many Talmudic references, Jesus is related to Balaam, a non-Israelite and foreteller of the future who was a contemporary of Moses. In the Book of Numbers (22–24), the fourth book of the Pentateuch, we find a long account of how the king of Moab sought Balaam's help in predicting the outcome of his conflicts with the Israelites and was disappointed when he replied that these conflicts would end in complete victory for the Israelites.

The name Balaam is sometimes used in the Talmud as a synonym for Jesus. For instance, of the mother of Balaam (Jesus is meant in this case) it says: 'She was the descendant of princes and rulers' (b. Sanh., 106a). The name of Balaam is also employed in establishing the age of Jesus at the time of his death: 'He was thirty-three or thirty-four when Pinhas . . . killed him' (b. Sanh., 106b). However, the Talmud also recognizes Balaam and Jesus as separate characters, as we sometimes find references to both of them in the same passage.[1]

One curious passage in the Talmud seems to go out of its way to stress that these Balaam–Jesus stories date from the time of Moses and the Exodus: 'Moses wrote his book and the section about Balaam' (b. B. Bathr., 14b). Why was it necessary to state the obvious when the Book of Numbers, where the Balaam story appears, is one of the five Old Testament books of which Moses is said to have been the author? Here we certainly have an attempt to refute indirectly the Gospel account of Jesus having lived in the first century A.D. at the time of Pontius Pilate by making the point that the Balaam–Jesus stories date to a much earlier period of history.

If Jesus lived fourteen centuries earlier than has been thought, it would throw a new light on an event described in the Gospels

of Matthew, Mark and Luke – the meeting of Jesus and Moses at
the time of what has become known as his Transfiguration: 'And
after six days Jesus taketh with him Peter, and James, and John,
and leadeth them up into an high mountain apart by themselves:
and he was transfigured before them. And his raiment became
shining, exceeding white as snow; so as no fuller on earth can
white them. And there appeared unto them Elias (Elijah) with
Moses: and they were talking with Jesus. And Peter answered
and said to Jesus, Master, it is good for us to be here: and let
us make three tabernacles; one for thee, and one for Moses, and
one for Elias . . . And there was a cloud that overshadowed them:
and a voice came out of the cloud, saying, This is my beloved Son:
hear him. And suddenly, when they had looked round about, they
saw no man any more, save Jesus only with themselves' (Mark, 9:
2–5, 7–8).

Christian authors avoided trying to interpret the meaning of this
account until the nineteenth century. It was then explained away
as not being a description of actual historical events, but rather
a matter of the psychology of Jesus and his disciples or having
been a 'spiritual experience'. However, the factual nature of the
Gospel narratives themselves does not permit this interpretation.
Unlike the confrontation with Satan, when Jesus was alone with
a fallen angelic being, the Transfiguration cannot be interpreted as
symbolic or a description of a vision. Here we have three disciples
who are said to be witnesses to a meeting between Jesus and Moses,
an event that is the only clue in the Gospels to the era in which Jesus
really lived.

An account in the Koran relates Jesus indirectly to Moses, not only
in terms of time but of blood. It tells how, after Mary had given
birth to her child, she went back to her own people, who rebuked
her for being an unmarried mother:

> O sister of Aaron!
> Thy father was not
> A man of evil, nor thy
> Mother a woman unchaste!
> (Sura, 19:28).[2]

In this case the Koran identifies Mary, the mother of Jesus, as
being the same person as Mary, the sister of Aaron and Moses.

Faced with this seemingly complete contradiction of the Gospel account, Muslim scholars have tried to find a logical explanation. Some have said that the real meaning of this passage is that it is *as if* Mary were a sister of Aaron, while others have attempted to relate the mother of Jesus to the tribe of Aaron. Neither of these approaches is convincing, however, since the Koran itself confirms the brother–sister relationship between Mary and Aaron by saying that they had the same father, Imram (Sura, 3:35).

We now have two contradictory eras for the life and death of Jesus – the traditional Gospel account, which places these events between the last years of the first century B.C. and the end of the third decade of the first century A.D., a chronology not supported by any outside evidence; and, supported by the Talmud, the Koran and the New Testament story of the Transfiguration, the indication that these events occurred fourteen centuries earlier. Where do the roots of this contradiction lie? For the answer we have to turn to the history and beliefs of the group of small and secret Gnostic sects, including the Essenes, that was scattered all over Palestine/Syria and Egypt for centuries prior to the start of the Christian era.

7

THE MAN SENT FROM GOD

THE Gnostic sects looked upon Jesus Christ as a historical character, a successor to Moses. They believed that the First Coming had already taken place, but that Jesus had been rejected by the Israelite hierarchy and executed by the Wicked Priest. Among these sects were the Qumran Essenes. They were the owners of the library of Dead Sea Scrolls which, as we saw earlier, date from the second century B.C., yet contain some elements of the Gospel account of the birth and life of Jesus.

The very name of the Essenes indicates that they were followers of Jesus. Philo Judaeus who wrote the earliest account of the sect around 30 A.D. called them Essaeans from the Greek *Essaios*, but made it clear that this was not originally a Greek word. Josephus, who, half a century later, included them among the Jewish divisions of his time, called them Essenes, the same term that is used in English. However, it was recognized that the word 'Essene' must have had a Semitic origin. Surprisingly, amid many unsatisfactory suggestions about its source, the obvious one was overlooked – *Essa*, the Arabic name of Jesus and the only one used in the Koran. 'Essaioi' would therefore mean 'a follower of *Essa*'. This meaning may in itself have been the main reason for its having been ignored: if the Essenes existed before the time of Jesus, they could not be looked upon as his followers. Essa was also the word used for Jesus in the Coptic Egyptian language in the first century A.D.

All of the Essene sects were closed and secret communities. Although part of the Jewish nation, they lived separate lives and took no part in Jewish feasts or temple rituals because of their belief that the Teacher of Righteousness had been rejected and killed centuries earlier by the Israelite priesthood. The strictly secret nature of the Essene sect was described by Josephus: 'If anyone hath a mind to come over to their sect . . . he is prescribed the same method of living which they use, for a year, while he continues excluded. They gave him a white garment for prayers, but did not allow him into their closed gatherings. If he had proved to be worthy of joining them, then he was baptized and "made a partaker of the water of purification". Yet even then he was not fully admitted to the sect and he had to wait for two more years under strict supervision before the profession and taking of the vow, which was mainly of absolute secrecy regarding all that concerned the order.'[1]

In the first century of what was to become the Christian era, the Essenes were expecting Jesus to return on the Day of Judgment at the end of the world. John, 'the man sent from God' (John, 1:6), was the first Essene to come out into the open and try to initiate all the Jews to a baptism of repentance, a confession of sin and the need for moral cleansing, a symbol of forgiveness. He commanded the Jews 'to come to baptism; for the washing (with water) would be acceptable to him (God), if they made use of it . . .'[2] John the Baptist was not, however, preparing the way for Jesus to be born, but for his Second Coming: 'In those days came John the Baptist, preaching in the wilderness of Judaea, And saying, Repent ye: for the kingdom of heaven is at hand. For this is he that was spoken of by the prophet Esaias, saying, Prepare ye the way of the Lord, make his paths straight' (Matthew, 3:1–3). John represented the prophet of the end of time, the eschatological messenger of the Old Testament prophetic books.

John's baptist movement aroused such enthusiasm, and such a large following, that Herod Antipas, the Tetrarch of Galilee and son of Herod the Great, as we saw earlier, fearing that John the Baptist might become a rallying point for Jewish dissidence, had him arrested, imprisoned and later executed. Had Herod Antipas not made this decision, the story of Jesus of Nazareth would almost certainly never have been written – for the life and violent death of John the Baptist are the cornerstone on which it rests.

At this time many rebellious Jewish leaders, inspired no doubt by these Messianic expectations, arose to confront the high priests in Jerusalem as well as the occupying Roman powers. Among them was Judas, a Galilean, who was to be cast in a rather different role when the four Gospels came to be written a generation later. Judas is, I believe, to be identified with Ben Stada, whom the Talmud describes in the same terms as it describes Jesus – 'a deceiver'. It also gives us some details of his trial and execution: 'And thus they did with Ben Stada in Lud (the town of Lydda in the Palestine plain south-east of Jaffa) . . . and they brought him to Beth Din (the Jewish court) and stoned him.'

Modern biblical scholars see in Ben Stada one of many false prophets of the first century A.D. and it has been suggested that he is the same person as an Egyptian rebel who, according to Josephus, led a rebellion against the Romans in the middle of the century.[3] I do not think this can be the case because Josephus assures us that this rebel was never caught: '. . . Felix (Antonius Felix, the Roman procurator, 52–60 A.D.) . . . ordered his soldiers to take their weapons, and came against them (the rebels) with a great number of horsemen and footmen, from Jerusalem, and attacked the Egyptian and the people that were with him. He also slew four hundred of them and took two hundred alive. But the Egyptian himself escaped out of the fight and did not appear any more.'[4]

This view is supported by the New Testament account of the arrest of Paul by the Romans, which took place at least two decades after the supposed date of the execution of Jesus: 'And as Paul was to be led into the castle, he said unto the chief captain, May I speak unto thee? Who said, Canst thou speak Greek? Art thou not that Egyptian, which before these days madest an uproar, and leddest out into the wilderness four thousand men that were murderers?' (Acts, 21:37–8).

It is therefore more likely that Ben Stada is to be identified as the prophet Judas, the Galilean who rose up 'in the days of the taxing, and drew away much people after him: he also perished; and all, even as many as obeyed him, were dispersed' (Acts, 5:37). Josephus wrote about how Judas called on the Jews not to pay the tax introduced by the Romans in the year 6 A.D. when the census was made to assess the amount of tribute. 'This taxation was no better than an introduction to slavery,' Judas said. Although the Jerusalem high priest had advised the Jews to pay the tax, Judas's opposition gathered a vast army of adherents, according to Josephus. This Galilean prophet seems, in fact, to have left a strong mark on Jewish history and caused a fundamental change in Jewish thought

in the first half of the first century A.D. At the time the Jews had
three philosophic sects, Sadducees, Pharisees and Essenes, but
'Judas . . . excited a fourth philosophic sect among us, and had
a great many followers'.[5] Josephus does not tell us how Judas met
his end after his uprising had been defeated, but it is known that
two of his sons, James and Simon, were crucified by the Romans
between 46 and 48 A.D. for following in their father's footsteps.

The killing of John the Baptist was a severe blow to his followers
and, in particular, his disciples, who were anxious to prove that
John's message about the return of the Messiah had been right.
They therefore not only continued with his teaching, but claimed
that his prophecy had been fulfilled and they had witnessed Jesus.

As nobody else had seen him, their story was not believed and
it was generally thought that the person who had risen from the
dead was actually John. We find two references to this belief in
the Gospel of Mark after the disciples had been sent out two by
two to preach repentance: 'And king Herod heard of him; (for
his name was spread abroad:) and he said, That John the Baptist
was risen from the dead . . .' (6:14), and: 'But when Herod heard
thereof, he said, It is John, whom I beheaded: he is risen from the
dead' (6:16).

We also find in Mark an important admission that nobody apart
from the disciples knew Jesus: '. . . he asked his disciples, saying
unto them, Whom do men say that I am? And they answered, John
the Baptist: but some say, Elias; and others, One of the prophets.
And he saith unto them, But whom say ye that I am? And Peter
answereth and saith unto him, Thou art the Christ. And he charged
them that they should tell no man of him' (8:27–30). This is not
only an important admission: the nature of Peter's reply is also
strange. Why is he reported to have said 'the Christ' rather than
'Jesus'? Jesus was the Lord's name; his disciples could not have
recognized him as Christ, the Redeemer, before he had died and
risen from the dead.

John never claimed to be the Christ and, once John's disciples
asserted that Jesus had been a contemporary of John's and they
had seen him, the only course open to them was to 'resurrect' the
Jesus whose memory had been preserved down the centuries by
the Prophets and draw on the Old Testament for the basis of his
Gospel. It proved an uphill task trying to have their claims

accepted. Around the year 53 A.D. 'a certain Jew named Apollos, born at Alexandria, an eloquent man, and mighty in the scriptures, came to Ephesus. This man was instructed in the way of the Lord; and being fervent in the spirit, he spake and thought diligently the things of the Lord, knowing only the baptism of John' (Acts, 18:24–5).

The baptism of John differed from the baptism of the Essenes and the baptism of Jesus. In John's case, the promise was that immersion in water would wash away sin. However, the baptism of the Essenes, which also featured the symbolic use of water, was looked upon as a baptism of the Holy Spirit that, in addition to erasing sin, initiated the person baptized, after a probationary period, into the New Covenant within the Community and carried the gift of eternal life. According to the Dead Sea text known as the Community Rule, the new adherent 'shall be cleansed from all his sins by the spirit of holiness uniting them to its truth . . . And when his flesh is sprinkled with purifying water and sanctified by cleansing water, it shall be made clean by the humble submission of his soul to all the precepts of God.'[6]

This baptism, always necessary in order to join the Essene Community, was applied to the now-open Christian Church. The apostles, attempting to convert not only Jews, but Gentiles, used the same baptism they had for their own Essene community: Jesus is quoted as saying: '. . . John truly baptized with water; but ye shall be baptized with the Holy Ghost not many days hence' (Acts, 1:5). In fact, according to the Gospels the apostles continued to practise baptism by water of the type administered by John, but they emphasized the necessity of its being preceded by an inner conversion. When Paul was converted, Ananias, one of the disciples, told him: '. . . Brother Saul, the Lord . . . hath sent me, that thou mightest receive thy sight, and be filled with the Holy Ghost . . . and he received sight forthwith, and arose, and was baptized' (Acts, 9:17–18).

Apollos therefore knew of John the Baptist and his form of baptism of repentance and the Gospel of Jesus, but, had he known of Jesus of Nazareth, who supposedly lived at the same time as John, he would also have known the new meaning that was attached to baptism by the Palestinian Church – a sign of unity in spirit with Christ and his Church. Other followers of Jesus are also described as having known only the baptism of John: 'And it came to pass, that . . . Paul having passed through the upper coasts came to Ephesus: and finding certain disciples, He said unto them, Have ye received the Holy Ghost since ye believed? And they said unto him, We have not so much as heard whether there be any Holy Ghost. And he said unto them, Unto what then were ye baptized? And they said, Unto John's baptism' (Acts, 19:1–3).

Therefore it seems that recognition of the Holy Spirit was the new element of early Christian baptism. Paul himself was the first to define its symbolic significance, joining the ritual to belief in the resurrected Christ. It was thus an initiation into the spiritual life with Christ: the stain of sin was not washed away by water, but by Jesus's death and belief in his Resurrection. The only fundamental difference between the baptism of the Essenes and the baptism of Christ was that the latter granted immediate membership of the Christian Church without the probationary period demanded by the Essenes.

In this context it is curious that three of the Gospels should give an account of Jesus being baptized by John. No Christian who believed in Jesus of Nazareth, let alone Jesus himself, the Son of the Holy Spirit, would have accepted the baptism of John as an alternative to the baptism of Christ because of their different significance. While Christian baptism, which confesses eternal life with Christ, could take place only after the historical Christ had died and was believed to have risen from the dead, John's baptism was intended as a sign of forgiveness for those who were responsible for Christ's actual death. The logical inference from the story of John the Baptist is that his disciples took the Jesus of the Essenes, who was a contemporary of Moses, placed him in the first century A.D. and, to establish him as a historical character, related the events of his life to those of John the Baptist.

8

THE SUFFERING SERVANT

NOBODY who reads the Old Testament closely can fail to see its influence upon the narratives we find in the Gospels. 'It may be conceded that the evangelists, especially Matthew, do sometimes . . . point to fulfilment of prophecy (e.g., Matthew, 2:15, 21:4–7) . . . But even if we write off all the sayings which are introduced by "It is written . . ." we are still left with the sayings about "cup" and "baptism", which, Jesus seems to say, are part of his destiny (Mark, 10:38ff, 14:36, Luke, 12:50 and parallels; cf. also Mark, 14:41, "the hour is come", and parallels). As he saw it, his death was neither a result of the circumstances in which he found himself, nor of the course of action he had taken. It was an irrevocable destiny ordained for him . . . And if we ask how this conviction came to him, the simplest and most likely answer is that he found it written in the Scripture, as the evangelists report of him . . .[1]

'Jesus of the Gospel seems as if he was following an earlier Old Testament text, not only for his movements but his sayings: on this point the words of the baptism, in the original form that they have in Mark 1:11, "Thou art my beloved Son, in thee I am well pleased", seem indicative, and determinative of the whole course of Jesus's ministry . . . They are a conflation of Psalms, 2:7, "Thou art my Son", and Isaiah, 42:1, "in whom I am well pleased" (lit., "in whom my soul delighteth, or is well pleased").'[2]

In 1924 the French scholar Couchoud was able to trace in his book *The Enigma of Jesus* the Old Testament roots of many of the chief events found in the Gospel accounts of the life and death of Jesus, including the Virgin Birth ('Behold, a virgin shall conceive, and bear a son, and shall call his name Immanuel,' Isaiah), the betrayal ('Yea, mine own familiar friend, in whom I trusted, which did eat of my bread, hath lifted up his heel against me,' Psalms), the casting of lots for his garments ('They part my garments among them, and cast lots upon my vesture,' Psalms) and the last cry of the crucified Jesus ('My God, my God, why hast thou forsaken me?' Psalms) (see Appendix A).

The dominating role given to Jesus in the Gospels is that of a messenger, sent by God as a light to the nations and a Redeemer, who is to suffer and be sacrificed like a lamb in order to wipe out the sins of his transgressing people. Such a figure had already existed in the prophetic Old Testament writings of Isaiah (Esaias), who lived during the second half of the eighth century B.C. His is the largest of the prophetic books, containing sixty-six chapters. Biblical scholars have come to the conclusion that the Book of Isaiah had at least two authors, Isaiah (I), who was responsible for chapters 1–39, and Isaiah (II), who was responsible for the rest of the book. However, some scholars have taken the view that yet a third author penned the last eleven chapters, which have been dated to the post-exilic period in the second half of the sixth century B.C.

In the character of the Servant, found in the Songs of Isaiah that form part of Isaiah (II), we find the original idea of the sufferings of Christ:

'Behold my servant, whom I uphold; mine elect, in whom my soul delighteth; I have put my spirit upon him: he shall bring forth judgment to the Gentiles' (42:1). 'And he said, It is a light thing that thou shouldest be my servant to raise up the tribes of Jacob, and to restore the preserved of Israel: I will also give thee for a light to the Gentiles, that thou mayest be my salvation unto the end of the earth' (49:6).

'All we like sheep have gone astray; we have turned every one to his own way; and the Lord hath laid on him the iniquity of us all. He was oppressed, and he was afflicted, but he opened not his mouth: he is brought as a lamb to the slaughter, and as a sheep before her shearers is dumb, so he openeth not his mouth. He was taken from prison and from judgment: and who shall declare his generation? for he was cut off out of the land of the living: for the transgression of my people was he stricken. And he made his grave with the wicked, and with the rich in his death; because he had done no violence, neither was any deceit in his mouth. Yet it pleased the Lord to bruise him; he shall put him to grief: when thou shalt make his soul an offering for sin, he shall see his seed, he shall prolong his days, and the pleasure of the Lord shall prosper in his hand. He shall see of the travail of his soul, and shall be satisfied: by his knowledge shall my righteous servant justify many; for he shall bear their iniquities' (53:6–11).

The title 'Servant' is used in the Scriptures to signify a prophet or king while the other title used in the songs, 'elect (chosen)' refers in the plural to the people of Israel, but its use in the singular was restricted to Moses and David. Thus we can see that the Servant was placed in a very special position, being related to both prophetic and royal titles. He is also endowed with the spirit of God, a description given to Jesus in the Koran.

It is also indicated that the Servant has already had a historical life in the past when, although he committed no violence nor uttered any deceit, he suffered oppression, was judged and taken 'out of the land of the living'. Like an innocent lamb he was sacrificed for the sins of the people. Yet he still has an eschatological mission to fulfil in the future when God will send him to raise the tribes of Israel, be a light to the Gentiles and bring judgment and salvation to the nations.

Some scholars have sought to interpret the Servant as being not an historical individual but the people of Israel as a nation. However, this cannot be supported by the text, which talks of a person who suffered and was oppressed by the people of Israel, and is to be sent to them and all nations on a future eschatological mission.

We find an echo of Isaiah's suffering Servant in the Gospel of Mark where Jesus is quoted as saying: '. . . it is written of the Son of man, that he must suffer many things, and be set at nought' (9:12). In fact, we find a reflection of this echo in all the Gospel passages where Jesus is represented as speaking of the sufferings of the Son of man. For example, in his account of how Jesus angered the Pharisees by healing on a Sabbath, Matthew makes a comment by quoting from the Songs of Isaiah: 'That it might be fulfilled which was spoken by Esaias the prophet, saying, Behold my servant, whom I have chosen; my beloved, in whom my soul is well pleased: I will put my spirit upon him, and he shall shew judgment to the Gentiles. He shall not strive, nor cry; neither shall any man hear his voice in the streets. A bruised reed shall he not break, and smoking flax shall he not quench, till he send forth judgment unto victory. And in his name shall the Gentiles trust' (Matthew, 12:17–21).

Luke, in his account of Jesus reading in the synagogue, has Jesus himself quoting Isaiah's prophecy: '. . . And when he had opened the book he found the place where it was written, The Spirit of the Lord is upon me, because he hath anointed me to preach the gospel to the poor; he hath sent me to heal the brokenhearted, to preach deliverance to the captives, and recovering of sight to the blind, to set at liberty them that are bruised, To preach the acceptable year of the Lord' (Luke, 4:17–19).

In order to emphasize that Jesus was the subject of this prophecy, Luke goes on to describe how he sat down and 'began to say unto them, This day is this scripture fulfilled in your ears' (Luke, 4:21). The insertion of the word 'anointed' in this use of the original Isaiah quotation is significant because there is no other reference in the Gospels to Jesus having been anointed, a completely different rite, with different implications, from baptism. Its use here, together with Jesus having been identified in the opening verse of Matthew as 'Jesus Christ, the son of David' and being addressed frequently as 'son of David' by ordinary people, provides a strong indication that the historical Christ was of royal descent.

We also find further allusions to Isaiah's Servant in the Gospel of John: 'The next day John seeth Jesus coming unto him, and saith, Behold the Lamb of God, which taketh away the sin of the world' (1:29); in Acts, where an Ethiopian eunuch, after a visit to Jerusalem, asks one of the apostles, Philip, who was meant by the Servant: 'Then Philip opened his mouth, and began at the same scripture, and preached unto him Jesus' (8:35); and again in the First Epistle of St Peter, who does not give any hint about his personal relation with Christ or about his life, teaching or death, but simply repeats the part of the Songs of Isaiah that relate to the Servant: '. . . Christ . . . Who did no sin, neither was guile found in his mouth: Who, when he was reviled, reviled not again; when he suffered, he threatened not; but committed himself to him that judgeth righteously: Who his own self bare our sins in his own body on the tree, that we, being dead to sins, should live unto righteousness: by whose stripes ye were healed' (2:21–4).

9

THE AFTER-LIFE

ISAIAH was the first Israelite prophet to present the Christ as the divinely appointed Saviour. Hitherto the Hebrew saviour was expected to be the victorious son of David, a living king who would defeat the nation's enemies, and the Israelites believed that life came to an end when a person went to Sheol, the underworld or grave. The account of the Servant in the Songs of Isaiah (II) also presents us for the first time in the Old Testament with the idea of spiritual salvation and a second life.

The rising of the Servant from the dead is very clear from these passages: 'He was . . . cut off out of the land of the living . . .' (Isaiah, 53:8); '. . . he made his grave with the wicked . . .' (the sense is that his grave was made for him with the wicked) (53:9); yet '. . . when thou shalt make his soul an offering for sin, he shall see his seed, he shall prolong his days, and the pleasure of the Lord shall prosper in his hand' (53:10). What was the source of these new ideas? On what authority did the prophet base these statements?

The argument of some scholars, that Isaiah (II) was here influenced by the Mesopotamian belief in Tammuz, a dying and rising agricultural deity, cannot be taken seriously: Tammuz rituals were used as a means of obtaining recovery from sickness in this life and had no connection with spiritual salvation or life after death.

The Talmudic rabbis, as we saw earlier, were in possession of some oral traditions about the sufferings of Jesus. Isaiah (II), more than six centuries earlier, was reporting traditions from the same source. Although we have to assume from the manner of his report that he accepted the truth of what he was saying, the belief in spiritual salvation and life after death can only have originated with the Servant himself. Isaiah could not have invented it.

The Songs of Isaiah (II) were written during the Babylonian

Exile. The Babylonians destroyed Jerusalem in 587 B.C., bringing the Jewish kingdom to an end. Most of its population became exiled in Babylon, a situation that continued until 538 B.C. when the Persian king, Cyrus, defeated Babylonia, freed the Jews and allowed them to rebuild their Jerusalem temple. Isaiah (II) represented the Israelite defeat and humiliation as a punishment by God for a crime they had committed a long time previously. All through the Old Testament books it can be sensed that there has been a cover-up, an attempt to destroy the evidence of a crime for which some Israelite leaders were responsible.

For instance, Ernest Sellin, the German biblical scholar, who found indications that an Israelite leader was killed in the wilderness during the time of the Exodus, suggested – wrongly, as we shall see – that the Servant represents Moses, murdered by his own followers. He goes on to say that 'despite the efforts of the priests to suppress the sordid story, it nevertheless lived on in prophetic circles, and that out of it Isaiah (II) developed the expectation that the once-slain leader would return from the dead, lead his people back through the desert, and then announce to all the world the salvation of God . . .' Sellin's inquiries led him to the conclusion that this is 'the scarlet thread' which runs through most of the prophets and binds them to one another.[1]

Sigmund Freud, who followed Sellin's identification of Moses as the murder victim, related this event to the later Christian idea of salvation: 'It seems that a growing feeling of guilt had seized the Jewish people – and perhaps the whole civilization of that time. Paul, a Roman Jew from Tarsus, seized upon this feeling of guilt and correctly traced it back to its primeval source. This he called original sin . . . The murderous deed itself, however, was not remembered; in its place stood the phantasy of expiation . . . A Son of God, innocent himself, had sacrificed himself – and had thereby taken off the guilt of the world.'[2]

Yet whatever changes and omissions were made in written accounts, the memory of these events remained alive in oral traditions, although confused and submerged in allegory. Isaiah (II), who could have been a secret believer in the Servant (that is, Christ), felt he had the opportunity to come out into the open and declare what, in his view, was the cause of God's anger with his nation. Thus, his Songs do not represent a personal vision or belief, but an ancient tradition of a real historical character, who suffered because of the ignorance of the people.

The fact that the resurrected Servant resembles an ancient dying and rising god has led some scholars to conclude that Isaiah's Christ was a mythological character, with no basis in history. However, this cannot be the case. When Moses delivered the Law to his people on Mount Sinai, declaring the unity of God, who had no graven image, he instructed his followers to abandon all the ancient gods and believe only in the living Lord.

At the time Egypt had many deities and sacred animals that were rejected by Moses and his followers. The God of Moses declared: '. . . against all the gods of Egypt I will execute judgment: I am the Lord' (Exodus, 12:12).

Osiris was one of the Egyptian gods abolished by Moses. From their very early history in the thirty-first century B.C., Egyptians believed that a human being consisted of spiritual as well as physical elements. They regarded death as the departure of the spiritual element from the body, but also believed that, if the physical being could be kept safe and protected by magic formulas, the spirit would return to the body at some point in the future and the person concerned would lead a second life. That is why they devoted such care to preserving a dead body by mummification and building secure tombs to keep it safe.

Osiris, whom they looked upon as one of their ancient kings, was said to have been killed on a Friday by his brother Set, who dismembered the body of Osiris in order to deny him a second life. However, his wife, Isis, was able to collect the various members and, with her magic, restore him to life three days later – not on earth but in the underworld, where he became the god and judge of the dead. When a Pharaoh died, Egyptian rituals conducted during the funeral processes were designed to ensure his eternal life. At the end of these rituals they believed that the dead king was to be identified as an Osiris.

The account of the Resurrection of Jesus is in many ways similar to that of Osiris. Like Osiris, he is said to have risen on the third day. 'The Osiris worshippers of ancient Egypt believed, as did the early Christians (Hebrews, 4:14), that "man cannot be saved" by a remote omnipotent deity, but by one who has shared the experience of human suffering and death.'[3] 'Osiris . . . became the saviour to whom men and women turned for assurance of immortality.'[4]

According to Apuleius,[5] the Latin author of the second century A.D., the rites of Isis – the ancient Egyptian wife and mother-of-god character – assured the mystae (followers who take part in the mystery drama of Isis) that they would see and venerate the goddess in their after-lives, which is an obvious parallel with Christians' expectations that they will see God in the next world: 'Blessed are the pure in heart: for they shall see God' (Matthew, 5:8).

The fact that the Old Testament has no Resurrection reference until Isaiah (II), writing in the sixth century B.C., makes it clear that he relied on another, non-biblical, tradition for his account of the risen Christ: 'External influence is perhaps to be conjectured for the rising of the Servant from the Dead, a thought which was otherwise foreign to contemporary Israelite religion.'[6] However, this does not require that the Redeemer figure should be a mythological character since, as in the case of the Osiride kings, the historical figure becomes identified as an eschatological being only in his second life.

Although Moses never spoke of an after-life, followers of Christ, the Essenes among them, believed – unlike the rest of the Jews – in life after death. This belief in the eternal existence of the spirit and judgment after death can be traced to the historical Jesus himself. There is a reference in The Damascus Document, one of the manuscripts found at Qumran, indicating that their Messianic leader as well as Moses delivered the commandments of God: 'They (Israelite leaders) preached rebellion against the commandments of God (revealed) by the hand of Moses and also by (the hands of the) Anointed [Messiah] of holiness.'[7] These commandments had to be obeyed – and obedience would have its reward.

In his account of the Essenes, Josephus says: 'Indeed, it is a firm belief among them that, although bodies are corruptible, and their matter unstable, souls are immortal and endure for ever; that, come from subtlest ether, they are entwined with the bodies that serve them as prisons, drawn down as they are by some physical spell; but that, when they are freed from the bonds of the flesh, liberated, so to speak, from long slavery, then they rejoice and rise up to the heavenly world.'[8] Those who 'clung to the commandments of God' revealed by the Messiah of holiness will be part of the New

Covenant, according to *The Damascus Document* of the Essenes, and they are promised 'everlasting life' and that 'theirs shall be the glory of Man'.[9] It is this 'Messiah of holiness' who taught them these commandments and offered the promise of eternal life. Thus they were awaiting 'the coming of the Teacher of Righteousness at the end of days'[10] as a fulfilment of this promise.

So it was the historical Messiah who, like Moses, handed God's commandments to the Israelites with the promise of eternal life. However, Christ's vision of the after-life differed from that of the Ancient Egyptians in that, while it was essential for the Egyptians to preserve the physical body by mummification and protected tombs, which could be afforded only by kings and rich men, in Christ's teaching all that was necessary to ensure spiritual survival was to believe.

Understandably, once his followers came out into the open, broke with the Jews and preached to the Gentiles, belief in Jesus spread rapidly throughout the world, particularly among the poor.

10

ECHOES FROM THE PAST

THE New Testament does not simply provide evidence that the Gospel stories are based on Old Testament stories, but that the events it describes occurred long before the start of the Christian era.

For example, after using a reference to Isaiah to report some of the activities of Jesus, the writer of the fourth Gospel goes on to say: 'These things said Esaias (Isaiah), when he saw his glory, and spake of him' (John, 12:41). Here the evangelist is saying that the prophet Isaiah, who lived six centuries before the start of the Christian era, saw Christ and spoke of him. Many scholars, puzzled by the implications of this passage, have suggested that Jesus must have had a spiritual pre-existence in Old Testament times: 'Where John appears to say that Isaiah saw Jesus's glory . . . commentators have agreed for the most part that there the pre-existent Christ seems to be envisaged as present in Old Testament events.'[1]

However, the historical evidence suggests that we are not dealing here with a spiritual, 'pre-existent' Christ, but that he had lived many centuries earlier and, after his death, believers were wont to experience some kind of spiritual encounter with him. This is clear from Paul's account of his own experience: '. . . I conferred not with flesh and blood' (Galatians, 1:16). In the same way, John is saying above that Isaiah saw the 'glory' of Jesus. The 'glory' of Christ indicates an eternal spiritual character, for Jesus is said to have achieved 'glory' only after his death and resurrection: '. . . God, that raised him up from the dead and gave him glory . . .' (I Peter, 1:21), and again: '. . . the sufferings of Christ and the glory that should follow' (I Peter, 1:11).

As with the Talmudic references to Jesus, there are strong

indications in the New Testament that the historical figure of Jesus was present with the Israelites in the wilderness of Sinai at the time of the Exodus. Paul makes this clear in his first Epistle to the Corinthians: 'Moreover, brethren, I would not that ye should be ignorant, how that all our fathers were under the cloud, and all passed through the sea; And were all baptized unto Moses in the cloud and in the sea; And did all eat the same spiritual meat; And did all drink the same spiritual drink: for they drank of that spiritual Rock that followed them: and that Rock was Christ' (I Corinthians, 10:1–4). This left no doubt in the minds of biblical scholars about what Paul was trying to say: 'It is much more likely that Paul here means that the Rock really was Christ . . . That is to say, he believed that the Messiah was in some form present with the people during this critical period in the wilderness . . .'[2] A. T. Hanson, Professor of Theology at the University of Hull in the post-war period, went even further: 'Paul frequently perplexes us by apparently throwing Christ's activity back into the Old Testament . . . he does not appear to be saying: "These texts were fulfilled centuries later in Christ." What he seems to be saying is: "This is what Christ says".'[3] Furthermore, commenting on II Corinthians, 3:7–18, where Paul refers to a passage in Exodus, 24:27–35, which describes what happened when Moses came down from the mountain with the two renewed tablets of the Law, he writes: 'Paul would read in this passage the narrative of the converse which Moses held with the pre-existent Christ in the tabernacle, and indeed he would probably draw the conclusion that it was Christ who had appeared to Moses on Mount Sinai . . .'[4] This would not only confirm the Gospel account of the meeting between Jesus and Moses on the mount, but make them meet again inside the Tabernacle, the tent for meetings that Moses built at the foot of Mount Sinai for worship.

The idea of the presence of Jesus having been with the Israelites in the Sinai wilderness is reinforced by Paul in his Epistle to the Hebrews where, after referring to the disobedient Israelites 'who left Egypt under Moses', he says: 'For unto us was the gospel preached, as well as unto them: but the word preached did not profit them, not being mixed with faith in them that heard it' (Hebrews, 4:2). Here 'we have a surprising inversion of what we would expect: we would quite understand if the author had said that the Israelites of old had heard the gospel (i.e., good news), just as we have. In fact, he says that we, too, have heard the gospel, just as *they* (my italics) had . . .'[5] The point Paul is making here is that the Gospel preached in the first century A.D. had been preached before.

John also confirms that Jesus was a contemporary of Moses when he quotes Jesus as telling the Jews of Jerusalem: 'For had ye believed Moses, ye would have believed me: for he wrote of me' (John, 5:46). He also attributes words to Philip, one of the disciples, mentioning the same fact: 'Philip findeth Nathanael, and saith unto him, We have found him, of whom Moses in the law, and the prophets, did write, Jesus of Nazareth, the son of Joseph' (John, 1:45). Therefore, Moses, according to John, did not prophesy concerning Jesus, but wrote about him in the Pentateuch, the first five books of the Old Testament.

Jesus – and this is particularly important – is also identified in the Bible as Joshua, who succeeded Moses as the leader of the Israelites. The most popularly used text of the Pentateuch concerning Christ is found in Deuteronomy: 'The Lord thy God will raise up unto thee a Prophet from the midst of thee, of thy brethren, like unto me; unto him ye shall hearken' (18:15). This is repeated in a slightly different form in the New Testament: 'For Moses truly said unto the fathers, A prophet shall the Lord your God raise up unto you of your brethren, like unto me; him shall ye hear in all things whatsoever he shall say unto you' (Acts, 3:22).

The Bible itself confirms that Moses was referring here to his successor, Joshua, which led early Christian authors to identify this Old Testament figure as the historical Christ. The Epistle to the Hebrews was the first New Testament book to name him: '. . . they to whom it was first preached entered not in because of unbelief . . . Today if ye will hear his voice, harden not your hearts . . . For if Jesus' – the King James Bible has the marginal note, 'That is, Joshua' – 'had given them rest, then would he not afterward have spoken of another day' (Hebrews, 4:6–8). This passage provides us with one Messianic character and two dates. There was a former time when the good news (about Joshua) was rejected, and those who hear his voice (his words) today should not do the same by hardening their hearts against his teaching.

The similarity of the names Joshua (*Ye-ho-shua* in Hebrew) and Jesus (*Ye-shua* in its short form), both of which have the same meaning, 'Yahweh (the Lord) is salvation', must have played a part in this identification. Greek translators of the Bible render both names as Jesus; in the later post-exilic period – after the return to Jerusalem from Babylon in the fifth century B.C. – and in the Books of Chronicles, Ezra and Nehemiah, the short form of Jesus is sometimes used for Joshua; the King James Bible, as we have seen, refers to Jesus with Joshua as a marginal note or vice versa, and many of the early Church Fathers of the second and third centuries A.D. accepted that they were one and the same person, including Justin Martyr, Irenaeus, Bishop of Lyon, Tertullian, Eusebius, Bishop of Caesarea and 'the father of Church history', and Origen, the most brilliant theologian of the third century A.D. Commenting on the passage (Exodus, 17:9) where Moses is first mentioned with Joshua, Origen makes clear his complete identification of Joshua as Jesus: '. . . let us observe what instructions Moses gave when war was imminent. It says: "He said to Jesus" – the King James Bible here gives Joshua with Jesus as a marginal note – "choose for yourself men and go and fight with Amalek tomorrow." Up to this point nowhere has there occurred a mention of the blessed man Jesus. Here first the brilliance of this name shone forth.'[6] Jesus and Joshua are also linked by various references to the latter in the Pentateuch as the 'son of Nun'. These are the only references in the Bible to 'Nun', a word which means 'fish', the traditional symbol of Christ.

11

DEATH IN THE WILDERNESS

THE Bible offers us two stories involving Jesus, Moses, a mountain and tabernacles, one in the New Testament, one in the Old. They are to be regarded as different versions of the same events.

In the New Testament account of the Transfiguration we are told that, shortly before his death, Jesus took the disciples Peter, James and John to a high mountain where 'he was transfigured before them', they saw him talking with Moses and Elias (Elijah), and Peter suggested that the disciples should make three tabernacles, one each for Jesus, Moses and Elijah. The Old Testament account is the one that relates how Moses received the Ten Commandments of the Lord on Mount Sinai, the holy mountain in the wilderness.

According to the Bible, the Israelites camped at the foot of Mount Sinai three months after the Exodus. There, says the Book of Exodus, Moses was summoned to meet the Lord on the mountain to receive tablets of stone bearing the Ten Commandments and 'Moses rose up, and his minister Joshua (Jesus): and Moses went up into the mount of God' (24:13). In his absence, the Israelites are said to have gathered together all their earrings, made a golden calf and worshipped it. As they descended from Mount Sinai, Moses and Joshua heard the noise of the subsequent celebrations and Joshua commented: 'the noise of them that sing do I hear' (32:18). Moses was so angry over what had happened while he was away that he cast down the tablets bearing the Ten Commandments and shattered them (32:19). The Lord therefore summoned him to a second meeting on the mountain to replace the broken tablets.

The God of Moses had neither shape nor image. In his first encounter with the Lord on the same mountain, before the supposed time of the Exodus, when Moses was attracted by the burning bush that was not consumed by the flames, he heard the voice of the Lord in his mind (3:4). Yet on the occasion of his journey to obtain replacement tablets inscribed with the Ten Commandments, we have an indication of a physical presence: 'And the Lord descended in the cloud, and stood with him there . . . And the Lord passed by before him' (34:5–6).

Here we have the Lord *standing* with Moses. The word for Lord in Hebrew (*Adon*) and Greek (*Kyrios*) can mean either the Lord in the sense of God or in the sense of master. In this case it has been taken by many scholars and by the apostle Paul, as we saw in the previous chapter, as indicating Jesus.

In addition to receiving the new tablets, Moses was told: 'The feast of unleavened bread' – the Passover – 'shalt thou keep. Seven days thou shalt eat unleavened bread, as I commanded thee, in the time of the month Abib (the Babylonian Nisan): for in the month Abib thou camest out from Egypt' (34:18). Moses again does not appear to have been alone when he came down from the mountain with the two new inscribed tablets. After their descent, Joshua entered the Tabernacle and Moses followed him a number of times, re-emerging to report to the Israelites what was happening inside. The account of these proceedings echoes the story of the Transfiguration found later in the New Testament: '. . . Moses wist not that the skin of his face shone while *he talked with him* (my italics). And when Aaron and all the children of Israel saw Moses, behold, the skin of his face shone . . . and Moses talked with them . . . And till Moses had done speaking with them, he put a vail on his face. But when Moses went in before the Lord to speak with him, he took the vail off, until he came out. And he came out, and spake unto the children of Israel that which he was commanded . . . and Moses put the vail upon his face again, until he went in to speak with him' (34:29–31, 33–5).

It was then, I believe, that Jesus was killed, *before*, not after, the actual Exodus, when Moses was in Sinai with only a handful of followers and some Midianite allies and the vast majority of Israelites were still in Egypt and cannot be said to have had any responsibility or even any possibility of being aware of events that have since haunted the Jewish race for more than three thousand years. Support for the view that this is where and when Jesus met his death is to be found in rabbinical tradition, which says of the occasion: 'According to . . . (Bava Batra 121a) it is the day on which Moses came down from Mount Sinai with the second tablets of the law'.[1]

In order to understand the circumstances, it is necessary to trace at this point the relationship between the Israelites and the royal house of Egypt and to identify some of the most important biblical figures by their Egyptian names.

Joseph the Patriarch, of the coat of many colours, who originally brought the tribe of Israel – his family – down to Egypt from Canaan in the fifteenth century B.C., was the grandson of Isaac and the favourite son of Jacob. He was sold into slavery in Egypt by his jealous half-brothers and was appointed as a minister early in the reign of the Pharaoh Tuthmosis IV (c.1413–1405 B.C.) after, according to the Old Testament, foretelling the seven good years that would be followed by seven years of famine. Joseph is to be identified as Yuya, who served as a minister to both Tuthmosis IV and his successor, Amenhotep III (c.1405–1367 B.C.).[2] Although there was no evidence to suggest that he might be of royal blood, the tombs of Yuya and his wife, Tuya, were found in the Valley of the Kings in the early years of this century.

Yuya's posts meant that he was resident in the royal palaces. The young prince who was to become Amenhotep III met and fell in love with Yuya's infant daughter, Tiye. On the death of his father, he married his sister, Sitamun, in order to inherit the throne, as was the Egyptian custom, but shortly afterwards also married Tiye and made her rather than Sitamun his Great Royal Wife (queen). Later, Tiye had a son, Tuthmosis, who disappeared in mysterious circumstances. Her second son – given the name Amenhotep, but remembered by the world as Moses[3] – was born, probably in 1394 B.C., at the fortified frontier city of Zarw on the eastern boundaries of Egypt proper. Zarw had been presented to Tiye by the king as a kind of summer palace where she could be near to her Israelite relations, who had been allowed to settle at Goshen in the Eastern Delta rather than Egypt itself because Asiatic shepherds had been 'anathema' to Egyptians since the successful invasion of Egypt by the Hyksos in the seventeenth century B.C.

The king gave instructions to the midwives in attendance upon Tiye that the child she was awaiting should be killed at birth if it proved to be a boy. The reason for the king's hostility was that Tiye was not the legitimate heiress and could not therefore, as was again the Egyptian custom, be accepted as the consort of the State god Amun. Furthermore, as she was of mixed Egyptian–Israelite

THE ISRAELITES AND THE ROYAL HOUSE OF EGYPT

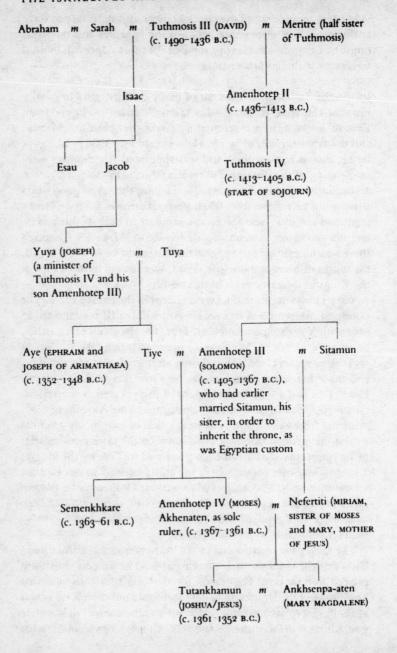

blood, her children could not, by Egyptian custom, be regarded as heirs to the throne. If her son succeeded to the throne, this would be regarded as forming a new dynasty of non-Egyptian, non-Amunite, part-Israelite rulers over Egypt. The midwives did not carry out the king's orders, and on learning – perhaps from the midwives themselves – of the threat to her new-born baby's life, Tiye sent him by water to the safe-keeping of her Israelite relations at nearby Goshen. This is the source of the biblical story of Moses being found by a princess in the bulrushes by the bank of the Nile: Zarw was largely surrounded by lakes and a branch of the Nile and connected by water with Goshen.

Amenhotep spent most of his youth in the Eastern Delta and at Heliopolis where he was educated by the priests of Ra, the ancient Egyptian solar deity, and also absorbed the traditional Israelite belief in a God without an image. The Aten, the God he would later introduce to Egypt, is depicted in paintings and sculptures as a circle sending rays that end in hands holding the Egyptian cross, the key of life, to the nostrils of the royal family. This is not a physical representation of the deity, but, like the Christian cross or Jewish star, a symbol, indicating salvation (as in Christianity), not the literal sun. At the Aten temple there was no physical representation to be addressed in prayer any more than the physical Ark of the Covenant, placed in the holy of holies in the Temple of Jerusalem, can be looked upon as an image of God. Nor can the Aten be identified with the sun god as this was either Ra or Atum.

It was not until he was a grown boy in his very early teens that Amenhotep was finally allowed to take up residence at Thebes, the capital city in Upper Egypt and the main centre of worship of the State god Amun. By this time the health of his father had begun to deteriorate and Tiye's power had increased correspondingly. In order to ensure her son's ultimate inheritance of the throne, she arranged for him to marry his half-sister, Nefertiti – the daughter of Amenhotep III by *his* sister, Sitamun, the legitimate heiress – and to be appointed co-regent, with special emphasis on Nefertiti's role in order to placate the priests and nobles.

The young Amenhotep, whose monotheistic religious ideas were already well developed, offended the Amunite priesthood from the start of the co-regency by building temples to his God, the Aten, at Karnak and Luxor. In a climate becoming increasingly hostile, Tiye eventually persuaded him to leave Thebes and found a new capital for himself at Tell el-Amarna, some two hundred miles to the north and roughly halfway between Thebes and modern Cairo. Amenhotep named his new city Akhetaten – the city of the horizon of the Aten – in honour of his new God. At Amarna his monotheistic ideas underwent further development and he also changed his name from Amenhotep IV to Akhenaten in honour of his deity. The co-regency came to an end upon the death of his father in Akhenaten's Year 12. At the start of his five years of sole rule in 1367 B.C., Akhenaten shut down the temples of the ancient gods of Egypt, cut off all financial support for them and sent the priests home. These actions caused such bitter resentment that in his Year 15 Akhenaten was forced to install his brother, Semenkhkare, as his co-regent at Thebes. This action served only to delay the eventual crisis. Although some Egyptians had been converted to worship of the Aten, Akhenaten was warned in his Year 17 by his minister Aye – who was also his uncle, the second son of Yuya – of the threat of an army rebellion and a plot against the king's life. Aye advised a compromise, allowing the old gods of Egypt to be worshipped alongside the Aten. The king refused. Instead, he abdicated – and fled to the safety of Sinai, accompanied by a small group of followers and taking with him his symbol of pharaonic authority, a staff topped by a brass serpent. Sinai was in those days a stone-mining area. Akhenaten (Moses), on arriving there, built his Tabernacle, the Tent of the Congregation, at the foot of the holy mountain.

His successor, Semenkhkare, did not survive him for long – perhaps only a few days – and was succeeded in his turn by the young king Tutankhaten, the son of Akhenaten (Moses). As can be seen from the scene on the back of the throne seat found in his tomb in the Valley of the Kings, the new Pharaoh followed his father in the worship of the Aten as the one God, but he reopened the ancient temples, allowed the worship of the old gods of Egypt and changed his name to Tutankhamun in honour of the State god Amun.

Tutankhamun ruled for at least nine, and perhaps ten, years (c. 1361–1352 B.C.) before meeting an early death, whereupon he was succeeded by Aye (Ephraim), his great-uncle and the last of the four Amarna kings. Aye ruled for only four years before he disappeared. Nothing much is known about his death as his mummy – if he was ever mummified – was never found, while the tomb he had excavated for himself in the Valley of the Kings, not far from that of Tutankhamun, was usurped by his successor, Horemheb, an army general who secured his seat on the throne by marrying Queen Nefertiti's sister, Mutnezmet.

The bitterness that divided the country at this period is indicated by the actions of Horemheb, who is to be looked upon as the biblical Pharaoh of the Oppression. Worship of the Aten was abolished. The names of the Amarna kings were excised from king lists and monuments in a studied campaign to try to remove all traces of their rule from Egyptian memory, and it was forbidden on pain of death even to mention the name of Akhenaten. Therefore, his followers referred to him as *Mos*, a term used in Egyptian legal cases at this period to signify the rightful son and heir.

The small group of followers who accompanied Moses into exile in Sinai – not to be confused with the later Exodus – included the Amarna priesthood. Among them was Panehesy, who had been the Chief Servitor and Second Priest of the Aten (the Lord) at Akhenaten's temple in Amarna. The Hebrew equivalent of this name is Phinehas (Pinhas), the priest named in the Talmud as having struck down Jesus.

12

THE SCARLET THREAD

THAT an Israelite leader was killed in Sinai – an event the German biblical scholar Ernest Sellin has described as 'the scarlet thread' running through Israelite history – is not a new idea. The identity of the victim has been obscured, however, by an elaborate attempt to hide the true facts. This is particularly clear from a chapter in the Book of Numbers, which was largely responsible for persuading Sellin that the assassination took place during the time of the Exodus from Egypt and that Moses was the victim.

The story in Numbers follows an account of how Israel was locked in combat with Moab and Midian (tribes living to the south and east of the Dead Sea and in Sinai) and Balaam's prediction of a victory over the Moabites. It goes on to relate how a number of Israelites began 'to commit whoredom' (25:1) with Moabite women, who invited them to 'the sacrifices of their gods: and the people did eat, and bowed down to their gods' (25:2). This, it is said, angered the Lord (25:3). Then 'one of the children of Israel came and brought unto his brethren a Midianitish woman in the sight of Moses, and in the sight of all the congregation of the children of Israel, who were weeping before the door of the tabernacle of the congregation. And when Phinehas, the son of Eleazar, the son of Aaron the priest, saw it, he rose up from among the congregation, and took a javelin in his hand; And he went after the man of Israel into the tent (Tabernacle), and thrust both of them through, the man of Israel, and the woman . . .' (25:6–8).

For these actions, Phinehas is presented to us as a hero. As a result, a 'plague' that had cost the lives of twenty-four thousand people was brought to an end, and the Lord spoke to Moses, saying: 'Phinehas, the son of Eleazar, the son of Aaron the priest, hath turned my wrath away from the children of Israel, while he

was zealous for my sake among them, that I consumed not the
children of Israel in my jealousy. Wherefore say, Behold, I give
unto him my covenant of peace; And he shall have it, and his
seed after him, even the covenant of an everlasting priesthood;
because he was zealous for his God, and made an atonement for
the children of Israel' (25:11–13). A few verses later the victims
are identified as minor figures – Zimri and Cozbi, the son and
daughter respectively of two chief houses.

If one analyses this account, it is easy to see why Sellin suspected
that it had been subjected to some priestly sleight-of-hand in the
editing in order to cover up what had actually happened. An
ordinary Israelite would not have taken a foreign woman into
the inner room of the Tabernacle, where only a king or high
priest was allowed; there is no mention of the man in this case
worshipping another god; making love to a woman was not
punishable by death; Moses, the Israelite leader, did not give any
orders for action against the man, and, if the male victim was a
minor figure, why would it require revenge in the form of the
death of twenty-four thousand people? It is no wonder that Sellin
commented that 'despite the efforts of the priests to suppress the
sordid story, it nevertheless lived on in prophetic circles'.

It is clear that, as what is described as a plague is mentioned only
after Phinehas had committed his killing, it was a punishment for
the assassination, not for consorting with foreign women. Paul
had this in mind when, after indicating that Christ was present
with the Israelites in Sinai, he went on to say: 'But with many of
them God was not well pleased . . . and fell in one day three and
twenty thousand' (I Corinthians, 10:5,8). This understanding is
reinforced by the evidence available from the Dead Sea Scrolls. The
Commentary on Habakkuk, one of the Qumran texts, tells us that,
after the Wicked Priest had killed the Teacher of Righteousness, 'he
(the Teacher) appeared before them to swallow them up'.[1]

'Swallow up' is a Hebrew metaphor for 'do away with' or 'kill'.
As for the appearance of the Teacher after death, 'the Hebrew
verb used here may also be translated as "he revealed himself to
them"'[2] – indicating a spiritual rather than a historical experience.

Further support for the theory that the 'plague' which followed
the Sinai assassination was a form of punishment is also to be
found in the Book of Hosea, where this punishment is said
to have been carried out by Ephraim: 'When Ephraim spake

trembling' – the sense here, given in other translations, is 'caused others to tremble' – 'he exalted himself in Israel . . .' (13:1).

It is also curious that Phinehas should have been rewarded with 'the covenant of a perpetual priesthood to him and his descendants after him' when we know from the previous book in the Pentateuch, Leviticus, that this promise had already been made to Aaron and his descendants.

Although Sellin was right in the dating of these events, he was mistaken about the identity of the victim. They occurred *before* the Exodus and Moses was not himself killed until two decades later. He was thirty-four or thirty-five when he fled to the safety of Sinai after his abdication in 1361 B.C. There, according to the Old Testament, he formed an alliance with the Midianites, who are to be identified in Egyptian history as the Shasu,[3] nomadic bedouin tribes of Sinai, some of whom were converted to worship of the Aten.

Back in Egypt in the meantime, Horemheb, the Pharaoh of the Oppression,[4] had turned the area around the fortified frontier city of Zarw, where Moses had been born, into a prison. There he gathered the mass of Akhenaten's followers, including the Israelites, who had embraced his monotheistic beliefs, and a variety of criminals, who lived in villages outside the city walls. Horemheb appointed Pa-Ramses, the head of his army, as mayor of Zarw as well as giving him responsibility for the local military garrison. It was Pa-Ramses, on Horemheb's orders, who inflicted harsh labour on the Israelites and other prisoners by forcing them to rebuild Zarw as well as a new residence for himself, known later as Pi-Ramses, the starting point of the Exodus, according to the Old Testament. Pi-Ramses also became the main residence in the Eastern Delta for Pharaohs of the Nineteenth and Twentieth Egyptian Dynasties.

The death of Horemheb left Egypt without a legitimate heir to the Eighteenth Dynasty. Pa-Ramses, by now an old man, therefore prepared to claim the throne for himself as the first ruler of a new dynasty, the Nineteenth. Moses, who had been in hiding in the wilderness for slightly more than a quarter of a century, decided to try to reclaim his throne from Ramses, who is described in the Old Testament as 'the king who knew not Joseph'. He made his way to Zarw where his challenge as the rightful ruler had to be decided by Egyptian priests and elders. With the aid of his sceptre topped by a brass serpent, the symbol of pharaonic authority,

Moses was able to establish his identity as the son of Amenhotep III, and the Egyptian priests and elders, who are called 'magicians' in the Bible, accepted his claim. However, Ramses, because of his military authority, was too powerful to be overthrown and became the first ruler of the Nineteenth Dynasty by a kind of *coup d'état*. At this point, realizing that his life was at stake, Moses fled again to the safety of Sinai, taking his followers with him, including the Israelite tribes, from the villages outside the walls of Zarw. *This* was the biblical Exodus.

Moses and his followers made their way to Sinai via the marshy area to the south of Zarw and north of Lake Temsah and present-day Ismailia. This watery route was chosen to hinder pursuit: Egyptian chariots would become stuck in the mud whereas the Israelites, travelling on foot, would be able to cross safely. This is the possible time and location for the biblical account of the pursuing Pharaoh who was drowned. Egyptian sources provide no evidence of this event, but it is certain that the short reign of Ramses I (c. 1335–1333 B.C.) came to an end upon his death at this very time.

Now faced with the problem of a large number of followers in need of food and water, Moses abandoned his plan to head for Mount Sinai and, instead, went north on the ancient Road of Horus that connected Zarw on the borders of Egypt with the Canaanite city of Gaza. Along the road were settlements with water wells, guarded by military posts. According to Deuteronomy, Moses was eventually not allowed to enter the Promised Land and was killed by the Lord because 'ye trespassed against me . . . at the waters of Meribah-Kadesh in the wilderness . . .' (32:51). Moses had not been forbidden to obtain water for his followers, which cannot in any case be regarded as a sinful act. The implication is that Moses secured water from the wells along the Road of Horus. This could have been done easily by force, although it seems more likely that force was not necessary: he still had his brass sceptre of authority, and it is hardly to be imagined that a garrison commander would challenge the wishes of a former king whom he regarded as the Son of Ra.

Realizing that a fertile land was needed to feed his large following, Moses next marched north towards Gaza and attempted to storm the city, seemingly joined by some of his bedouin Shasu allies in the assault. News of these events was reported to Egypt. Seti I, the son and successor of Ramses I, did not even wait for his late father's mummification, a process that took seventy days, before marching against Moses, the Israelites and the Shasu. He met and defeated them at many locations on the Horus road as well as in central Sinai. There was great slaughter among the Shasu, large numbers of whom were also captured and taken back to Egypt to be sacrificed at the feet of the god Amun-Ra at the Karnak temple. It is likely that Moses was killed by Seti himself in the course of these military operations.

The introduction of Ephraim, whom I have identified[5] as Aye, into the story of the slaughter that followed the assassination of the Israelite leader in Sinai, is a further indication that these events took place between the flight of Akhenaten (Moses) to the safety of Sinai after his abdication and his return to Egypt a quarter of a century later in a vain attempt to reclaim his throne. Aye disappeared from the Egyptian scene in 1348 B.C., thirteen years before Ramses I came to the throne. During the reign of the young king Tutankhamun, when he was the king's vizier and Master of the King's Horses, Commander of the Chariots and Chief of the Bowmen, and again during his own reign, he was the most powerful man in Egypt, and thus in a position to inflict heavy punishment on those responsible for the death of Jesus.

If we now take a closer look at some of the events described in the Book of Exodus we find further indications of the true identity of the Israelite leader who met his death at the foot of Mount Sinai. At the time that Moses made his first journey, accompanied by Joshua (Jesus), up the mountain to receive the Ten Commandments, there is an indication that a measure of discord existed as a result of the behaviour of the occupants of the Israelite camp below. The Lord is quoted as saying to Moses: 'I have seen this people, and, behold, it is a stiffnecked people' (32:9).

The absence of the name of Joshua (Jesus) from the account of Moses's second visit to the mountain, to replace the broken tablets from his first visit, is suspicious when we also have the suggestion that Moses met and talked with the Lord on the mountain. It seems a somewhat clumsy attempt to remove Joshua from the scene, although we are at the same time assured that 'Joshua . . . did not depart from the tent (Tabernacle)'. The admonition to Moses by the Lord on this occasion that 'seven days shalt thou eat unleavened bread' also echoes the story in the Bible and the Talmud that Jesus met his death on the eve of the Passover (the Jewish day lasted from one sunset to the next).

Once Moses returned to the foot of Mount Sinai, the attempt to remove Joshua (Jesus) from the scene collapses. Moses, whose face shone and was 'vailed' when he spoke to the Israelites, is depicted as acting as a go-between, talking to the Israelites outside the Tabernacle, wearing his veil, but removing the veil when he enters the Tabernacle. Who was he talking to inside this sacred shrine? We have already been told that Joshua (Jesus) 'did not depart from the tent (Tabernacle)'. Yet it is clear from the sequence of events that the person within the Tabernacle had a higher authority than that of Moses, otherwise the latter would not have been acting as a go-between. When Moses was the acknowledged leader of the Israelites, who could the person in the Tabernacle have been other than Jesus?

Finally, it is also strange that, from this point, both Joshua and Phinehas disappear from the Exodus account, despite the promise to the latter that he and his descendants would enjoy the covenant of an everlasting priesthood. Yet both surface again later as part of the elaborate priestly attempt to conceal what actually happened at the foot of Mount Sinai in the fourteenth century B.C.

13

COVER-UP

THE killing of Joshua (Jesus) was always remembered by those who believed in him and later became his followers. On the other hand, the official priesthood subsequently made deliberate efforts to conceal both the killing and the date when it took place.

After Moses and his closest followers left Egypt they observed in celebration, as the Lord commanded them, the feast of the Passover: 'Thou shalt keep the feast of unleavened bread: (thou shalt eat unleavened bread seven days . . . in the time appointed of the month Abib (Nisan); for in it thou camest out from Egypt . . .)' (Exodus, 23:15). The Passover, originally an Egyptian spring festival, was observed for seven days, from the fifteenth to the twenty-first day of Abib, Babylonian Nisan, then the first month of the Israelite year. Later, after the death of Jesus, on the eve of the Passover, the fourteenth day of Abib, the Israelites offered, in accordance with the instructions of Moses, a sacrificial lamb in atonement for the killing of their Messiah and asked for God's forgiveness: 'Thou shalt therefore sacrifice the passover unto the Lord thy God, of the flock and the herd . . . thou shalt sacrifice the passover at even (evening), at the going down of the sun, at the season that thou camest forth out of Egypt' (Deuteronomy, 16:2,6).

For their part, the Essenes, who took the view that they had nothing to feel guilty about and looked upon Christ as their sacrificial lamb, did not offer a sacrifice of atonement. Instead, on the same day – the fourteenth day of Abib – they held a Messianic Banquet in anticipation of the return of their dead Teacher of Righteousness at the end of the world when he would celebrate the meal with them. This Messianic Banquet bears a strong resemblance to the Last Supper when, on Maundy Thursday, the eve of the Crucifixion, Christ is said to have instituted the

Christian sacrament of Communion. According to the Qumran
texts the priest '. . . [will bl]ess the first of the bread and win[e and
will stretch forth] his hand on the bread first. And after[wards] the
Messiah will str[etch forth] his hands upon the bread, [and then]
all the Congregation of the Community [will give bles]sings, each
[according to] his rank. And after this prescription shall they act
for every ass[embly where] at least ten men are assembled.'[1]
Christians, too, later rid themselves of animal sacrifice because they
regarded Jesus himself as the sacrifice: 'For even the Son of man
came not to be ministered unto, but to minister, and to give his
life a ransom for many' (Mark, 10:45) and '. . . Behold the Lamb
of God, which taketh away the sins of the world' (John, 1:29).

After the death of Moses and their entry into the Promised
Land, the Israelites spent centuries as small groups, scattered
around Canaan without any central authority or central place of
worship. During these years, as the great majority of Israelites
forsook the God of Moses for Canaanite and Phoenician deities,
the Passover feast was not observed except by a few people who
celebrated it privately. This changed after the Babylonian exile in
the sixth century B.C. In exile, the priestly scribes put down in their
present form the books of the Pentateuch which had originated at
the time of Moses. Some of them gave the date of the Passover
as 'the first month', others as Nisan. This would not have caused
any confusion had the priests not, in exile, adopted the Babylonian
lunar calendar in place of the solar calendar used previously. As a
result, for purposes of this calendar, Tishri (September–October),
originally the seventh month of the Israelites' year, became the first
month of a new calendar.

Originally, both the Day of Atonement and Passover were
observed as one feast in Abib (Nisan), the previous first month
which had now become the seventh month. No separate date is
given for Atonement in the feast list of Ezekiel, the priest and
prophet who served in the Jerusalem Temple before its destruction
by the Babylonians in 586 B.C. (Ezekiel, 45:18–25). However, recognizing that confusion existed about which was the right *month* in
which to observe the two religious occasions – the old first month,
Nisan, or the new first month, Tishri – Ezekiel divided the year
into two parts with the religious observances of the first month
repeated in the seventh. Then, about half a century after the return
from Babylon, priests took advantage of the situation to establish a

separate Atonement day from the Passover. While the Passover continued to be celebrated in Nisan, the Day of Atonement was observed in Tishri: 'Now in the twenty and fourth day of this month (Tishri) the children of Israel were assembled with fasting, and with sackclothes, and earth upon them' (Nehemiah, 9:1). The significance of the Day of Atonement was also changed. Whereas it had been introduced originally as a day of repentance for the killing of the Messiah, it now became the occasion for general repentance for sin.

Today, the Day of Atonement, Yom Kippur, the most solemn day of fasting in the Jewish calendar, is observed on the tenth day of Tishri. This is the result of editors adding two passages to the Pentateuch in which they reverted to the old calendar in which Tishri had been the seventh month: '. . . on the tenth day of this seventh month there shall be a day of atonement: it shall be an holy convocation unto you; and ye shall afflict your souls . . .' (Leviticus, 23:27),[2] and: '. . . ye shall have on the tenth day of this seventh month an holy convocation; and ye shall afflict your souls . . .' (Numbers, 29:7). This attempt to cover up the crime of Phinehas would probably have succeeded but for the Essenes working in secret to keep the memory and precepts of their Teacher of Righteousness alive until the day of his return.

If Jesus (Joshua) died at the foot of Mount Sinai, we should not expect to hear of his being alive after this date. However, Joshua then disappears entirely from the scene until the last book of the Pentateuch, Deuteronomy, mentions him as the leader who succeeded Moses: 'And Joshua the son of Nun was full of the spirit of wisdom; for Moses had laid his hands upon him: and the children of Israel hearkened unto him . . .' (34:9). This is followed by an entire book devoted to an account of Joshua's exploits, including the conquest of Canaan as a result of a swift military campaign at the head of the united tribes of Israel in the thirteenth century B.C. Although this account has gained popular acceptance, it is – as we shall see – a complete fiction, void of any historical validity, and simply part of the plan to cloud the circumstances surrounding his death. It cannot be supported by either modern biblical criticism or archaeological evidence.

The Book of Joshua is the first of what are known as the Former Prophets or Historical Books. It consists of three main sections – the conquest of Canaan (chapters 1–12); division of the conquered territory between the twelve tribes of Israel (13–21); and negotiations with tribes to the east of the Jordan, followed by the covenant at Shecham (22–24). Modern biblical scholars have recognized, for example, that the military campaigns described in the opening twelve chapters do not represent a single unified campaign but are a compilation of several ancient battle stories, originally not related and some pre-dating the Israelite period.

Martin Noth, the German biblical scholar, was the first to expose the fact that there had been a priestly cover-up. He demonstrated in 1966 that the fifth book of the Pentateuch, Deuteronomy, and the books of the Former Prophets or Historical Books, from Joshua to Kings, are the product of a priestly editor, who became known as the Deuteronomic redactor. This work was carried out during the sixth century B.C. at the time of the Babylonian exile. This was about the same time that Isaiah (II) was claiming that the defeat, humiliation and exile of the Israelites was a punishment for their killing of the Servant of the Lord, their Messiah.

What better way to refute this charge than to produce the Servant, still alive after the death of Moses and the victorious conqueror of the Promised Land? Even Phinehas, who all the indications suggest was among the thousands said to have been slaughtered on the Day of Atonement, was kept alive. He is named as one of Joshua's followers in the account of the latter's conquest of the Promised Land. His death was never reported and he even surfaces again in the Book of Judges, which deals with events that took place nearly three and a half centuries later: 'And Phinehas, the son of Eleazar, the son of Aaron, stood before it (the Ark of the Covenant) in those days saying, Shall I yet again go out to battle against the children of Benjamin my brother, or shall I cease? And the Lord said, Go up; for tomorrow I will deliver them into thine hand' (20:28).

Although more than seven centuries had passed, the Deuteronomic editor must have known of the traditions that lay behind Isaiah's account of the death of the Servant and the claim of the Talmudic rabbis that 'Pinhas killed Jesus'. Yet he chose to exclude such traditions from his work and rearranged events to suggest that Joshua was still alive at the time of the conquest of Canaan. Apart from modern biblical criticism, the archaeological evidence also makes it clear that the account of Joshua's conquest of the Promised Land as part of a swift military campaign cannot be a true recital of events.

14

AND THE WALLS CAME
TUMBLING DOWN

THE swift military campaigns ascribed to Joshua cannot have taken place in the thirteenth century B.C. because two of the cities said to have been sacked by him had been destroyed earlier and the other two were not destroyed until later.

The accounts of these campaigns in the first twelve chapters of the Book of Joshua tell us that the Israelites began by crossing the River Jordan from east to west opposite the ancient city of Jericho, which was in a state of siege. They took it and 'utterly destroyed all that was in the city' after, in a seemingly miraculous manner, its walls came tumbling down (Joshua, 6:20–1). Another ancient Canaanite city, Ai, west of Jericho and north of Jerusalem, became the next target of the Israelite invaders. At the first attempt, when about three thousand men tried to take the city, they were defeated and forced to flee. Joshua then resorted to another plan. He divided his army into two. Part of it lay in ambush between Bethel, another fortified city a few miles north-west of Ai, and Ai itself. In the ensuing battle, Joshua, pretending that his forces had been defeated, withdrew, pursued by the men of Ai. At a signal, the army waiting in ambush fell upon the city, entering from the west through the open and now unprotected gate, set it on fire and sacked it. In the meantime, Joshua advanced to renew the battle with the King of Ai's army and defeated them (Joshua, 8:21).

After this campaign, Joshua is said to have been approached to make a peace covenant with the Hivites, who dwelled in the four cities of Gibeon – Gibeon, Chepirah, Beeroth and Kiriath-Jearim – to the south-west of Ai and north-west of Jerusalem. Once this covenant had been completed, however, Joshua found himself facing a new threat from Adoni-Zedek, the King of

Jerusalem, who arranged an alliance of five Amorite kings of the Judaean hills and lowland – Jerusalem, Hebron, Jarmuth, Lachish and Eglon – to fight the united Israelite tribes. Joshua, who had returned to his base city of Gilgal, a few miles north of Jericho, marched against the alliance in another successful campaign, which included the destruction of Lachish. He took the city 'on the second day, and smote it with the edge of the sword, and all the souls that were therein . . .' (Joshua, 10:32).

After returning to his camp at Gilgal, Joshua learned that the opposition to the Israelites was not yet over. He found himself facing another alliance, this time of the northern kings of Hazor, Madon, Shimron and Achshaph: 'And when all these kings were met together, they came and pitched together at the waters of Merom, to fight against Israel' (Joshua, 11:5). In the subsequent battle, Joshua recorded another distinguished victory in the course of which he 'took Hazor, and smote the king thereof with the sword: for Hazor beforetime was the head of all those kingdoms. And they smote all the souls that were therein with the edge of the sword, utterly destroying them: there was not any left to breathe: and he burnt Hazor with fire' (Joshua, 11:10–11).

The description of these battles concludes with a list of the conquered Canaanite cities and their kings, numbering in all thirty-one, whose territory was divided among the tribes of Israel.

The remains of Jericho, now known as Tell el-Sultan, are about a mile north-west of modern Jericho and four and a half miles to the west of the River Jordan on the road to Jerusalem. Jericho was a very ancient city, dating back as far as 8000 B.C. It was surrounded by a stone wall six and a half feet thick and guarded by a thirty-foot stone watchtower, and is the earliest known example of a city with such massive fortifications.

In the course of its long history, the city and its walls were destroyed and rebuilt many times. In the Middle Bronze Age II (nineteenth–seventeenth century B.C.), for example, its defences included a huge bank of beaten earth on the slopes of the tell (hill), supported at its foot by a massive stone retaining wall, twenty feet high. These kinds of fortifications are typical of the time of the Hyksos, who invaded Egypt around 1659 B.C., ruled for slightly more than a century and had Jericho under their control at this period. After the kings of Egypt's Eighteenth Dynasty expelled the Hyksos and pursued them into western Asia, they destroyed

Jericho and its fortifications during the fifteenth century B.C. There is no evidence that the city itself or its walls were rebuilt for many centuries after this destruction: 'Thus there was settlement on the tell from about 1400 to 1325 B.C., or even for a generation or so longer. Thereafter the earliest evidence for renewed settlement is isolated pottery vessels dating from *the eleventh into the tenth century* B.C.'[1] (my italics).

So, at the time of the supposed invasion by Joshua in the second half of the thirteenth century B.C., neither the city of Jericho nor its walls existed. Accordingly, some scholars came to the conclusion that the biblical tradition was a story attempting to provide a cause for the earlier destruction of the city.

A similar problem arises over Joshua's next campaign – the conquest of Ai (modern el-Tell). Excavations have shown that a large city existed there in the early Canaanite period, but it was destroyed in the Early Bronze Age, in about 2350 B.C., and was not resettled until the Early Iron Age (twelfth century B.C.) when a village was established on the site. The newcomers were then mainly farmers, trying to secure a living in the inhospitable hills of central Canaan: 'This discovery indicates that, in the time of Joshua, the site was waste (also implied by the name Ai, literally ruin). Scholars explain the discrepancy in various ways. Some consider the narrative of the conquest of Ai contained in the Book of Joshua an aetiological story which developed in order to explain the ancient ruins of the city and its fortifications.'[2]

After early excavation of the site of Lachish (modern Tell el-Duweir) in southern Canaan between 1932 and 1938 it was thought that the evidence unearthed made it possible for destruction of the city to have taken place during the reign of Merenptah (c. 1237–1227 B.C.), fourth ruler of the Nineteenth Dynasty, during the second half of the thirteenth century B.C., which would have made it possible to argue that Joshua's account was correct. However, when 'Professor Ussishkin renewed excavations at Lachish in 1973 establishing the correct date for this destruction was one of his main objectives. He was to be unusually lucky in this respect. In 1978 a deep probe into destruction levels of the last Canaanite town at the site of a city gate revealed a cast-bronze fragment bearing the name of the Egyptian Pharaoh Ramses III in a cache of bronze objects sealed by production debris. Thus the destruction could not have occurred before the accession of Ramses III to the throne of Egypt

(c. 1182 B.C.) . . . Such a substantial bronze fitting, likely to be from an architectural setting, even if allowed a minimum life, makes it likely that Lachish was devastated some time in the second quarter of the twelfth century B.C.'[3]

After defeating Jabin, king of Hazor and head of the coalition against the Israelites, Joshua is said to have burned his city – and his city alone (Joshua, 11:10–13). Hazor (modern Tell el-Qidah) was a large Canaanite city nearly nine miles north of the Sea of Galilee and strategically situated to dominate the main branches of the Way of the Sea, the road leading from Egypt to Syria, Mesopotamia and Anatolia. Yigael Yadin, an Israeli archaeologist and former Chief of Staff of the Israel Defence Forces, who is also one of those scholars who believes that every word in the Bible is to be taken literally, carried out excavations in the area from 1955 to 1958 and again in 1968.

On the basis of some tenuous arguments about ashes from an incense-altar and the absence of Mycenaean pottery at the site (see Appendix B), Yadin placed the time of the destruction of Hazor as 'most probably . . . some time in the second third of the thirteenth century B.C. (that is, during the reign of Ramses II)'.[4] This is at odds with all historical records, which snow that Palestine was completely under Egyptian control at the period in question, with a number of military posts in the area.

Yadin has not produced a shred of evidence to prove that Hazor was conquered by Joshua during the second half of the thirteenth century B.C. The fact that Hazor was mentioned by Ramses III (c. 1182–1151 B.C.) in his Temple of Amun at Karnak indicates both that the city was still in existence and under his control during his reign as well as the possibility that Hazor, like so many other sites in Syria/Palestine, was actually destroyed later by the Peoples of the Sea, the Philistines, against whom Ramses III fought a war in the same area.

Of the story of Joshua's supposed swift military campaign, the *Encyclopaedia Judaica* says: 'Most scholars believe that the stories of the battles (mentioned in the Book of Joshua) originally were related to individual tribes and were only associated with Joshua, and with Israel as a whole, at a later period.'[5]

And commenting on the destruction of the Canaanite cities, the British archaeologist John Romer had this to say as recently as 1988: '(Kathleen) Kenyon (the British archaeologist) had also found that during the Early Iron Age, the period which was the only possible time for the first Israelite Settlements in Canaan, the city of Jericho had been largely deserted, having been in a state of destruction since the destruction of the last Bronze Age city 300 years before. Joshua and his Israelites would have found little more than a poor village atop an ancient hill, when they arrived at Jericho, a state of affairs that has since been confirmed in excavations at other cities which, the Bible tells us, were also visited by Joshua and his army.

'All of this was a serious blow to the historians who had long been carefully gathering up archaeological evidence of a systematic invasion and destruction of all the cities of Canaan, and keying their evidence in with biblical accounts of the Israelite invasion. Now it appeared that the destruction of these cities had been earlier and more random than had previously been imagined. Several attempts have been made to salvage their theory by what might best be described as moving the goalposts; the archaeology was re-dated so that Joshua and the Israelites would find someone to fight on their arrival. But most scholars were agreed that the known archaeological facts called for a fresh look at our understanding of these Bible stories.'⁶

The doubts about Joshua's campaign have led some scholars to question whether he ever existed. However, what is to be doubted is the Deuteronomic account. The aim of Deuteronomic history has been explained as an attempt to show that God's promise, already found in the Pentateuch, of Israelite possession of the Promised Land, had been fulfilled. The compiler recalled ancient traditions to illustrate God's work through history, not to present history itself. It was a theological interpretation designed to renew faith at a time of great difficulty.

It is no wonder that the Qumran Essenes took the view that the Jerusalem priests were falsifying the Scriptures.

15

THE GOSPELS

THE four authors of the Gospels were evangelists, not historians. Their purpose was to preach the basic Christian message – Christ has died, Christ is risen, Christ will come again – and to show that every event in the life of Jesus Christ came as a fulfilment of an earlier Old Testament prophecy.

Although many gospels of Christ existed in the early history of the Church, only the four included in the New Testament – those of Matthew, Mark, Luke and John – were finally accepted as authentic by the Council of Trent in 1546. Even the Gospel of Thomas, discovered in the Upper Egyptian town of Nag Hammadi in 1945, has been rejected by the Vatican as heretical.

Mark, who is named in Acts and in four epistles as a companion of Peter and Paul, is thought to have been the author of the earliest of the four canonical Gospels. The exact date is not known, but biblical scholars generally tend to place it in the last quarter of the first century A.D. As there is evidence that both Matthew and Luke relied on Mark, plus other sources, it has come to be accepted that they should be dated after him. Matthew has been dated to the first half of the second century A.D. Lucan references, especially those relating to the birth of Jesus, did not feature in the writings of the Church Fathers until the second half of that century, followed in the same period by John, the least historically minded of the four evangelists.

Yet it is evident that all of them must have relied on an earlier common source and a variety of traditions for their accounts. Mark, for instance, if the first of the four authors, cannot have been an eye-witness of the events he was describing. Neither can Matthew, Luke and John, who followed him later. Mark could, of course, have had the benefit of second-hand information from

Peter and third-hand from Paul. Yet his Gospel account includes information that is absent from the writings of Peter and Paul. Where did he obtain it?

'It has been argued since the end of the last century that there existed in the Church from the very beginning collections of Old Testament quotations which were used by the Fathers in debate and teaching. The theory has some backing from similar collections in use by the Church of later times, which may well . . . be based on much earlier documents . . . It now seems that we have from Qumran important support for the idea in a pre-Christian collection of eschatological testimonia.'[1]

It is clear from the evidence that we have examined so far that the four authors of the canonical Gospels must have drawn on a variety of sources – Israelite traditions, the Old Testament, the practices of the Essenes and their belief in an after-life, the life and death of John the Baptist, the claim by John the Baptist's followers that they had seen Jesus, which they may have done in a vision, and the political upheavals of the first century A.D. – to compile their stories, in which they placed the life of Jesus in Galilee at this period and related him to Herod, Caiaphas and Pilate.

Naming Bethlehem as the birthplace of Jesus was the result of a desire to demonstrate fulfilment of one of the Old Testament prophecies. There was a strong Jewish tradition that the Christ would be born as a descendant of King David, who was known to have been born at Bethlehem in Judaea. Therefore, both Matthew and Luke, who provide accounts of the nativity of Jesus, place his birth in Bethlehem and Matthew (2:5) cites the account in Micah (5:2) in support of his statement. Here again we also find another example of the extent to which the Gospels rely on the Old Testament for their content. The Old Testament does not provide any details of the birth of Jesus: Matthew therefore adapted the Old Testament account of events surrounding the birth of Moses, with Herod instead of Pharaoh ordering the death 'of all children from two years old and under'.

The association of Jesus with Galilee, which has no echo in the Old Testament, is connected to the political situation in the first century A.D. Paul, who was converted to Christianity about 35 A.D., never related Jesus either to Galilee or to John the Baptist: nor did Peter in his Epistles. It was Mark, writing in the last quarter of the first century A.D., who, not having mentioned Bethlehem at all, locates the ministry of Jesus in Galilee and describes his going to Judaea only once – when he entered Jerusalem to meet his end.

This brings us to the curious account of the role that Judas Iscariot is said to have played in the betrayal of Jesus. The narrative tells us that Christ had been in Jerusalem for days prior to his arrest, teaching in the Temple. The Jewish authorities could therefore have laid hands upon him whenever they wanted to. It is not possible to justify their failure to do so by arguing that they feared the anger of the people: only a day later, after Jesus had been arrested and imprisoned, these same people are said to have refused to have him set free, demanding instead that he be crucified.

No mention of Judas as the betrayer is to be found in any of the Epistles, indicating that attribution of this act to him was a later interpretation of events. Furthermore, Iscariot has been taken as indicating the location to which Judas belonged. This is not the correct meaning. As the corresponding Greek verb means 'to deliver up', the word can only have been used as an epithet, 'Judas the Deliverer'. This meaning is reinforced by the fact that 'the Syrian *skariot* is an epithet equivalent to the Hebrew *sikkarti*, I shall deliver up'.[2]

All the indications are that Judas was an Essene leader. As the Last Supper, with the blessing of bread and wine, echoes the Messianic Banquet of the Essenes, the twelve disciples mentioned in the Gospels find an echo in the practice of the same sect that long pre-dates the Christian era. Their *Community Rule*, one of the documents found at Qumran, says that, at that time: 'In the Council of the Community (there shall be) twelve men and three priests' – the ambiguous text allows two meanings: either that three of the twelve should be priests or that three extra priests were to be included – 'to practise truth, righteousness, justice, loving charity, and modesty, one towards the other, to guard the faith upon the earth with a firm inclination and contrite spirit, and to expiate iniquity among those that practise justice and undergo distress of affliction, and to behave towards all men according to the measure of truth and the norm of the time.'[3]

These were the leaders responsible for guarding and spreading the truth about the Teacher of Righteousness – and, as we saw before, it can only be they who, after the execution of John the Baptist, decided to carry on with his movement and confirm his prophecy.

On the evidence available the probability is that Judas Iscariot is to be identified with Judas the Galilean rebel, one of the twelve members of the Essene Council of the Community, which he left to lead a political rebellion against the Romans and the Jerusalem authorities in 6 A.D. Since the rebellion of Judas, Galilee had remained notorious for its opposition to both Roman and Jerusalem authorities. If Jesus were placed in Galilee, it would be easier to accept the conflict between him and the authorities as a political reality of the time. However, Mark, in placing the ministry of Jesus in Galilee, does not appear to have been acquainted with the geographical scene: no mention is found of the main towns of Galilee, and there is no convincing topographical background: 'The link with Galilee, because it is invention, remained thin; just as the conflict with the Jerusalem authorities remained implausible.'[4]

The nature of Jesus's mission is also reflected in the Songs of Isaiah, which the Qumran Essenes interpreted as referring to their Teacher of Righteousness. In the *Hymn Scroll*, one of the Dead Sea manuscripts containing Psalms in the first person, 'the Psalmist (the Teacher) repeatedly applies Isaiah's Servant Songs to himself, as Christian writers were to apply them to Jesus a century later'. For instance, both the Psalmist and Jesus declare themselves to be the person whom Isaiah says (61:1–2) was 'sent to bring good tidings to the humble . . . to proclaim the year of the Lord's favour . . . to console the afflicted' (repeated in Luke, 4:16–22). In the hymns the Psalmist repeatedly appears as 'the man of sorrows, overwhelmed by blows and sickness, despised and rejected'.[5] The Qumran Essenes, like John the Baptist, were talking of the anointed Christ, a Saviour who would return on the Day of Judgment when the world came to an end.[6]

The Gospel authors collected information from all these separate sources, including the claim by the disciples that, as a fulfilment of John's prophecy, they had witnessed Jesus. In relating such information to Jesus, it obviously cannot have been their intention to mislead their readers. Uppermost in their minds was the idea of being faithful to their Lord, whom they regarded as being alive and with them all the time. It was not historical fact they were interested in conveying, but rather proclamation of the hidden truth about Christ.

However, one aspect of their story – and of the Old Testament account as well – leaves us facing another curious anomaly. Both sources assure us that the Messiah would be descended from the royal House of David. The David whose exploits are described in the Bible is thought to have lived in the tenth century B.C. If the historical Jesus was a contemporary of Moses and lived and died in Sinai four centuries earlier, how could David be his ancestor?

Book Two

THE HOUSE OF THE MESSIAH

16

CHILD OF SIN

THE task of establishing the identity of the David from whose House the promised Messiah would one day appear has been complicated by the fact that the Old Testament provides us with two contrasting characters for David. One is a mighty warrior king, who fought a series of major wars in Asia and established an empire that stretched from the Nile to the Euphrates; the other a tribal king, who ruled over the traditional Promised Land – from Dan in the north to Beersheba in the south of the Israel–Judaean upland – and spent much of his life in a running conflict with the Philistines. A further complication is that biblical scholars have reached the conclusion that the warrior David established his massive empire during the early years of the tenth century B.C.

Acceptance of this dating, plus some confused archaeological evidence, has led scholars to identify the tribal David (1000–960 B.C.) as the biblical King David. Yet, lacking any historical evidence pointing to the creation of such an empire at this time they have had to explain – or, rather, explain away – the empire story. The course they have chosen is to say that the biblical narrator simply invented it as an act of aggrandisement towards an important biblical figure.

That we are, in fact, dealing with two separate characters, both named David, can be simply established at this point by comparing their military campaigns. The key to the identity of the warrior king is contained briefly in II Samuel, 8:3 and 8:13: 'David smote also Hadadezer . . . as he went to recover his border at the river Euphrates . . . And David gat him a name (erected a stele) when he returned from smiting of the Syrians in the valley of salt . . .' This account is repeated in I Chronicles, 18:3: 'And David smote Hadadezer . . . as he went to stablish his dominion by the river

Euphrates.' In the Book of Kings we find many mentions of the fact that Solomon, David's son and successor, had control of an empire that stretched from the Nile to the Euphrates. Yet it is known that Solomon did not take part in any military campaigns – the fact that they were apparently unnecessary is an ingredient of the legend of his wisdom – and it is an element of Jewish tradition, and a logical deduction from the story of Solomon, that he inherited an empire which had existed before he came to the throne.

History and archaeology also indicate that the David who created the empire inherited by Solomon can have been only one person – his ancestor, Tuthmosis III (c. 1490–1436 B.C.), the greatest king of the ancient world. (David is *dwd* in the Bible, which, in transliteration into Egyptian, becomes *twt*, the first part of the name of Tuthmosis III.) The empire that he went 'to recover' had been established initially by his grandfather, Tuthmosis I (c. 1528–1510 B.C.), who had himself erected a stele by the Euphrates. However, Tuthmosis did not have time to consolidate his position in western Asia. Later, during a somewhat confused era in Egyptian history, Tuthmosis III shared the co-regency with his aunt-stepmother, Queen Hatshepsut.

A rebellion in Syria during Year 21 of the co-regency between Queen Hatshepsut and Tuthmosis III resulted in the loss of the empire that had been established by his grandfather. However, on becoming sole ruler twelve months later on the death of the queen, Tuthmosis III, in his Year 22, set out to restore his empire and, in his Year 33, crossed the Euphrates and erected his own monument next to that of his grandfather.

No other king of the ancient world can be said to have matched this feat up to this time. Nor, according to our knowledge from historical and archaeological sources, did anyone else rule the whole of this area subsequently until the second half of the sixth century B.C. when Cyrus of Persia conquered both Mesopotamia and Egypt. It is also significant that both the Old Testament and the historical evidence describe the recovery of an empire *between* the Nile and Euphrates, indicating that Egypt must have been securely under David's control at the time these events took place.

Historical and archaeological evidence, as we shall see, also makes it clear that the David who re-established this vast empire in the fifteenth century B.C. cannot have been the same David who is said to have become involved in recurrent conflict with the Philistines five centuries later. Apart from anything else, Tuthmosis III had been dead for the better part of three hundred years before the mass invasion of the coastal areas of Canaan by the Philistines – the Peoples of the Sea – in the middle of the twelfth century B.C. brought Egyptian control of the territory to an end.

What persuaded the biblical scribes to take two characters who lived five centuries apart and treat them as one? The clue lies, I think, in the answer to another question. Who was the father of Isaac?

The Old Testament assures us repeatedly that Abraham was the father of Isaac and also the founder of the twelve tribes of Israel. I believe Abraham was merely the adoptive father: the child's real father – and the founder of the twelve tribes of Israel – was Tuthmosis III.

I have argued elsewhere[1] that Abram and his wife Sarai – both renamed by the Lord later as Abraham and Sarah – made their way to Egypt from Canaan at a time of famine when the young Tuthmosis III was sharing a co-regency with his aunt-stepmother Queen Hatshepsut. On their arrival, fearing he might be killed because of Sarai's good looks, Abram took the precaution of introducing her as his sister (Genesis, 12:11–12). The precaution proved wise. On hearing of her beauty, Tuthmosis III took Sarai as his wife, having paid Abram her bride-price. However, his transgression in having married another man's wife resulted in what the Bible describes as 'a plague' descending on Pharaoh's house. When he eventually discovered the reason, he sent Abram and Sarai back to Canaan.

As marriage in those days meant having sexual intercourse with a woman after having paid her bride-price with the intention of keeping her, there is no question of sex not having taken place. The very fact that the Bible confirms the marriage also means that it had been consummated. This idea is reinforced, moreover, by the punishment of the plague said to have descended on Pharaoh's house. The question therefore arises whether Isaac, the son born to Sarai after her return to Canaan, was Abram's or Pharaoh's. A number of events that followed, including the changing of Abram's name to Abraham and Sarai's to Sarah, confirm that Pharaoh was Isaac's father.

- Genesis, 15:13 speaks of Abram's descendants (in fact, only the descendants of Sarai are meant for, although Abram fathered seven other sons, none of them is included here), and promises that they will return to Egypt.

- Genesis, 15:18 contains the further promise that Isaac's descendants will inherit the Egyptian empire existing at the time of Tuthmosis III, 'from the river of Egypt unto the great river, the river Euphrates'. In this case God's Covenant is not to be transferred to all of Abram's children, but only to those of Isaac.

- According to Genesis, 16:3 Sarai had an Egyptian maid named Hagar. The only reasonable way for Sarai to have had an Egyptian maid in those days was if her royal husband had presented her with one – and he would have been more likely to do that had he expected her to give birth to his child.

- Abram's name is now changed by the Lord to Abraham, 'for a father of many nations have I made thee' (Genesis, 17:5). (From the point of view of Egyptian hieroglyphics, the insertion of *ha* into Abram's name gives us *ham* [majesty], and his new name can be translated as 'heart of the majesty of the sun god Ra'.)

  At the same time, Sarai's name was changed to Sarah, which meant 'queen' in the ancient languages of western Asia: '. . . thou shalt not call her name Sarai, but Sarah shall her name be . . . and she shall be a mother of nations; kings of people shall be of her' (Genesis, 17:15–16). (The Amarna letters, which are basically the foreign archives of the Eighteenth Dynasty of Egypt, make it clear that the Pharaoh was sometimes addressed as *sar*, the masculine form of Sarah: it was the term, for instance, that Tarkhun Dara, the Hittite prince, used in addressing Amenhotep III, the great-grandson of Tuthmosis III.)[2] This foretelling of the royal character of Sarah's descendants confirms the royal nature of their father, and therefore Abraham must be the adoptive father.

- Before the account of the change in Sarai's name, we are told that part of the Lord's covenant with Abraham involved the stipulation that, before the birth of the child to be born to Sarai, all male children should be circumcised when eight days old, a practice that had been confined until then solely to the Egyptians among ancient nations.

- A further indication that the line of descent from Abraham will be through Isaac rather than any of his other sons is to be found in Genesis, 21:12 where the Lord instructs him '. . . in all that Sarah hath said unto thee, hearken unto her voice; for in Isaac shall thy seed be called.'

- Genesis, 22:9–12 records how Abraham took Isaac to the top of a mountain where he proposed to sacrifice him as a burnt offering – a scarcely credible action if Isaac was his own son – until the Lord intervened. (A tradition in the Talmud relates that Sarah's death, reported in the Bible after this event, came as a result of someone telling her of Abraham's intention to kill Isaac.)[3]

- When Esau, the elder of Isaac's twin sons, sold his 'birthright' to his younger brother Jacob (Genesis, 26:33), he seems to have transferred to him some honorary position or title rather than material inheritance. This, in turn, appears to have been transferred from Jacob to Joseph, his favourite son, when he presented him with his many-coloured coat (Genesis, 37:3), a gift which helped to increase the enmity of the half-brothers who, shortly afterwards, were to sell him into slavery in Egypt.

17

HIDING THE SINFUL TRUTH

THE view that Isaac was not the son of Abraham does not rest solely on interpretation of these biblical texts. Since that time, for instance, and even to the present day, a child cannot be regarded as a Jew no matter who the father may have been, unless the mother was herself Jewish – again indicating that descendants of Sarah were not descendants of Abraham. Other non-biblical sources point to the same conclusion.

• The Talmud preserves a tradition that nobody who knew Abraham believed that Isaac was his son: 'On the day that Abraham weaned his son Isaac, he made a great banquet, and all the peoples of the world derided him, saying: "Have you seen that old man and woman who brought a foundling from the street, and now claim him as their son? And what is more they make a great banquet to establish their claim."

• A verse in the Koran (The Prophets, Sura XXI:72) says of Abraham:

> . . . We bestowed on him Isaac
> and, as an additional gift,
> (A grandson), Jacob . . .

The verse indicates that Isaac and Jacob were not Abraham's originally. Muslim scholars interpret the passage by claiming that what it really means is: 'We gave him Isaac because he was asking for a son, and another as a gift whom he was not asking for.' It is easy to see, however, that this cannot have been the case. In the first place, Jacob had not been born when Abraham died. Furthermore, at the time Jacob was born Abraham already had seven other sons – one, Ishmael, by Hagar, Sarah's Egyptian maid, and six by another wife, Keturah. A third point is that Jacob was not the first-born of Isaac's twin sons, but gained importance when Esau sold him his birthright.

• Another Sura of the Koran, having mentioned three of the prophets – Moses, Aaron and Ishmael – speaks of them in Mary, Sura XIX: 58, as being:

> The posterity of Abraham
> And Israel (Jacob) . . .[1]

The only possible explanation of this verse is that some of these three prophets were descendants of Jacob, but not of Abraham. To elaborate on this point, we have two named ancestors (Abraham and Jacob) and three named descendants (Moses, Aaron and Ishmael). It is obvious that, had Jacob been a descendant of Abraham, he would have been named in the list of descendants rather than, together with Abraham, as an ancestor. However, the fact that Jacob's name is placed in an equal position as an ancestor signifies that we are dealing with two separate lines of descent, in which case Jacob himself could not have been descended from Abraham. The correct interpretation is that Ishmael was descended from Abraham, and Aaron and Moses were descended from Jacob.

The fact that the Koran gives Abraham and Jacob equal position as ancestors – the former of the Ishmaelites, the latter of the Israelites – is also a strong indication that the Israelites were not to be regarded as descendants of Abraham.

The confusion that surrounds the identity of Isaac's father has, I believe, historical roots that go beyond the 'sinful' marriage between Sarah and Tuthmosis III.

The biblical account of these events was not put down in writing until many centuries after the Israelites' Exodus from Egypt. By that time Egypt and its Pharaoh had become a symbol of hatred for the Israelites. The biblical narrator was therefore at pains to conceal any blood connection between Israel and Egypt. He was faced with a difficult task, for the information available confirmed that Sarah had been married to an Egyptian Pharaoh, then returned with Abraham to Canaan, where she gave birth to Isaac. Anyone who reads the story, told in this form, would conclude automatically that Pharaoh must have been Isaac's father. However, at a time when the cornerstone of biblical teaching was to emphasize how God saved the Israelites from their Egyptian oppressors, the narrator had to find some means of separating the two events – the departure of Sarah from Egypt and the birth of Isaac – thus hiding the identity of the real father.

Hence, once Sarah and Abraham had resettled in Canaan, the narrator interrupted events by interpolating another story, in which he described how Abraham sought to free his nephew, Lot, who had been captured by some enemies. Next we have the appearance of the Lord to Abraham, foretelling what can only be the birth of Isaac, whose descendants would return to Egypt. We should expect an account of Isaac's birth to follow, but no. It is stressed (Genesis, 16:1) that Sarah was unable to bear children. Consequently, after ten years had elapsed since the return to Canaan, she gave Abraham her Egyptian maid, Hagar, as a wife, and Ishmael was born of their union. Another fourteen years are allowed to pass by, according to the biblical narrator, who again stresses that Sarah was barren, and adds the information that, at ninety, she was too old to give birth. Yet we now learn that three messengers of God appear and announce that Sarah will have a son the following year.

Even then the biblical narrator did not feel safe in introducing the birth of Isaac, fearing that someone might still relate him to his real father, so he presents us with yet another character, Abimelech, king of Gerar. On a visit to Gerar, we are told, Abraham again took the precaution of claiming that Sarah was his sister and – although we have been assured that she was an old woman of ninety – Abimelech fell in love with Sarah and was about to marry her when the Lord appeared to him in a dream and warned him not to marry a woman who was already someone else's wife. And it is only at this point – with a great deal of time having been made to pass, and a number of other events having taken place – that the narrator felt it at last safe to introduce the birth of Isaac.

These delaying tactics are not really convincing. In fact, in tinkering with part of the chronology and not with others, the biblical narrator has betrayed himself. If, as we saw earlier, Sarah had an Egyptian maid, she must have been given the maid as a gift, and it seems likely that the reason for the gift was that she was expecting Pharaoh's child. Therefore, one would expect Isaac to be older than Ishmael, the child born to the maid, Hagar, after Sarah had given her to Abraham as a wife. Yet the biblical narrator tries to persuade us that the opposite is true by a wide margin. We are told (Genesis, 17:25) that Ishmael was thirteen years of age when he was circumcised, a year before the birth of Isaac.

However, the biblical account four chapters later of Hagar's flight with her son, after Sarah had sent them away, gives quite a different impression of his age: 'And Abraham rose up early in the morning, and took bread, and a bottle of water, and gave it unto Hagar, putting it on her shoulder, and the child, and sent her away: and she departed, and wandered in the wilderness of Beersheba. And the water was spent in the bottle, and she cast the child under one of the shrubs. And she went, and sat her down over against him a good way off, as it were a bowshot: for she said, Let me not see the death of the child. And she sat over against him, and lift up her voice, and wept.

'And God heard the voice of the lad; and the angel of God called to Hagar out of Heaven, and said unto her, What aileth thee, Hagar? fear not; for God hath heard the voice of the lad where he is. Arise, lift up the lad, and hold him in thine hand; for I will make him a great nation. And God opened her eyes, and she saw a well of water; and she went, and filled the bottle with water, and gave the lad drink' (Genesis, 21:14–19).

If his mother had to carry Ishmael, and when she placed him under a bush he was unable to move, he cannot – unlike Isaac – have yet reached walking age. Although this story is not mentioned in the Koran, Islamic tradition agrees with the Bible in this account, representing Ishmael as a mere baby, carried by his mother and unable to move from the spot where she placed him; but a fountain of water, identified with the present Zamzam in Mecca, appeared suddenly beneath his feet.

To summarize briefly, therefore, what seems to have been the correct sequence of events . . .

When she left Egypt with Abraham, Sarah was already pregnant by Tuthmosis III, who gave her Hagar as a maid to assist in the birth and subsequent nursing of Isaac. Abraham later took Hagar as another wife and she gave birth to Ishmael. Sarah – who now regarded herself as a king's wife and her son, Isaac, as a prince – was not prepared to grant equal status to Ishmael. That is why she sent Hagar and Ishmael away – and why only Isaac of Abraham's sons is to be regarded from the Israelite point of view as his heir.

Despite all the efforts of the biblical narrator to distort his account of these events, the Israelites never lost sight of the true identity of their great ancestor, Tuthmosis III. Not long after Abraham's death, we are told, Jacob assumed the role of this ancestor when the Lord changed his name to Israel: 'And God appeared unto Jacob again . . . And God said unto him, Thy name is Jacob: thy name shall not be called any more Jacob, but Israel shall be thy name: and he called his name Israel' (Genesis, 35:9–10). The significance of this passage lies in the name. The Hebrew term *el* is the short form of *Elohim* (God) and *Ysra* or *sar* indicates a prince or a ruler. Therefore *Ysrael* means *Elohim* rules, like Egyptian gods (Pharaoh, too, was looked upon as a ruling god).

In the early centuries, Abraham appeared in Israelite writings as their great ancestor. However, from the time of Saul's subsequent Israelite kingdom, five centuries later, and even into Christian times, the warrior King David came to be regarded as the only accepted ancestor for any legitimate king or Messiah.

18

PEOPLES OF THE SEA

EVIDENCE about how and when the Israelites eventually reached the Promised Land of Canaan – a fragmentary process that lasted over an extended period of time – also makes it clear that the warrior king who founded a great empire is a different person from the tribal chief who spent a large part of his life in conflict with the Philistines.

Canaan was still firmly under Egyptian control when Ramses III (c.1182–1151 B.C.), the second ruler of Egypt's Twentieth Dynasty, came to the throne. A papyrus found in Thebes – known as the Papyrus Harris and now in the British Museum – relates that, at this comparatively late date, Ramses III built a temple of Amun in the land of Canaan, and the 'foreigners of Retenu come to it, bearing their tributes before it'. Furthermore, an ivory model pen-case, found at the Palestinian city of Megiddo and belonging to an Egyptian envoy to foreign countries, bears the name of Ramses III.[1]

After the reign of Ramses III, Egypt lost control over Palestine. The main reason was the mass invasion of Canaan by the 'Peoples of the Sea'. This invasion had begun around 1174 B.C. – Year 8 of Ramses III – about the same time that, according to the *Iliad*, the Greek war against Troy was taking place. The invaders' story is recorded in the best-preserved inscriptions and reliefs on the walls of Ramses III's funerary temple in western Thebes. The reliefs depict people who were after permanent settlement, whole families on the move, travelling by ox-cart with women, children and household possessions: 'Their confederation consisted of Peleset, Tjekker, Sheklesh, Danu and Weshesh, united lands.'[2]

The Peleset are the Philistines, who later gave their name to the land of Palestine. They are shown with feathered headdresses and round shields. The Danu are thought to have been the Danaoi of the *Iliad*. Some other groups were also able to land in Phoenicia. The Hittite empire, as well as northern Syria, was swept away, and the Hittite capital, Hattushash, burned to the ground: 'The foreign countries made a plot in their islands. Dislodged and scattered by battle were the lands all at one time, and no land could stand before their arms, beginning with Khatti (the Hittite country), Kode, Carchemish, Arzawa and Alasiya . . . A camp was set up in one place in Amur (Syria), and they desolated its people and its land as though they had never come to being. They came, the flame prepared before them, onwards to Egypt.'[3]

Ramses III succeeded in defeating the invaders in a naval battle, described by Alan Gardiner, the British Egyptologist, in the following terms: 'For the details . . . we turn rather to the reliefs than to the verbal descriptions . . . The artist has managed to combine into a single picture the various phases of the engagement. First we see Egyptian soldiers attacking imperturbably from the deck of their ship; opposite them in a vessel held fast with grappling irons the enemy is in the utmost confusion, two of them falling into the water while one looks towards the shore in the hope of mercy from the Pharaoh. Another of their vessels, however, displays them met with a shower of arrows from the land. The Egyptian fleet now turns homeward, taking with it numerous captives helpless and bound; one of them seeking to escape is caught by a soldier on the bank. On the way upstream, a capsized vessel is encountered, with its entire crew flung into the water. The defeat of the invaders is complete; nine separate ships have sufficed to tell the tale, and there remains to be recounted only the presentation of the prisoners to Amun-Ra and the other details of the triumph.'[4]

Although Ramses III was able to repulse the attack on Egypt itself and we have textual and archaeological evidence showing that Egypt's control over Canaan continued at least until the middle of the twelfth century B.C., there are also indications that some 'Peoples of the Sea' had settled in the area prior to this date. The archaeological feature (or evidence) consists of a class of painted Mycenaean pottery that has been found in south-west Canaan at levels dating from the first half of the twelfth century B.C. Despite the fact that it follows in colour, shapes and painted motifs the long-established Mycenaean–Greek tradition, chemical and physical analyses have indicated that it was made locally. Thus it seems clear that it was the potters rather than the pots that were intrusive. This suggests that their original homeland was in the Aegean or western Turkey, which agrees with the Bible in naming the original homeland of the Philistines as 'Caphtor' (Amos, 9:7; Jeremiah, 47:4). Scholars have associated this region with the Egyptian term 'Keftiu', which is taken to denote Crete or possibly the Aegean region in general.

Another indication of Philistine settlement in south-west Canaan is the discovery of weapons and tools of iron – unknown to the Canaanites at the time – that can be dated to the twelfth century B.C. Two views have emerged to explain the apparent contradiction that some 'Peoples of the Sea' were dwelling in the area while Canaan was still under Egyptian control: that after defeating the Peleset in the naval battle, the Egyptians settled them in south-west Canaan, the area that was to become Philistia; or that some of them had already landed in the coastal part of Canaan before the attack on Egypt and had been allowed by the Egyptians to settle there.

Whichever of these theories is correct, these Peleset, who became Egyptianized in their customs, seem to have enjoyed some kind of *détente* with their Egyptian rulers until about the middle of the twelfth century B.C. when they entrenched themselves more firmly in and around Gaza in city states largely independent of Egyptian rule: 'It was in the second half of the twelfth century B.C. that the Philistines really established themselves by rebuilding older towns and founding new ones, often no doubt in close association with the Canaanite population they now ruled. Ashdod was remodelled to a new layout and strongly fortified. At Tel Qasile, in the northern suburbs of modern Tel Aviv on the Yarkon river, a new maritime settlement was established. Elsewhere there is a varied archaeological record of urban recession, as at Aphek and Lachish, or of richly equipped cemeteries, as at Azor, where the contemporary settlement remains unknown.'[5]

Where were the Israelites when these events were taking place?

The Old Testament provides us with two contradictory accounts of the arrival of the Israelites in the Promised Land of Canaan. The version that has gained most popular acceptance, despite the evidence that Canaan remained firmly under Egyptian control until the latter part of the twelfth century B.C., is that Canaan was conquered as a result of a swift military campaign led by

Joshua nearly a century earlier, in the latter part of the thirteenth century B.C. Thus the Israelite occupation would have taken place *before* the Philistines appeared on the scene. However, as we saw in the first section of this book, the supposed campaign by Joshua is part of the priestly effort to conceal the crime of Phinehas by keeping Joshua alive.

The alternative – and correct – view is that the Israelite occupation was a fragmentary process by individual tribes, accompanied by various local conflicts, that took place over a long period of time *after* the Philistine invasion.

19

THE PROMISED LAND

THE Book of Judges, which follows the Book of Joshua, suggests that occupation of Canaan was a gradual process by separate tribes that took place over a long period of time. The Israelite personalities and tribes involved in these various fragmentary campaigns, fought over a wide area of Canaan, include Judah and his brother Simeon; the descendants of Jethro the Kenite, the father-in-law of Moses; Caleb; Benjamin; the House of Joseph, Joseph's two sons, Manasseh and Ephraim; Zebulun, Asher, Naftali and Dan.

In trying to establish the truth about this matter, it is important to be clear about when the Israelites arrived in Egypt, how long they stayed and when they left. The majority of Egyptologists still cling to the view that Joseph the Patriarch, his family and the tribes of Israel arrived in Egypt at the time of the Hyksos occupation of the Eastern Delta in the middle of the seventeenth century B.C., remained in the country for four centuries and did not leave until late in the reign of Ramses II (c. 1304–1237 B.C.) or possibly early in that of his successor, Merenptah. My own view, argued elsewhere[1] and now gaining increasing acceptance among biblical scholars as opposed to the majority of Egyptologists, is that Joseph arrived in Egypt some time before the reign of Tuthmosis IV (c. 1413–1405 B.C.) and later brought the tribes of Israel down from Canaan to join him. They settled at Goshen in the Eastern Delta where they remained for four generations, not four centuries, until the time of the Exodus during the last year of the short reign of Ramses I (c. 1335–1333 B.C.), the elderly first king of the Nineteenth Dynasty.

The Old Testament and Egyptian history provide us with contradictory accounts of what happened immediately after the Exodus. Initially, according to the Bible, the Israelites made their way into Sinai where they allied themselves with Sinatic bedouins, the Shasu (the Midianites of the Bible). Then the biblical account of the Israelite entry into Palestine describes how, still under the leadership of Moses, they left northern Sinai by way of the top end of the Gulf of Aqaba before skirting the borders of Edom, south and south-west of the Dead Sea, and Moab, to the east of the Dead Sea. After that, when they were refused permission to pass westwards through the territory of the Amorites, they fought their way, capturing the area to the north of the Jordanian River Arnon, which was assigned to the Rubenites for settlement. According to the Book of Deuteronomy, the death of Moses followed on a mountain to the east of the River Jordan before Joshua, his successor, led the Israelites across the Jordan and into the Promised Land.

In contrast, Egyptian evidence indicates that, after leaving the city of Pi-Ramses, near modern Kantara in northern Sinai, Moses led the Israelites southward towards Lake Timsah, a marshy area inaccessible to chariots, which simply became stuck in the mud. This is possibly the origin of the Exodus story of the parting of the waters and the death of the ruling Pharaoh – in this case, Ramses I – in pursuit of the Israelites. Certainly, his son and successor, Seti I (c. 1333–1304 B.C.), did not wait for the burial of his father or even his own coronation before himself setting out in pursuit of them.[2]

His war scenes on the exterior north wall of the great Hypostyle Hall at Karnak show that his first campaign against the Shasu took place when they (and the Israelites)[3] made their initial attempt to reach Canaan via the Road of Horus, the ancient highway connecting Egypt with western Asia. This occurred immediately after the Exodus from Egypt, almost certainly because of their efforts to obtain water from military settlements that guarded the road (which, in its turn, is almost certainly the origin of the biblical story of Moses being punished by the Lord for striking a rock with his rod to obtain water for his followers). Seti I pursued them as far as the city of Canaan, Gaza, and, in the process, killed their leader, Moses, and caused great slaughter among his followers. As a result the Israelites and the Shasu were forced back into Sinai for what the Old Testament calls 'the forty years of wandering'.

From Seti I's war scenes, we know that, a short time after the above campaign, he began a series of wars in western Asia to consolidate Egyptian positions and regain those that had been lost. After these campaigns, it is about forty years – in the second decade (1294–1284 B.C.) of the long reign of Seti I's son and successor, Ramses II – before we encounter another mention of the Shasu, who had by then left Egypt. Many texts have been found to confirm these wars. In an article published by the *Journal of Egyptian Archaeology* in 1964, Dr Kenneth Kitchen, Professor of Egyptology at Liverpool University, described how a stele from Wadi Tumilat in the Eastern Delta speaks of the king as 'making great slaughter in the land of (the) Shasu, He plunders their tells, Slaying their (people) and building (anew?) with towns bearing his name.'4 An obelisk from Tanis describes Ramses II as a 'terrible and raging lion who despoils the Shasu-land, Who plunders the mountains of Seir with his valiant arms . . .' Dr Kitchen makes the point: 'Here Shasu is by parallelism equated with Mount Seir, which is Edom.'5 Subsequently he adds: 'This evidence suggests that Ramses or troops of his raided the Negeb, the uplands of Seir or Edom, and perhaps part of the intervening Araba rift valley.'6

From the war reliefs of Ramses II on the east wall of his court in the Luxor Temple we also have evidence that he fought in the land of Moab around the same time: 'The new evidence is sufficient to show that the forces of Ramses II penetrated the territory north of the (river) Arnon (taking Dibon) and probably the heartland of Moab between the Arnon and (river) Zered.'7 No mention of the Shasu occurs, however, in accounts of Ramses II's Moabite wars.

The above evidence signifies that, during the second decade of the thirteenth century B.C., the Israelite tribes – evidently still semi-nomadic – had left Egypt but, far from posing the suggested threat to Egyptian power in Canaan, were still located in the area of Mount Seir in Edom, south and south-west of the Dead Sea, between Elath, at the head of the Gulf of Aqaba, and the southern end of the Dead Sea, and that Moab was still under Egyptian control and had not yet been penetrated by the Israelite tribes.

Even as late as the reign of Ramses III (c. 1182–1151 B.C.) we find an account of military activity against nomadic bedouin tribes in the Edomite area of Seir, which seems to be the only campaign of this Pharaoh in Palestine. The Papyrus Harris, mentioned at the start of the previous chapter about the Philistines, describes how he 'destroyed the Seirites among the Shasu-tribes. I plundered their tents of people and goods.'8

All the evidence indicates that after the Exodus the Israelites dwelt in the area of Mount Seir in Edom for a long time. Memory of those days can be seen in the Song of Deborah: 'Lord, when thou wentest out of Seir, when thou marchedst out of the field of Edom, the earth trembled, and the heavens dropped, the clouds also dropped water' (Judges, 5:4). It was only when Egypt lost control over Palestine in the second half of the twelfth century B.C. that the Israelite tribes started to infiltrate the land from Dan (ancient Lachish in Upper Galilee, a mere village at the time, situated some eighteen miles north of Hazor, near the source of the River Jordan) in the north to Beersheba in the Negeb desert to the south, where archaeological excavation has shown evidence of new settlement during the twelfth century B.C. They were still semi-nomadic, living among the ruins of ancient cities or among other Canaanite inhabitants. The Philistines had already established their city states of south-west Canaan and were attempting to expand towards the Dead Sea and the River Jordan when the Israelites, too, were trying to establish themselves in the area. Thus conflict between the two new arrivals became the main preoccupation of both Saul and the tribal David. To summarize the main points made in these two chapters:

- The David who established an empire that stretched from the Nile to the Euphrates can only have lived in the fifteenth century B.C. . . . the Israelite infiltration of Canaan, the Promised Land, was a fragmentary process that did not gather pace until after Egypt lost control over Palestine in the second half of the twelfth century B.C. . . . the David whose main campaigns were against the Philistines cannot have lived before the twelfth century B.C. because that was when the mass invasion of the coastal plain of Canaan by the Philistines took place.

20

THE TWO DAVIDS

THE tribal David who lived in the first half of the tenth century B.C. is clearly a minor figure. He is presented to us in a number of guises – shepherd, rival to Saul and later Ishbosheth, one of Saul's surviving sons, for the Israelite leadership, an accomplished harpist and 'a man of war', engaged in recurrent battles with the Philistines. An attempt to enhance this last trait, as part of the plan to disguise the true identity of David, is the introduction of the epic fight between David and Goliath. However, this account was actually borrowed from a popular and much-admired Egyptian literary work, *The Autobiography of Sinuhe*, describing events that took place a thousand years earlier, and has no relevance to the stories of either of the biblical Davids (see Appendices C and D).[1]

The narration of the warrior King David's life that we find in II Samuel is comparatively straightforward. His first campaign is described in the fifth chapter. We learn that 'the king and his men went to Jerusalem unto the Jebusites, the inhabitants of the land . . . (and) took the strong hold (fortress) of Zion: the same is the city of David.' David dwelled in the fort and built fortifications around it, and 'Hiram king of Tyre sent messengers . . . and cedar trees, and carpenters, and masons; and they built David an house' (II Samuel, 5:6–11).

Although this achievement is credited to the tribal David in II Samuel immediately after he became sole ruler over the Israelites, this cannot have been the case. Firstly, we are told that, as *soon* as they heard of David's appointment, the Philistines set out to do battle with him, and 'spread themselves in the valley of Rephaim', situated to the north-west of Bethlehem. This resulted in two encounters, in the second of which he 'smote the Philistines from

Geba . . . to Gazer', one of the coastal Philistine cities north of Ashdod. Yet the taking of Jerusalem, the building of fortifications and the despatch of materials and craftsmen from Tyre which form part of this story would have taken a considerable time. Secondly, at the time of King David (Tuthmosis III) in the fifteenth century B.C. the mass invasion by the Philistines of the coastal plain of Canaan had not yet taken place.

The next chapter of II Samuel describes how David gathered together the thirty thousand chosen men of Israel and set out from Baale in Judaea to Gibeah in Benjamin 'to bring up from thence the Ark of God'. This is supposed to have been the Ark that Moses placed in the Holy of Holies in the Tabernacle he built in Sinai, the Ark in which he placed the Ten Commandments and which is said to have been taken by the Israelites to the Promised Land. Now it was brought in procession to 'the city of David' where it was placed 'in the midst of a tabernacle that David had pitched for it' on Mount Moriah, north of the ancient fortress of Jerusalem.

Three chapters later we have an account of a whole series of wars in northern Palestine, Syria – up to the limits of the Mesopotamian river, the Euphrates, where King David's control was being threatened – as well as Moab, to the east of the Dead Sea. It is said that he:

- 'smote Moab . . . And so the Moabites became David's servants, and brought gifts' (II Samuel, 8:2).

- David 'smote also Hadadezer . . . King of Zobah (towards Hamath in northern Syria), as he went to recover his border at the river Euphrates' (II Samuel, 8:3), and 'gat him a name' (erected a stele) (8:13).

- The Syrians of Damascus then came to help Hadadezer, who was the leader of the confederate Syrian kingdoms, but David defeated them, slaying twenty thousand of the enemy before putting garrisons in Aram of Damascus, and the Syrians became his servants and paid tribute.

- When the king of Hamath learned that David had defeated Hadadezer, he sent his son to David bearing congratulations and gifts.

- Another war then followed in southern Canaan – at Edom, bordering Egyptian Sinai – where David's army slew eighteen thousand men and he put garrisons in Edom, which became his servant.

- When the king of the Ammonites died and was succeeded by his son, David sent messengers to offer his condolences, but the messengers were treated badly because the Ammonites suspected that the real purpose of their visit was to spy on their city, which is not named at this point. The Ammonites gathered their allies from Syria and Mesopotamia and prepared for war. When David's army responded to this challenge by marching on their city, his troops found the opposing forces divided into two: the Ammonites had gathered at the city gate while their allies waited on open ground. David's army was similarly divided into two forces. The Ammonites' allies on the open ground were soon defeated and fled, whereupon the Ammonites sought refuge behind the gates of their city.

- The Syrians gathered a new army, which seems to have been located to the east of the River Jordan. David crossed the Jordan and again defeated the Syrians, slaying 'the men of seven hundred chariots . . . and forty thousand horsemen' (II Samuel, 10:18). As a result of this defeat, all the kings who were allies of Hadadezer, king of Zobah, who seems still to have been the leader of the Syrian alliance, made peace with David and became his servants.

- Then David's army returned to lay siege to the city – here identified as Rabbah (II Samuel, 11:1) – in which the Ammonites had taken refuge in the earlier campaign. David himself remained in Jerusalem. It is at this point that his liaison with Bathsheba is introduced.

While David was enjoying an evening stroll on the roof of his house in Jerusalem, we are told, his eye was taken by the sight of a beautiful woman bathing. She was Bathsheba, the wife of Uriah the Hittite, who was absent from home, serving with the king's army at the siege of Rabbah. David sent messengers to bring her to him, they made love and, not long afterwards, Bathsheba announced: 'I am with child.' David ordered the return of Uriah to Jerusalem and, after hearing his report on how the campaign fared, ordered him to go to his home, clearly hoping that he and his wife would make love and David's part in the parenthood would be concealed. However, Uriah did not follow the king's wishes and slept instead with the royal servants outside David's house. On learning this, David sent Uriah back to the front with a letter to his commander, Joab, saying: 'Set ye Uriah in the forefront of the hottest battle, and retire ye from him, that he may be smitten, and die' (II Samuel, 11:15). Once news was brought of the subsequent death of Uriah in the fighting at Rabbah, David sent again for Bathsheba and married her, and she bore him a son, Solomon.

David joined his troops when it was clear that Rabbah was about to fall, and he led them in the final successful assault. Then he took 'their king's crown from off his head, the weight whereof was a talent of gold with the precious stones: and it was set on David's head. And he brought forth the spoil of the city in great abundance.' David also took a large number of prisoners of war to work for him, and, before finally returning to Jerusalem, subdued the rest of the Ammonite cities.

The biblical accounts of these campaigns fought by the warrior King David match precisely the historical accounts of the wars fought by Tuthmosis III, the greatest king of the ancient world.

21

JOURNEY TO HEAVEN

TUTHMOSIS III, the son of a concubine, came to the throne of Egypt as the fifth ruler of the Eighteenth Dynasty in odd circumstances. The dynasty had been founded nearly a hundred years earlier when, after just over a century of rule by the invading Hyksos shepherds, the princes of Thebes united in the sixteenth century B.C. in a successful attempt to drive them out of Egypt, and Ahmosis (c. 1575–1550 B.C.) was crowned as the dynasty's first ruler. In all, the new king spent fifteen years battling to ensure that no part of Egypt remained under foreign control, including the pursuit of the remnants of the Hyksos into the region of Gaza.

He was followed by his son, Amenhotep I (c. 1550–1528 B.C.), who pushed further into Palestine and Syria in continuing campaigns against the Hyksos. He, in turn, was followed on the throne by Tuthmosis I (c. 1528–1510 B.C.), one of his generals, after the king had arranged for him to be married to the royal heiress and appointed him as his co-regent. Despite his short reign, Tuthmosis I was the original founder of the Egyptian Empire. He marched into western Asia at the head of his army and reached the River Euphrates in the area between northern Syria and Mesopotamia, south of Anatolia. There they succeeded in crossing the river into the territory of Mitanni (the ancient kingdom of northern Mesopotamia) where Tuthmosis I erected a stele commemorating his victory. At this time, however, the Egyptians were satisfied simply to crush their enemies and never tried to establish control over the vanquished territories.

At this point we enter on a mysterious period in Egyptian history. The next ruler was the king's son, Tuthmosis II (c. 1510–1490 B.C.), born of a minor wife and not the Great Royal Wife (Queen Ahmose). In order to inherit the throne he married – as was the custom – his half-sister, Hatshepsut, the heiress daughter of his father and Queen Ahmose. In *his* turn, Tuthmosis II chose his son, Tuthmosis III (c. 1490–1436 B.C.), by a concubine named Isis, to be his successor. Shortly before the death of Tuthmosis II, Hatshepsut gave birth to a daughter, Neferure. The normal method of ensuring the right of Tuthmosis III to inherit the throne would have been marriage to Neferure, *his* half-sister, who was the heiress. This marriage did not take place. Was it because Queen Hatshepsut refused her consent? We do not know. We do know, however, that she continued to insist that Neferure was the only legal heir, 'Lady of the Two Lands, mistress of Upper and Lower Egypt'.[1] In the circumstances, Tuthmosis II had to have his son 'adopted' by the State god Amun in order to ensure his right to the throne.

The story of the god's choice of Tuthmosis III to be king is found in an inscription at Karnak, on the east bank of the Nile in Upper Egypt, written long after the king had come to the throne. It describes how the selection ceremony took place on a day of festival when he was just an acolyte in the Temple of Amun at Thebes and the barque of Amun was proceeding around the hall: '. . . [the god] made the circuit of the hypostyle on both sides of it, the heart of those who were in front did not comprehend his actions, while searching for my majesty in every place. On recognizing me, lo, he halted . . . [I threw myself on] the pavement, I prostrated myself in his presence. He set me before his majesty: I was stationed at the "Station of the King" (the place in the holy of holies where the king stood in the performance of the prescribed State ritual) . . . Then they (the priests) [revealed] before the people the secrets in the hearts of the gods . . . there was none who knew them, there was none who revealed them [beside him].'

At this point, the story describes how the young prince was whisked off to Heaven to be appointed as king: '[He opened for me] the doors of Heaven; he opened the portals of the horizon of Ra. I flew to Heaven as the divine hawk, beholding his form in Heaven; I adored his majesty . . . I saw the glorious forms of the Horizon-God upon his mysterious ways in Heaven.'[2] Now, after being allowed into the holy of holies, Tuthmosis III is permitted to behold the majesty of god himself: 'Ra himself established me.

I was dignified with the diadems which [we]re upon his head, his serpent diadem, rested upon [my forehead] . . . I was sated with the counsels of the gods, like Horus, when he counted his body at the house of my father, Amun-Ra . . . His own titulary was affixed for me.'3

Tuthmosis III, who had been given the throne name Menkheper-Ra ('established in the form of Ra'), was still a young boy, aged about five, when his father died. Although he had been chosen by the State god Amun himself to succeed his father on the throne, he was not allowed by his aunt-stepmother, Queen Hatshepsut, to rule. Instead she appointed herself as his guardian, allowing him only to appear behind her in reliefs of the period. Soon, as early as his Year 2, she even took the step of sharing kingship with the young king, posing and being dressed as a man. For as long as she lived she kept Tuthmosis III in the background and regarded her daughter, Neferure, as the real heiress *and* heir. Her plans were undermined, however, when Neferure died in Year 16 of the co-regency, and from this point onward Tuthmosis III gained increasing importance. He seems to have joined the Egyptian army as a young man, and there is evidence to suggest his having fought in the area of Gaza towards the end of the co-regency.

The chance for Tuthmosis III to rule Egypt on his own came in the middle of Year 22 of the co-regency when Hatshepsut died. It seems that the first task he undertook was to deface many of the monuments erected to his aunt-stepmother: her reliefs were hacked out, her inscriptions erased, her cartouches obliterated, her obelisks walled up. So now, technically speaking, as he was not the son of the Egyptian queen, nor had he married the heiress to inherit the throne, but had been chosen to rule by the State god Amun, Tuthmosis III was not the legal descendant of the earlier Ahmosside dynasty. From now until the end of the Amarna rule in Egypt – the rule of Akhenaten, Semenkhkare, Tutankhamun and Aye – it was the dynasty founded by Tuthmosis III that sat on the throne of Egypt.

The sarcophagus in the tomb of Tuthmosis III (No. 34 in the Valley of the Kings) was found to be empty when it was discovered. His mummy eventually came to light, together with thirty-two other royal mummies, hidden in a chamber, three metres wide and nearly 300 metres long, at the bottom of a narrow shaft dug in the slopes

Kings of the Later Eighteenth
and Early Nineteenth Dynasties[4]

King	Length of reign	Dates
Tuthmosis III (DAVID)	54	1490–1436 B.C.
Amenhotep II	23	1436–1413 B.C.
Tuthmosis IV	8	1413–1405 B.C.
Amenhotep III (SOLOMON)	38	1405–1367 B.C.
Akhenaten (MOSES) (alone)	6	1367–1361 B.C.
Semenkhkare	–	–
Tutankhamun (JESUS)	9	1361–1352 B.C.
Aye (EPHRAIM)	4	1352–1348 B.C.
Horemheb	13	1348–1335 B.C.
Nineteenth Dynasty		
Ramses I	2	1335–1333 B.C.
Seti I	29	1333–1304 B.C.
Ramses II	67	1304–1237 B.C.

of the necropolis of western Thebes. They had been hidden there more than three thousand years earlier by Egyptian priests who feared for their safety after many cases of tomb-robbing had come to light. Ironically, this new secret hiding place was also found by tomb robbers, and it was only when the antiquity authorities noticed the appearance of a number of funerary objects on the market that they started to look for the source. When at last they were found, the mummies were removed to the Cairo Museum.

The mummy of Tuthmosis III had been torn from its coffin when it was discovered, and robbers had done considerable damage in stripping it of its jewels. The head, which had broken free from the body, showed that the king was almost completely bald at the time of his death apart from a few short white hairs behind the left ear. All four limbs had also become detached from the torso, the feet had become detached from the legs and both arms had been broken in two at the elbow: '. . . before re-burial some renovation of the wrapping was necessary, and, as portions of the body became loose, the restorers, in order to give the mummy the necessary firmness, compressed it between four oar-shaped slips of wood . . . Happily, the face, which had been plastered over with pitch at the time of embalming, did not suffer at all from this rough treatment, and appeared intact when the protecting mask was removed.'5

The author of these words, Gaston Maspero, director-general of the Cairo Museum at the time, went on to say: 'His statues, although not representing him as a type of manly beauty, yet give him refined, intelligent features, but a comparison with the mummy shows that the artists have idealized their model.'6 Another view of the king's appearance has been provided by the American scholar William C. Hayes: 'Incontestably the greatest pharaoh ever to occupy the throne of Egypt, Tuthmosis III appears to have excelled not only as a warrior, a statesman and an administrator, but also as one of the most accomplished horsemen, archers and all-round athletes of his time . . . (Yet) physically he cannot have been very prepossessing. His mummy shows him to have been a stocky little man, under five feet four inches in height, and his portraits are almost unanimous in endowing him with the . . . most beaked of all the Tuthmosside noses.'7

His lack of stature and the physical appearance which Hayes found not 'very prepossessing' did not have a deleterious effect on the domestic life of Tuthmosis III. His chief wife and the mother of his successor, Amenhotep II (c. 1436–1413 B.C.), was his half-sister, Meryt-Ra. Nothing much is known about her, but she was certainly not the heiress. In addition, he had at least three Syrian wives, whose tomb was found in western Thebes, and a large harem.

We find no evidence of the relationship with the visiting Sarah that resulted in the birth of Isaac. Egyptian scribes must have regarded it as an unimportant episode or as a great sin whose memory should not be preserved in official records in the same way that biblical scribes, while admitting the marriage, tried to obscure the identity of the father of the child born of it.

22

ARMAGEDDON

At the time Tuthmosis III became sole ruler of Egypt in his Year 22 after the death of Hatshepsut, four decades had passed without a major Egyptian military campaign in western Asia. Now the situation changed completely. The King of Qadesh, a strong fortified city on the River Orontes in northern Syria, led a Syrio–Canaanite confederacy in a general rebellion against Egypt. In response, Tuthmosis III marched into western Asia to regain the territories between the Nile and Euphrates that had been conquered forty years earlier by his grandfather, Tuthmosis I. In the next twenty years he led a total of seventeen campaigns in western Asia, at the end of which he had earned himself the reputation as the mightiest of all the kings of the ancient world. The account of these various wars, copied from the daily records of the scribe who accompanied the army on its campaigns, is to be found in the Annals, a 223-line document that covers the inside of the walls enclosing the corridor surrounding the granite holy of holies Tuthmosis III built at Karnak. The account begins with his departure at the head of his troops from the fortified border city of Zarw during the last days of his Year 22.

Ten days later he arrived in Gaza, where he celebrated the start of his Year 23 with festivals in honour of his 'father', Amun, whose image he carried inside an Ark at the head of the marching army. He stayed there for the night before pushing on northward towards central Canaan where he paused in a town called Yehem to the south of a mountainous ridge he had to cross in order to reach Megiddo, the city where the Qadesh enemy had gathered. Here he was faced with a choice of three routes, but the shortest, called the Aruna Road, was narrow and dangerous, and he therefore summoned a Council of War, in which he said to his officers: 'That vile enemy of Qadesh . . . has gathered to himself the princes of all lands who were loyal to Egypt . . . And he says (so they say): "I shall stand to fight against His Majesty here in Megiddo." Tell me what is in your hearts.'

To this choice of which road to take for the approach to Megiddo, his officers replied: 'How can one go on this road which is so narrow? It is reported that the enemy stand outside and are numerous. Will not horse have to go behind horse, and soldiers and people likewise? Shall our own vanguard be·fighting while the rear stands here in Aruna (the starting point of the narrow road) and does not fight?' However, in the light of fresh reports brought in by messengers Tuthmosis III decided that he would make his way to Megiddo by the unappealing – but, to his enemies, unexpected – narrow road, a choice to which his officers replied: 'Thy father Amun prosper thy counsel . . . The servant will follow his master.'[1]

Thus was set the scene for the first battle of Armageddon.

The military importance of Megiddo and its long history as an international battleground is 'aptly reflected in the Apocalypse of John (Revelation, 16:22ff) in which Armageddon (*Har Meggiddon*, the Mount of Megiddo) is designated as the site where, at the end of days, all the kings of the world will fight the ultimate battle against the forces of God'.[2] This underlines the belief up to the Christian era that the Messiah born of the House of David will one day have to re-enact the battle of his great ancestor who conquered Megiddo, where the final battle between Good and Evil will take place.

In his assault upon Megiddo, Tuthmosis III marched at the head of the narrow mountainous road from Aruna, with the image of Amun pointing the way. When he eventually emerged into the valley south-east of Megiddo, he could see that the enemy forces – as in the biblical account of the attack on Rabbah – had been divided. Having apparently expected him to take one or other of the two broader roads available to him, one group had been stationed at Taanach to the south and the other nearer to Megiddo, but, as a result of his unexpected choice of route, Tuthmosis and his troops appeared on the scene between them. On the advice of his officers, the king encamped for two days while he waited for the rear echelon of his army to arrive. Then, having divided his army into separate units, he attacked: 'His Majesty set forth in a chariot of fine gold, adorned with his accoutrements of combat, like Horus, the Mighty of Arm, a lord of action like Montu (Egyptian god of war), the Theban, while his father Amun made strong his arm. The southern wing of His Majesty's army was at a hill south of [the] Kina [brook], and the northern was to the north-west of Megiddo, while His Majesty was in their centre, Amun being the protection of his person . . .'

The Egyptian forces prevailed in the ensuing battle and the kings opposed to Tuthmosis fled to the sanctuary of Megiddo, where, as the gates of the city had been shut, they were hauled to safety by citizens who let down 'garments to hoist them up'. The account of the battle complains that the enemy had 'abandoned their horses and their chariots of gold and silver' and 'if only His Majesty's army had not given up their hearts to capturing the possessions of the enemy, they would [have captured] Megiddo at this time'.[3] Instead, they had to lay siege to the city for seven months, the occupants having surrounded it with a protective ditch and fence: 'They measured [this] city, which was corralled with a moat and enclosed with fresh timbers of all their pleasant trees.' However, the king was not with them: 'His Majesty himself was in a fortress east of this town.'[4]

A stele from Gebel Barakal in Nubia describes the ultimate surrender of the city at the end of this protracted campaign: 'Then that enemy and the princes who were with him sent out to My Majesty, with all their children carrying abundant tribute, gold and silver, all their horses which were with them, their great chariots of gold and silver, as well as those which were painted, all their coats of mail, their bows, their arrows and all their weapons of warfare. It was these with which they had come from afar to fight against My Majesty, and now they were bringing them as tribute to My Majesty, standing on their walls, giving praise to My Majesty, seeking that the breath of life might be given to them.'[5]

On the fall of Megiddo, most of the city states situated between the Jordan and the sea, as well as some northern Syrian cities, including Hamath (north of Qadesh), recognized the suzerainty of Egypt, and their lords, bringing presents with them, came to Tuthmosis III's camp to do homage to him.

The attack upon Megiddo, followed by a protracted siege during which Tuthmosis III left the scene to live in a 'fortress to the east' before returning to lead the final assault on the city, was the start of

ABOVE: Amenhotep III: the historical Solomon, in whose time peace prevailed in western Asia. It was he who stationed a garrison north of Jerusalem and built the Millo and the Temple in the 14th century BC.

BELOW: Modern Jerusalem. The ancient city occupied only the small lower rock on the right of the picture. Behind it, on the higher and wider rock, was Solomon's Temple – now occupied by the Dome of the Rock.

BELOW: Tuthmosis III: the historical David, great ancestor of Tutankhamun and mightiest of all the kings of the ancient world, who re-established the Egyptian empire between the Nile and the Euphrates during the 15th century BC.

Tutankhamun emerges from a lotus flower, the symbol of holy birth.

Nefertiti, the mother of Tutankhamun: the biblical Madonna, whose image was used by her husband Akhenaten to replace the goddess Isis in his tomb.

The 6th-century BC statue of Isis and her son (left), now in the Turin Museum, which inspired the 15th-century painter Masaccio in his representation of *The Virgin and Child* (below).

The three wise men portrayed on a plaque that was found early this century near the tomb of Tutankhamun in the Valley of the Kings. It shows three types of foreigners (as represented by Egyptians) paying homage to King Aye's name.

ABOVE: The scene on the back of the throne of Tutankhamun shows his wife Ankhsenpa-amun (the biblical Mary Magdalene) anointing him with perfume exactly as the gospels say. Although the king is named after Amun, he is still shown under the protection of the Aten.

LEFT: An alabaster triple lamp, in the form of three lotus flowers, that belonged to Tutankhamun.

RIGHT: The funerary mask of Tutankhamun, the finest representation of a pharaoh ever found, which appears to be an exact likeness of the king. The eyes indicate suffering.

LEFT: One of two ritual robes belonging to Tutankhamun which Howard Carter identified as the same as the priestly dalmatic worn by Christian deacons and bishops.

BELOW: The 'ankh' or Egyptian cross, used by ancient Egyptians in the Osarian rituals of the dead to represent eternal life. Although he abolished Osiris along with the other gods, Akhenaten kept the cross as a symbol of life given by the Aten, his God. After the killing of Tutankhamun, it became a symbol of his resurrection. This wooden mirror case was found in his tomb.

RIGHT: The priest Panehesy from a scene in his Amarna tomb. He was never buried there and is to be identified with the biblical Phinehas, the Aaronite priest. It was he, according to the Talmud, who killed Jesus.

BELOW: The monastery of St Catherine, built in the sixth century AD at the foot of Mount Sinai, in the same spot where Moses had his Tabernacle and where the historical Jesus was killed.

ABOVE: Aye (right), the biblical
Ephraim, second son of Joseph and
great-uncle of Tutankhamun as well
as his successor. Here he is shown
on the wall of Tutankhamun's
burial chamber performing the
ritual of Opening the Mouth, at
which Tutankhamun is believed to
have risen from the dead.

LEFT: John the Baptist was ordered
to be put to death by Herod
Antipas in the early years of the
Christian era: painting by Puvis de
Chavannes (1824–98).

a long and successful military career for the king. After the capture of Megiddo, he proceeded to south Lebanon, where he captured three cities by the River Litani before returning to Egypt. However, it was not until his sixth campaign in his Year 30 that he was finally to vanquish his persistent enemy, Qadesh in northern Syria, which had survived the defeat of its allies at Megiddo and continued to instigate rebellion against Egypt. Three years after laying siege to Qadesh and capturing it, he crossed the Euphrates – as part of the continuing campaign to restore his empire between the Nile and the Euphrates – and defeated the King of Mitanni: 'My Majesty crossed to the farthest limits of Asia. I caused to be built many boats of cedar on the hills of the God's Land (Phoenicia) in the neighbourhood of the-mistress-of-Byblos. They were placed on chariots (wheeled wagons), oxen dragging them, and they journeyed in front of My Majesty in order to cross that great river which flows between this country and Nahrin (Mitanni) . . . Then My Majesty set up a stele on that mountain of Nahrin taken from the mountain on the west side of the Euphrates.'6

Maspero says: 'He entered the country (Mitanni) by the fords of Carchemish (between Syria to the west, Mesopotamia to the east and the Hittite land of Anagol in the north), near the spot where his grandfather, Tuthmosis I, had erected his stele a century previously. He placed another beside this . . . to mark the point to which he had extended his empire.'7

Yet, although he had now succeeded in re-establishing the empire stretching from the Nile to the Euphrates that his grandfather had created originally, Tuthmosis looked back on the battle of Megiddo as the most important military campaign of his life. That is why in all his military inscriptions, not only those carved on the walls of the temple at Karnak, he gives more details about that first military campaign than the others. It was a theme he returned to in the granite stele at Gebel Barakal, near the fourth cataract in Nubia, that he erected in his Year 47, when his days of battle were over, to give a summary of his achievements during his reign: 'I repeat further to you – hear, O people! He (the god) entrusted to me the foreign countries of Retenu (Canaan/Syria) on the first campaign when they had come to engage with My Majesty, being millions and hundred-thousands of men, the individuals of every foreign country, waiting in their chariots – three hundred and thirty princes, every one of them having his (own) army.'8

23

A TALE OF TWO CITIES

BIBLICAL narration often confuses the names of places and people, as well as the chronology of events, no doubt as a result of its long oral tradition. In the matter of chronology, for example, we saw how David attacked the Syrian city of Zobah, whose king is named as Hadadezer, won the battle and, after this success, put his own military garrisons into Syria (Aram) and the Syrians became his servants, paying him tribute. Two biblical chapters later, however, we have the Ammonites, in fear of David, asking the Syrians for military support. Moreover, Zobah is mentioned as being among the Syrian allies. This situation could not have existed if Zobah had already been defeated and David had established garrisons in Syria, and the clear inference to be drawn is that these events took place chronologically in the reverse order to that described in the biblical account.

In the matter of place-names, we do not find any mention in the annals of Tuthmosis III of two cities that are a prominent feature of the military exploits of David in the Old Testament – Rabbah and Zobah. Rabbah is to be identified as present-day Amman, capital of the Hashemite kingdom of Jordan. However, in naming Rabbah as the city attacked and besieged by David, the biblical editor has made another error and the city meant is Megiddo. For its part, Zobah is to be identified as Qadesh, once a northern Syrian stronghold on the River Orontes. The archaeological evidence once again makes it clear that the battles over these cities were fought by Tuthmosis III rather than the tribal David who lived in the tenth century B.C. because, by then, both Megiddo and Qadesh had already been destroyed and modern Amman was a settlement of minor importance.

*   *   *

Megiddo is modern Tell Megiddo, also known as Tell el-Mutesellim, one of the most important city mounds in Palestine, rising forty to sixty metres above the surrounding plain and covering an area of about fifteen acres. This area was enlarged at various periods by a lower city.

Its strategic situation at the junction of two busy highways in the Jezreel valley made it important for both trade and military purposes. Megiddo commanded the Way of the Sea, which branched off the main coastal Way of the Land of the Philistines that started at Zarw, the border city of Egypt in northern Sinai, and led eventually to Upper Galilee and northern Syria. At Megiddo, this highway bisected an east–west route leading from the Mediterranean and across the River Jordan to the land of the Ammonites. After capturing Megiddo, Tuthmosis III made it into the major Egyptian base in the valley, and it remained under Egyptian control until at least the end of the first half of the twelfth century B.C. when Ramses III occupied the Egyptian throne.

The excavations carried out at Megiddo at various times since the start of this century have been the most extensive in Palestine's history. They showed that the city, whose site had been occupied since 3300 B.C., suffered total destruction and was rebuilt in the twentieth century B.C. During the seventeenth century B.C. it seems to have fallen to the Hyksos, who ruled both Egypt and Canaan. The city's defence system at that time was 'typical of the fortifications of the Hyksos period'.[1]

During the second half of the fifteenth century B.C., the time of Tuthmosis III's siege of Megiddo, evidence of some destruction of the city was found, but 'no signs of decline . . . In fact, this is one of the periods of the greatest material wealth in Canaanite Megiddo. The palace was greatly enlarged (to fifty metres in length) and was enclosed by a two-metre-thick wall . . . A rich treasure, including ivory plaques, gold vessels, jewellery and gold and lapis lazuli beads, was found in the palace. This treasure . . . hidden beneath the floor of one of the smaller rooms in the north end of the palace . . . is a clear indication of the great wealth of the kings of Megiddo in the Amarna Age (fourteenth century B.C.).'[2]

So, after it was taken by Tuthmosis III, Megiddo became an even more important city under Egyptian control. This situation continued until the latter third of the twelfth century B.C. when there is evidence of another destruction. The date has been determined by discovery of the cartouches of both Ramses III and Ramses VI (c. 1141–1134 B.C.), which were found on objects at the last level before 'a sudden and total destruction. This is evident . . . by the signs of devastation wrought upon the (stratum) VII–A buildings and by the numerous objects . . . found strewn over the floors of this level. If the pedestal bearing the cartouche of Ramses VI does indeed belong to stratum VII–A, then the end of this stratum can be dated to approximately 1130 B.C.'[3]

This destruction of Megiddo, therefore, occurred at the same time as the destruction of Hazor and other Syrian and Canaanite cities by the Philistines, the 'Peoples of the Sea', which, as we have seen, has nothing to do with the infiltration of the Promised Land by the Israelites. Megiddo was settled again before the end of the twelfth century B.C.: 'The buildings were very poor, and the city seems to have been unfortified.'[4] This was followed by a period when some building activity was evident. Some Philistine pottery was found, and there are indications that the site was used by the Philistines in the last half of the eleventh century B.C. That settlement, too, seems to have been destroyed in the second half of the eleventh century B.C., to be replaced by poorly built buildings that indicate a period of decline. Now 'modest dwellings replaced the large buildings of the previous level. The houses were built of rubble and sun-dried brick. Some of the walls were coated with a mud plaster from the same clay used for the bricks. The city gate of level VI–A (the previous level) did not apparently . exist . . . Indeed, it seems that the city was entirely unfortified during this period.'[5]

This was the city – unfortified, not needing a siege to subdue it – that existed when the tribal chief David is said to have lived in the first half of the tenth century B.C.

In the details of the biblical account of David's Ammonite campaign we find similarities with Tuthmosis III's battle for Megiddo. While the Ammonites wait near the gate of their city – although the name is not mentioned here, it could only have been Megiddo – their Syrian allies wait further away in the open country. Then, 3s was the case at Megiddo, David's enemies fled and sought refuge in their city, which was then subjected to siege. In contrast

to the Megiddo account found at Karnak, II Samuel suggests that
the subsequent long siege of the city did not start until 'after
the year was expired', but, as in the battle for Megiddo, it
ended in triumph. However, with the exception of the time
lapse between the battle and the siege, the biblical account of
these events matches exactly the historical details of Tuthmosis
III's successful campaign against Megiddo. What strengthens this
conclusion is that Solomon, David's successor, simply inherited the empire without becoming involved in any military
campaigns and Megiddo is found among his possessions. In
I Kings, 9:15 we are told that one of the purposes of his
raising a levy was 'to build . . . the wall . . . of Megiddo' and
it is also mentioned as one of his possessions in I Kings, 4:12.

At present-day Amman, expansion of the capital after the Second
World War revealed remains, including a temple and the residue of
an ancient wall, dating from the ninth century B.C., a century later
than the time of the tribal chief David. Most of the other buildings
and tombs unearthed belonged to the period between the ninth century B.C. and Roman times. Therefore archaeology has not offered
any evidence to justify the biblical claim that the tribal chief David
conquered Rabbah (Amman) after a long siege in the first half of
the tenth century B.C. No walls dating from this period have been
found, and it would seem then to have been a minor settlement.

As we saw earlier, the Old Testament itself casts doubt on the
authenticity of the Rabbah story. Hanun, son of Nahesh, is said
to have been its king when David took the city (II Samuel, 10:2).
Yet, five chapters later, when the tribal chief David fled out of fear
of his son Absalom, we find that Rabbah was still independent
under its king, Shobi, son of Nahas, and, far from behaving like
a vassal who would have welcomed his master to the city, he took
pity on David and his followers and sent them food, drink and
utensils because they were 'hungry, and weary, and thirsty, in the
wilderness' (II Samuel, 17:28–9).

As for Tuthmosis III, although Rabbah is mentioned by him
as being among the subdued cities when he reigned,[6] there is no
indication that he personally conducted any military campaigns
against Rabbah and it appears that Rabbah, like many other
Canaanite and Syrian towns, sent tribute to Tuthmosis III without
the need for war.

What of Zobah? No trace of a locality with this name has been found in either Syria or Canaan at the time of either Tuthmosis III (fifteenth century B.C.) or the tribal David (tenth century B.C.). Yet its conquest, as we saw earlier in this chapter, must have *followed* rather than preceded that of Rabbah. This fits in precisely with the sequence of events described in the war annals of Tuthmosis III where the taking of Megiddo preceded the triumph over Qadesh, which was always at the head of rebellion, both at Megiddo and in northern Syria. As with Tuthmosis III, who put garrisons in Syria after conquering Qadesh, David was unable to control Syria until after he had defeated and taken Zobah. Furthermore, David's defeat of Hadadezer, the king of Zobah, took place as he 'went to recover his borders at the River Euphrates' and the defeat of Qadesh by Tuthmosis III was followed three years later by the campaign that carried him to the banks of the Euphrates and the subsequent defeat of the King of Mitanni after crossing the river with his boats of cedarwood.

Qadesh, the northern Syrian stronghold on the River Orontes in the Canaanite period, has been identified with modern Tell Nabi Mind, south of Lake Homs. Together with Megiddo, Qadesh headed the coalition of Canaanite kings against Tuthmosis III and, although confined with the other defeated kings within the walls of Megiddo, the King of Qadesh managed to escape and continued, as we saw, to lead rebellions against Egypt until Tuthmosis III finally conquered Qadesh in his Year 30. Qadesh remained under Egyptian control until it came under the influence of the Hittite inhabitants of Anatolia in the fourteenth century B.C., the Amarna period. Subsequently, it was conquered again by Seti I, the second king of the Nineteenth Dynasty, but it soon slipped from Egypt's grasp because of its geographical proximity to Hittite influence. Ramses II, the son of Seti I, later fought a great war at Qadesh, but had in the end to accept a peace treaty leaving Qadesh under Hittite control.

Evidence of these various wars has been found by archaeologists excavating at the site of Qadesh. This evidence also makes it clear that the final destruction of this Syrian stronghold, like that of Megiddo, occurred in the twelfth century B.C. at the hands of the Philistines. The fortified city of Qadesh therefore no longer existed at the time of David the tribal chief in the early part of the tenth century B.C.

To summarize the main conclusions that can be drawn from this chapter:

- The war annals of Tuthmosis III and the biblical account of David's campaigns agree that the king fought against a major fortified city in Canaan that was supported by a Syrian confederation under the leadership of one Syrian city;

- The king's army defeated the coalition near the city gates and the enemy sought sanctuary within its fortified walls;

- The king's army laid siege to the city for a long time before he was eventually able to take it;

- Despite the earlier defeat of the Syrian confederation, the main Syrian city went on threatening the king until conquered just before he went on to achieve his main goal with the regaining of his borders at the River Euphrates and the erection of a stele in celebration of this triumph.

Historical and archaeological evidence confirms that these events took place in the reign of Tuthmosis III. Apart from the biblical account, there is not a shred of evidence that points to their having happened five centuries later, at the time of the tribal David in the first half of the tenth century B.C. The only possible conclusion is that, despite the discrepancies over place-names, the annals used by the biblical narrators were inspired by the deeds of Tuthmosis III.

24

JERUSALEM, CITY OF DAVID

JERUSALEM, the 'city of David', sacred to three faiths – Judaism, Christianity and Islam – because of him, offers the clearest evidence about King David's identity. It is situated in the Judaean hills, thirty-five miles east of the Mediterranean, at an elevation of 2,440 feet, and consists of an ancient walled Old City and a New City, extending outside the walls and largely built since 1860. Jerusalem began as an obscure fortress on the southeast hill, on the edge of the wilderness of Judah and looked down upon from the neighbouring heights. The present walls of the Old City, to which seven gates provide access, were last restored and rebuilt by the Ottoman sultan, Suleiman the Magnificent, in the first half of the sixteenth century A.D. The first settlement of Jerusalem dates back to the Stone Age, when families dwelt in caves, and there is evidence of continuity of settlement from the Early Bronze Age in the third millennium B.C.

The second Book of Samuel describes the taking of Jerusalem as a military operation carried out by the tribal David: 'And the king and his men went to Jerusalem unto the Jebusites, the inhabitants of the land . . . David took the strong hold (fortress) of Zion: the same is the city of David' (II Samuel, 5:6–7). The account in II Samuel goes on to indicate that the city was taken by David's men penetrating the fortress through a water shaft (gutter): 'So David dwelt in the fort, and called it the city of David. And David built round about from Millo and inward' (II Samuel, 5:9). However, the evidence makes it clear that the operation was actually a peaceful one, carried out by Tuthmosis III, the historical King David, five centuries earlier.

The link between Tuthmosis III and Jerusalem derives from the time when he based himself there while his army was besieging Megiddo. His annals, as we saw earlier, refer to his having stayed 'at a fortress east of this town'. Although the name of the fortress is not mentioned at any point in the Egyptian text, all the indications are that Jerusalem, which lies to the south-east of Megiddo, is the location meant here. Leaving the besieged city and travelling east, the only route was the Way of the Sea, joined near the River Jordan by the road leading south to Jerusalem. It seems that we have an incomplete account of the fortress where the king stayed because the scribe concerned remained with the army, recording details of the military campaign at Megiddo, rather than accompanying Tuthmosis III.

The biblical reference to 'the king and his men' indicates that it was the ruler and his bodyguard, not his entire army, that was involved. As for the 'gutter' by which they obtained entry to the fortress, this is thought to have been a shaft dug to ensure supplies of water from a spring known as the Gihon – the Christian Virgin Fountain – that lay in the valley some 325 metres below Jerusalem (see Appendix E).

Shortly after David's arrival, we have a description of how the Israelites 'brought in the ark of the Lord, and set it in his place, in the midst of the tabernacle that David had pitched for it . . .' (II Samuel, 6:17). The consequence of bringing the Ark to Jerusalem is said to have made the city the holy centre for the Israelite tribes. However, there is a further element of confusion here because we are dealing not only with two Davids but with two Arks – the Ark of the Covenant, in which Moses placed the Ten Commandments, and the Ark in which Tuthmosis III carried his god, Amun-Ra, into battle before him at Megiddo, as described in his annals at Karnak: 'Year 23, first month of the third season, day 19 – awakening in [life] in the tent of life, prosperity and health, at the town of Aruna. Proceeding northward by my majesty, carrying my father Amun-Ra, Lord of the Thrones of the Two Lands [that he might open the ways] before me.'[1]

As I have shown elsewhere,[2] the idea of a holy Ark was introduced to the Israelites by Moses (Akhenaten) from Egyptian practices of worship. In his festivals and on other occasions, the Egyptian deity used to be carried by the priests in an Ark, usually in the form of a boat. When the king went to live in the fortress in the form of a boat. When the king went to live in the fortress of Jerusalem at the start of the protracted siege of Megiddo, the only possible location for the god Amun-Ra in his Ark was where the king was in residence. In fact, we know that there were some rituals in Egyptian religion that only the king and high priests could perform before the deity.

The peaceful nature of events is also indicated by the fact that Araunah, the Jebusite king, was still in control of Mount Moriah, the high holy ground to the north of the city. We have an account of how David bought the threshing-floor of Mount Moriah 'for fifty shekels of silver' in order to build an altar to the Lord. In the course of these negotiations Araunah said to David: 'Let my lord the king take and offer up what seemeth good unto him: behold, here be oxen for burnt sacrifice, and threshing instruments and other instruments of the oxen for wood. All these things did Araunah, *as a king* (my italics), give unto the king . . .' (II Samuel, 24:22–3).

The choice of a threshing-floor on Mount Moriah may seem a curious one for the site of an altar, but it is 'clear that this site was held sacred even prior to David for an elevated, exposed spot used as a threshing-floor at the approaches to a city often served as the local cultic spot. The sanctity of Jerusalem, atop the Temple Mount, is inferred (*sic*) already in the Book of Genesis (Mount Moriah) . . .'[3] This earlier biblical reference describes how Abraham is said to have received holy blessing on this same piece of ground: 'And Melchizedek king of Salem (Jerusalem) brought forth bread and wine: and he was the priest of the most high God. And he blessed him, and said, Blessed be Abram of the most high God, possessor of heaven and earth: And blessed be the most high God, which hath delivered thine enemies into thy hand . . .' (Genesis, 14:18–20). Therefore, from the time of Abraham this high ground to the north of Jerusalem had been regarded as holy ground, not just for the inhabitants of the city but for other peoples in Canaan as well.

However, the threshing-floor was not bought by the tribal David to build an altar for the Lord, but by Tuthmosis III as the site for a shrine to his State god, Amun-Ra. This is made clear in the Book of Psalms where David, like Egyptian kings, is spoken of as being the 'Son of God': 'Yet have I set my king upon my holy hill of Zion. I will declare the decree: the Lord hath said unto me,

Thou art my Son; this day have I begotten thee. Ask of me, and I shall give thee the heathen for thine inheritance, and the uttermost parts of the earth for thy possession' (Psalms, 2:6–8).

The new name of Zion makes its first appearance in the Bible as soon as we learn of King David's entry into Jerusalem – 'David took the strong hold of Zion: the same is the city of David' (II Samuel, 5:7) – and assumes more importance from this time onward.

 · The name Zion, whose meaning is not known, originated in the Bible and has not been found in any historical source. What confuses the matter further is that the name is not always used to indicate the same location. In some cases, as the one cited above, it seems to signify the fortress of Jerusalem itself. Yet, at the same time, we have the suggestion that the fortress was named after the king himself: 'So David dwelt in the fort, and called it the city of David . . .' (II Samuel, 5:9). In other cases, Zion refers only to the sacred area that was used to build the Temple: 'So shall ye know that I am the Lord your God dwelling in Zion, my holy mountain: then shall Jerusalem be holy . . .' (Joel, 3:17). Here, while Zion refers clearly to the holy area of the Temple Mount, Jerusalem is clearly separate, although related to it. We have also the reference: 'The Lord hear thee in the day of trouble; the name of the God of Jacob defend thee; Send thee help from the sanctuary, and strengthen thee out of Zion' (Psalms, 20:1–2). It is clear in this case that by Zion only the sanctuary is meant.

Further complications have arisen from the fact that Mount Zion was later believed not to have been in the area of the Temple, high to the north of ancient Jerusalem, but on the western mount. Here, in the first century A.D., a small church was built on the southern end of the hill, which became identified as the Coenaculum (the room of the Last Supper of Jesus). This was followed many centuries later – in 1936 – by a Christian monastery known today as the Church of Mary. Nevertheless, modern archaeology has confirmed that this western mount did not form part of ancient Jerusalem and was not occupied at the time of the tribal chief David.

All the indications are, in fact, that by Zion the ancient holy ground of Jerusalem was meant, the artificially flattened ground on Mount Moriah where Solomon built his Temple and which today includes two of the holiest shrines of Islam – the Dome of the Rock, built by Muhammad's second Calif, Omar, and al-Aqsa Mosque. The Temple area is surrounded by the colossal Herodian enclosure wall, preserved in the east, south and west: a larger section of the western wall (the Wailing Wall), which survives today, is regarded as the most venerated site in Jewish tradition. In ancient times, before David entered the fortress, this area was regarded as holy ground, not only by the Jebusites but by Abraham. In fact, Mount Moriah is identified as the area where the Temple was first built: 'Then Solomon began to build the house of the Lord at Jerusalem in mount Moriah, where the Lord appeared unto David his father . . .' (II Chronicles, 3:1). It is the same location where, in the account of Abraham's intention to slay Sarah's son, Isaac, until he was forbidden to do so by the Lord, we have the obscure reference: 'And Abraham called the name of that place Jehovah-jirah: as it is said to this day. In the mount of the Lord it shall be seen' (Genesis, 22:14). As we saw before, Abraham also received the blessing from the king, Melchizedek, on the same holy ground.

However, it was when King David brought *his* Ark and placed it in the same area that this ancient holy ground was transformed into a holy centre believed to be the abode of the Lord: 'For the Lord hath chosen Zion; he hath desired it for his habitation. This is my rest for ever: here will I dwell; for I have desired it' (Psalms, 132:13–14). Once Tuthmosis III had taken the image of Amun-Ra in his Ark to Jerusalem, the logical resting place for it, at a time when religious bigotry did not exist, was on the existing holy high ground of Mount Moriah where, one would expect, Tuthmosis III worshipped during his seven-month stay.

We have another case of Tuthmosis III appropriating a local holy spot for his own worship. Number 41 of the Tell el-Amarna letters, which are basically Egypt's foreign archives of the Eighteenth Dynasty, was sent by the inhabitants of the Syrian city of Tunip to Akhenaten. Here there is reference to Tuthmosis III, having captured the city, entering its temple and making a sacrifice to Egyptian gods: 'Was it not Manakhbirya (Tuthmosis III) who saved the abode of this people? His gods and his rule our region chose; exalting the gods of the king of Egypt our Lord, they dwelt in the city of Tunip.'[4]

*   *   *

After Tuthmosis III left Jerusalem at the end of his seven-month stay, the holy ground where he had worshipped became Egyptianized because of him. This can be seen easily from the name it acquired, Zion. Although found for the first time in the Bible, it is not an original Hebrew word but consists of two elements, one Hebrew, the other Egyptian. The Hebrew first element, 'Zi', means 'a land of drought, a barren place'.[5] It is the Egyptian element whose meaning has hitherto escaped recognition.

'On' is the biblical name of the ancient Egyptian holy city known from Greek as Heliopolis, a short distance to the north of modern Cairo. In the Old Testament account of the life of Joseph the Patriarch, who brought the Israelites to Egypt, we are told that Pharaoh, having appointed Joseph to a high position, gave him an Egyptian wife, 'the daughter of Potipherah priest of On' (Genesis, 41:45). Although Heliopolis was the original Egyptian holy city, the emphasis changed during the Eighteenth Dynasty when Thebes in Upper Egypt became the new capital city of the Empire as well as the holy city of the State god Amun-Ra. From this time it became the custom to refer to Thebes as 'the southern On' and Heliopolis as 'the northern On', with the word 'On' being used in the sense of 'holy city'.

In English the word 'On' has only two letters: in Hebrew it has three – *aleph* (which, like the French 'h', does not have any strong vocal value and therefore takes on the vocalization of the vowel), 'o' and 'n'. I think the fact that the *aleph*, which can only precede or follow a word, was omitted when 'Zi' and 'On' were joined together has served to obscure the original meaning of the name – the On (holy place) of the desert.

Thus the very word 'Zion', used to designate the holy ground to the north of Jerusalem from the time King David entered the city, in itself reveals its Egyptian origin. From that time, Mount Moriah, until then holy to the inhabitants of Jerusalem, became holy for all the Asiatic kingdoms of the Empire. By introducing the earlier story of Abraham being blessed by El Elyon, which is one of the names of the Israelite God, on the same Mount Moriah, the biblical narrator wanted to stress that the area was related to the God of Israel even before King David used it for his own worship.

After his seven-month stay, Tuthmosis III returned to Megiddo for his successful assault on the city, then made his way to Thebes.

We have no means of knowing whether he visited Jerusalem again during one of his many campaigns in western Asia. Nevertheless, his descendants, the children of Sarah, never really forgot their great ancestor and, after leaving Egypt and eventually settling in the Promised Land of Canaan, they made his holy ground the most venerated and holy part of their new home.

25

JERUSALEM, CITY OF PEACE

IT has been suggested – wrongly, I believe – that the name Jerusalem appeared in Egyptian records as early as the nineteenth and eighteenth centuries B.C. at the time of the Twelfth Dynasty. Without going into the rather complex semantic arguments over this, we do have a clear reference to Jerusalem, however, in the Tell el-Amarna letters, dating from the fourteenth century B.C., which contain six communications from the ruler of Jerusalem to the Egyptian king, written in Akkadian, the diplomatic language of the period. The source of these letters was given as '*mat Urusalim*', 'the land of Jerusalem', and they make it clear that Jerusalem was by then under Egyptian control, with an Egyptian military garrison stationed locally. Yet, despite this, the name Jerusalem does not appear in the western Asiatic city-lists of Tuthmosis III or any of his successors during the Empire period when Canaan was part of Egypt's empire. This absence of the name Jerusalem has not hitherto been explained. My own view is that the Egyptians recognized Jerusalem by another name – Qadesh.

Among the historical records of Tuthmosis III found at Karnak was a list that included more than a hundred names of Palestinian locations subdued during his first Asiatic campaign. Southern Palestine seems to have offered no military resistance, for the localities mentioned are to be found north of this territory in an area between Gezer (south), Damascus (north), the Mediterranean (west) and the River Jordan (east). Jerusalem is not mentioned. Yet, at the top of the Palestinian (or Megiddo) list, we find the name Qadesh.

As there was more than one location bearing that name at the time, scholars have disagreed about which one was being referred to here. The text introducing this list states: 'List of the countries of Upper Retenu . . . shut up by His Majesty in the city of the wretched *m-k-i* (Megiddo) . . . on his first victorious campaign, according to the command of his father, Amun, who led him to fortunate paths.'[1] The basic argument was about whether the Qadesh mentioned here should be identified with the northern Syrian city on the River Orontes that, as we have seen, was defeated by Tuthmosis III in a later campaign, or with a minor location of the same name in Upper Galilee, north of Hazor.

Neither of these views is, I think, to be taken seriously in the light of the available evidence. Firstly, although many of the names in the Palestine list have not been identified, of those that *have* been identified none is to be found further north than Damascus, the line reached by Tuthmosis III in his first campaign. This argues that the Syrian city on the River Orontes, which is north of Damascus, should not be identified as the Qadesh of this first campaign. Furthermore, the fact that Qadesh is given precedence in the list, followed by Megiddo, as the main object of this first campaign, excludes identification of the northern Palestine city as Qadesh. Both from archaeological and historical evidence it seems to have been a small, unfortified settlement at the time, no mention of which has ever appeared in Egyptian sources. According to Yohanan Aharoni, the prominent Israeli archaeologist, the 'rough, hilly and relatively inhospitable terrain of Upper Galilee was almost uninhabited in the Late Bronze Period (1550–1200 B.C.)'.[2]

The modern Arabic name for Jerusalem is *al-Quds*, which becomes *ha-Qudesh* in Hebrew. This word means, both in Arabic and Hebrew, the holy (ground), and is used in the first verse of chapter 11 of the Book of Nehemiah where it speaks of 'Jerusalem the holy city' (in Hebrew, *Yurushalayim ha Qudesh*). As we saw earlier, the area where David built his altar, and later Solomon his Temple, was sacred ground even before David bought it from Araunah, the Jebusite king of Jerusalem, and Abraham is said to have received holy blessing on this same piece of ground: 'And Melchizedek king of Salem (Jerusalem) brought forth bread and wine: and he was the priest of the most high God. And he blessed him, and said, Blessed be Abram of the most high God, possessor of heaven and earth. And blessed be the most high God, which hath delivered thine enemies into thy hand . . .' (Genesis, 14:18–20). Therefore, from the time of Abraham this high ground to the north of Jerusalem had been regarded as holy ground, not just for the inhabitants of the city but for other peoples in Palestine as well, and the Nehemiah mention of *Qudesh* for Jerusalem indicates that the city itself was also referred to by this name.

Urusalim, the Akkadian name for Jerusalem found in the Tell el-Amarna letters, can be divided into two elements, *Uru* and *Salim*. The first element, *Uru*, is derived from the verb *yarah*, meaning 'to found' or 'to establish'. The second element, however, has caused some misunderstanding. A number of scholars have argued that here we have a reference to a Western Semitic or Amorite god, Shulmanu or Shalim. Thus Urusalim would, in their view, mean 'Shalim has founded'. However, no textual or archaeological evidence has ever been found to indicate, either directly or indirectly, that the Amorite god Shalim was a deity worshipped at Jerusalem, which could not have been the case if the very founding of the city was related to him.

When we abandon this unsupported explanation of the second element in the word Urusalim we find that *Salim* – as was correctly understood by the early Jewish rabbis in the Haggadah, the legendary part of the Talmud – means 'peace' (Hebrew *shalom* and Arabic *salam*). Thus the meaning of Urusalim would be 'foundation of peace' or 'establishing peace', an interpretation that is supported by the historical evidence – the lack of any mention of Urusalim in Egyptian sources outside the Tell el-Amarna letters . . . the fact that Qadesh, used in both the Bible and the Koran as a synonym for Jerusalem, is mentioned in the lists of subdued Asiatic cities of most Egyptian kings of this period . . . and that the Qadesh in question cannot have been either of the other two locations whose claims have been canvassed.

The only name we have from historical documents for the King of Jerusalem during the Eighteenth Dynasty is Abdi-Kheba, who wrote to Amenhotep III (c. 1405–1367 B.C.). Yet why should he have written from Urusalim rather than Qadesh? The answer lies in the fact that he was 'establishing peace' – and confirming a tradition of peace – with Pharaoh much as the French declared Paris to be an open city in the Second World War to ensure that it would not be destroyed by Hitler's advancing forces. In the case of Qadesh, peace did not mean simply a desire not to fight the Egyptian king, but represented submission to Tuthmosis III without the need for war. In this respect, the word 'Islam', which is from the same root as *salam*, also means submission – in this case to the will of God. We find another example in the concluding section of the Israel Stele – 'The princes (of Canaan) are prostrate, saying "Mercy!"' – where the word translated as 'mercy' is indeed *salam*, indicating their submission to the will of Pharaoh.

The relationship is made quite clear from letters that Abdi-Kheba sent later to Akhenaten, the son and successor of Amenhotep III, one of which says: 'Behold, this land of Jerusalem, neither my father nor my mother gave it to me; the mighty arm [of the king] gave it to me', while in another letter he confirms his royal ancestry: '. . . the mighty arm of the king set [me] in the house of my father'. This echoes the relationship we find in the biblical account of David's purchase of the threshing-floor on Mount Moriah as a shrine for the Ark of the Lord from the local king, Araunah, who said: 'All these things did Araunah, as a king, give unto the king . . .' (II Samuel, 24:23). It seems that, after the King of Jerusalem had placed his land peacefully under Egyptian control, Tuthmosis III kept him and his descendants as rulers. Thus, when Tuthmosis III went out to fight against the confederation of Canaanite and Syrian princes at Megiddo, Jerusalem did not take part in the rebellion. The king faced no need to take control of the fortress and, instead, was able to make his way straight from Gaza to Megiddo and, without need for military action, to seek safe sanctuary in Jerusalem during the long months that Megiddo was under siege. Although Egyptian scribes continued to use Qadesh – the name still used in Arabic (*al-Quds*) to indicate Jerusalem – the city always reminded Pharaoh of their submission by using the name Urusalim. This was also the name used later by the biblical narrators, from which the Greek version, Hierosolyma (the first element indicates holiness), was derived and thus transmitted to the western world.

26

DAVID AND ABRAHAM

IF Tuthmosis III, whom I have identified as the biblical King
David, was the real father of Isaac, then he and Abraham must
have lived at the same time – in the fifteenth century B.C. A careful
examination of the biblical story of Abraham provides evidence to
support this view.

The main details of Abraham's story are to be found in a series
of isolated traditions in the Book of Genesis, 11:26 to 25:10. Since
the latter years of the last century, biblical scholars have come
to accept the opinions of the German scholar Julius Wellhausen
(1844–1918), who regarded the Pentateuch, the first five books of
the Old Testament that have been ascribed to Moses, as being – in
the form we know them today – of composite origin. Five sources
were thought to have been used to assemble the books of the
Pentateuch: a Jehovistic source, in which God is referred to as
Jehovah, dating from the ninth century B.C. (J); an Elohistic
document, in which God is referred to as Elohim, dating from the
eighth century B.C. (E); the Book of Deuteronomy, to be regarded
as a separate source, dating from the seventh or sixth century B.C.;
a priestly source dating from about the fifth century B.C. (P); and
the work of an editor who revised and edited the entire collection
between the fifth and second centuries B.C.

It was believed that most of the Abrahamic story in Genesis
comes from the (J) source of the ninth century B.C. Nevertheless,
although not challenging the general ideas of Wellhausen, modern
biblical scholars have been persuaded to think that the Abrahamic
story we find in Genesis could have been first developed only
during the time when the empire of King David, stretching
from the Nile to the Euphrates, was re-established. As they
thought – wrongly – that this happened during the first half of

the tenth century B.C., they are now arguing that this is the date when the first account of the life and times of Abraham was composed. However, as we have already seen, the re-establishment of this empire, while certainly a historical fact, can have occurred only during the reign of Tuthmosis III five centuries earlier. Some scholars have even made the point that the story of Abraham reflects conditions that can be identified as having existed *only* during the reign of King David: 'H. W. Wolff notes that certain peoples are mentioned in Genesis – Philistines, Moabites, Ammonites, Aramaeans, Edomites, Amalekites and Canaanites – the very peoples which, according to II Samuel, 8, were incorporated in David's empire.'[1]

Some scholars have put forward the view that Abraham lived during the seventeenth century B.C., two centuries before Tuthmosis III. However, the reference to Jerusalem in the Abrahamic story as *Salem* (Genesis, 14:17) – a name which was given to the city only from the time of Tuthmosis III – contradicts this theory. Yet, to leave what are basically minutiae of the argument . . . .

It is in the promise or covenant found in the stories of both David and Abraham that we can see clearly the historical connection between the two characters. The different traditions used to make up the story of Abraham are linked into one composition mainly by means of the promises that the Lord keeps giving to Abraham from his first appearance to the end of the story. These promises are of varied kinds:

• Of an heir,

• Of many descendants,

• Of royal descendants,

• Of the land of Canaan,

• Of the land from the Nile to the Euphrates.

Scholars have been locked in argument about which of these various promises is central to the story: 'In more recent years debate has centred on whether it was the promise of land or of numerous seed which served as the basic theme. Claus Westermann has shown the inadequacy of this method of investigation by turning to the literary structure of the various promises. He attempts to isolate those promises which are capable of standing on their own from those which appear in various combinations. He feels that the former are original whereas the latter have been built up over a period of time. When he comes at the problem this way he discovers that the promise of an heir alone fills the bill.'[2]

It is true, as Westermann has shown, that the promise of an heir was the main connecting element in the story of Abraham. Even before he left Ur, immediately after we are given the information about his marriage, we are warned that 'Sarai was barren' (Genesis, 11:30). Yet, as if to make the plot of the story more interesting, we are given only a few verses later the Lord's promise to Abraham: 'I will make of thee a great nation' (Genesis, 12:2) – and we are left to wonder how, if his wife is barren, he is to become the founding father of a great nation?

Wagner makes the point: 'No reader of the Abraham story could really miss the absolutely basic theme of the promise of an heir. In fact, the whole Abraham story hinges on this point, which constantly seems in danger of frustration. Beginning with the barren wife . . . Abraham is assured that he will have a son . . . and it begins to appear as if this will become a reality by means of Hagar, the Egyptian slave girl (Genesis, 16:4). The expulsion of Hagar, however, frustrated that hope. Finally, it is stated that Sarah is to become pregnant (Genesis, 17:16). After this long-awaited son is born, Abraham is called upon to sacrifice him as a burnt offering. Only by means of the promised heir are the separate episodes of the Abraham narrative strung together . . . the theme itself is of such importance that the story falls apart without it.'[3]

However, careful examination of the Abraham story makes it clear that the promised heir is not Abraham's own son, but Sarah's. For Abraham had Ishmael: 'Hagar bare Abram a son: and Abram called his son's name, which Hagar bare, Ishmael' (Genesis, 16:15). After Sarah's death: 'Abraham took a wife, and her name was Keturah. And she bare him Zimran, and Jokshan, and Medan, and Midian, and Ishbak, and Shuah' (Genesis, 25:1–2). Yet none of these seven sons was the expected heir whose birth had been foretold. He was Sarah's son by David (Tuthmosis III).

So it was because of the birth of Isaac that the promises to Abraham were made and, in fact, it was also made very clear that they were not meant for Abraham's descendants, but for Isaac's: 'I will establish my covenant with him (Isaac) for an everlasting covenant, and with his seed after him' (Genesis, 17:19). Abraham even appeared unwelcoming when the birth of Isaac was foretold: 'And Abraham said unto God, O that Ishmael might live before thee!' (Genesis, 17:18), meaning that Ishmael was enough without Isaac, but God insisted: 'Sarah thy wife shall bear thee a son . . . and thou shalt call his name Isaac' (Genesis, 17:19). The birth of Isaac is made more important because of the royal element attached to it: 'Kings of people shall be of her (Sarah)' (Genesis, 17:16). This is confirmed by other promises given to Abraham about Isaac's descendants: '. . . and thy seed shall possess the gate of his enemies. And in thy seed shall all the nations of the earth be blessed . . .' (Genesis 22:17–18). The royal nature of Isaac and his descendants supports my argument that he was the son of Tuthmosis III. This can also be seen from the description of the land that Isaac's descendants were promised:

- '. . . from the river of Egypt unto the great river, the river Euphrates' (Genesis, 15:18);

- '. . . all the land of Canaan, for an everlasting possession . . .' (Genesis, 17:8).

The first promise, of the land between the Nile and Euphrates, I interpret as being meant for those descendants of Isaac who went down to Egypt at the time of the Sojourn. Before the promise about the land between the Nile and Euphrates, the Lord told Abraham that his descendants (Isaac's) would be 'strangers in a land that is not theirs' but would return to Canaan 'in the fourth generation'. Therefore, it was meant for those descendants who went to Egypt with the Patriarch Joseph, whom I have identified as Yuya.[4] When Yuya's daughter, Tiye, was married to Amenhotep III, the great-grandson of Tuthmosis III, this part of the prophecy was fulfilled as the following four kings – Akhenaten, Semenkhkare, Tutankhamun and Aye, known as the Amarna kings – ruled the land between the two great rivers before the Israelites returned to the Promised Land of Canaan. It was not until Cyrus of Persia had conquered Egypt after defeating Babylonia in the second half of the sixth century B.C. that another king established his control over the land between the Nile and Euphrates. Thus the promise given to Abraham because of the forthcoming birth of Isaac differs from the promise or covenant made between the Lord and the Israelites in Sinai. There the covenant was between two sides, God and the Israelites; the Abrahamic promise, made to Isaac's descendants even before Isaac's own birth, is an inheritance promise with no conditions attached to it.

In Egypt, in contrast, the Lord told Moses: '. . . I will bring you out from under the burdens of the Egyptians, and I will rid you out of their bondage . . . And I will take you to me for a people . . . And I will bring you in unto the land (Canaan), concerning the which I did swear to give it to Abraham, to Isaac, and to Jacob; and I will give it to you for an heritage . . .' (Exodus, 6:6–8). Later, in Sinai, the Lord asked Moses to tell the Israelites: 'Ye have seen what I did unto the Egyptians, and how I bare you on eagles' wings, and brought you unto myself. Now therefore, if ye will obey my voice indeed, and keep my covenant, then ye shall be a peculiar treasure unto me above all people . . .' (Exodus, 19:4–5). The Israelites replied: '. . . All that the Lord hath spoken we will do . . .' (Exodus, 19:8), thus binding themselves by the covenant.

This story is followed by an account of the Ten Commandments, the laws that the Lord asked them to observe. Subsequently, however, during the absence of Moses, we are told that the Israelites resumed their relationship with the ancient Canaanite gods and made themselves a golden calf to worship. This rebellious act breached the covenant and the Lord, angry with the Israelites, refused to accompany them to the Promised Land: '. . . I will not go up in the midst of thee; for thou art a stiffnecked people . . .' (Exodus, 33:3). It was only after Moses had pleaded for pardon, and on condition that the Israelites would always observe his commandments, that the Lord renewed his covenant with them. In the words of Ronald E. Clements, Professor of Old Testament Studies at King's College, London: 'In the Sinai covenant, the Law entered as a demand upon Israel, and so provides a condition for the continuance of the covenant.'[5]

The promise made to David, unlike the Sinai promise with its conditions, is the same as the promise made to Abraham – a straightforward matter of inheritance. After stating that it was the Lord who had appointed David to rule his people, the account continues: '. . . the Lord telleth thee that he will make thee an house' (II Samuel, 7:11); '. . . I will set up thy seed after thee . . . and I will establish his kingdom' (II Samuel, 7:12); '. . .

thine house and thy kingdom shall be established for ever . . .'
(II Samuel, 7:16).

As the borders of his empire, from the Nile to the Euphrates, are
found in other parts of the David story, as well as in the story of
Solomon, the promise we are considering here consists basically
of two elements – establishing his throne and establishing the
throne for his descendants after him: '. . . the tradition of the
covenant with Abraham became the pattern of the covenant
between Jehovah and David, whereby Jehovah promised to main-
tain the Davidic line on the throne (II Samuel, 23:5). Jehovah
bound Himself, exactly as in the Abrahamic . . . covenant, and
therefore Israel could not escape responsibility to the king. The
covenant with Abraham was the prophecy and that with David
the "fulfilment" . . . the form of the Davidic covenant is similar
to that made with Abraham, but is different from the Sinai-Horeb
law covenant form.'[6]

The main difference, however, between the promise made to
David and the promise made to Abraham is that, while the
kingdom is allotted to David and his sons, it is not promised to
Abraham at all, nor to any of the descendants of his seven sons
apart from Isaac. It is not even promised to Isaac himself, for he is
instructed: 'Go not down into Egypt . . .' (Genesis, 26:2), and thus
forbidden to seek his real father's inheritance. But it is to be given,
as we said before, to his descendants, who would be returning to
Egypt and would spend four generations there.

Recognizing the similarity between the two promises made
to Abraham and David, Professor Clements commented: 'It is
perfectly possible that the Jehovist's account of the covenant with
Abraham in Genesis 15 has itself been moulded by the form of
the covenant between Jehovah and David as part of a conscious
attempt to relate the two. Secondly, we have already noted that
there are traces in Genesis 15 of royal motifs which suggest that
Genesis 15 has been influenced by the Jerusalem court theology.'[7]
Here Clements has been able to see what really happened. Not
only is the Abrahamic promise similar to the Davidic one: it was
composed to agree with it. Thus the Davidic promise existed first.
To try to put the matter in simple terms, in the Book of Genesis,
where the ancestral role of Tuthmosis III (King David) is disguised,
the promise is attributed to Abraham. However, once the tribal
David entered the scene, when the (J) source of the first five books

of the Old Testament was put down in writing during the ninth century B.C., the promise was attributed to him (which would, of course, have excluded the Israelites from the inheritance promise as no empire existed for them to inherit at that time or for many centuries later).

The biblical account of the inheritance promise to King David finds an echo in the story we find in Egyptian records of the way Tuthmosis III came to the throne. As we saw before, he was not supposed to become a king. He was neither the son of the heiress nor the husband of the heiress. It was because the god Amun chose him that the historical King David became a king. The promise made to Tuthmosis III is recorded on a stele that was found by Mariette Pasha, the French Egyptologist, and is now in the Cairo Museum: 'I grant thee by decree the earth in its length and breadth. The tribes of the East and those of the West are under the place of thy countenance . . .

'Thou hast crossed the water of the great curve of Nahrain (the Euphrates) in thy strength and thy power, and I have commanded thee to let them hear thy roaring, which shall enter their dens . . . I have granted to thee that thy deeds shall sink into their hearts, that my uraeus (the serpent on his forehead, the sign of royal power) is upon thy head . . . I grant to thee that thy conquests may embrace all lands, that the uraeus that shines upon my forehead may be thy vassal, so that in all the compass of the heaven there may not be one to rise against thee, but that the people may come bearing their tribute on their backs and bending before Thy Majesty according to my behest; I ordain that all aggressors arising in thy time shall fail before thee, their heart burning within them, their limbs trembling.'[8]

The correct course of events, I believe, is that, after the birth of Isaac, Abraham did not want him to survive, looking upon him as illegitimate. However, he was persuaded to spare his life and is said to have been given many promises, confirming the royal status of Isaac and his descendants. Abraham then accepted the role of Isaac's adoptive father and, although the Israelite descendants of Isaac regarded Abraham as their great ancestor, they also knew who the *real* founding father of the tribes of Israel was. In fact, as I have argued elsewhere, Amenhotep III would not have made Tiye, the daughter of Joseph the Patriarch (Yuya), his queen unless he accepted that his own great-grandfather, Tuthmosis

III, was also hers.[9] Later, descendants of the Israelites wanted to restore their real ancestor, King David, in their traditions. The biblical narrators, writing many centuries later, therefore grafted the exploits of the mighty King David on to the life of an ordinary chief from the tribe of Judah.

The view that the promise said to have been made to Abraham is actually the promise made to David is supported by the fact that, once the Israelite scribes had restored their real ancestor by attributing the feats of King David to the tribal chief who lived five centuries later, Abraham disappears from the biblical scene: 'In the (J) and (E) history, as well as in the introductory sections to the Code of Deuteronomy, the Abrahamic covenant is given a position of importance, whereas in the pre-exilic prophets it plays no part at all. It is not until we come to the great prophets of the exile . . . that appeal is made to Abraham as the ancestor who received a divine promise of possession of the land of Canaan . . . How are we to explain this indifference to the Abrahamic covenant in the pre-exilic prophets . . . ?'[10]

From the point at which David appears, therefore, the promise originally related to Abraham passes to David and his descendants and it is from the House of their now-remembered great ancestor that the Messiah, the expected Redeemer, would come.

27

DAVID AND BATHSHEBA

THE similarities in the stories of Abraham and David are again reflected in the fact that both concern married women who went through second marriages with a king.

In the Book of Genesis we are told that Abraham introduced his wife Sarah to the court of Egypt as his sister and she was taken in marriage by the ruling Pharaoh, who, I have argued here, was Tuthmosis III and the father of Isaac. The story of King David and Bathsheba, to be found in II Samuel, is slightly different. While David was staying at the fortress of Jerusalem at the time of the siege of the fortified city, he saw Bathsheba bathing and made inquiries about her identity. On learning that she was the wife of Uriah the Hittite, who was serving with the king's forces at the siege, David sent messengers to bring her to his house where 'he lay with her' (II Samuel, 11:4). As a result of this liaison, Bathsheba became pregnant. In the hope of disguising his guilt, David had Uriah brought to Jerusalem, but the warrior refused to sleep in the comfort of his own home while the king's army suffered the hardships of having to live in tents before the besieged city. David therefore sent him back to the battle with orders that he should be placed in a dangerous position. As expected, Uriah was killed in the fighting.

After the mourning period, David married Bathsheba, who bore him a son: 'But the thing that David had done displeased the Lord' (II Samuel, 11:27).

This last verse and the first twenty-five verses of the chapter that follows are clearly a later insertion as they have the prophet Nathan being sent by the Lord to reprove David for his sin and go on to describe the illness and death of the unnamed child born to Bathsheba and the birth of another son to be called Solomon.

This is followed by the account of the fall of the besieged city to David.

The main line of the stories of Abraham and Uriah is the same. Both are foreigners, Abraham a Canaanite in Egypt, Uriah a Hittite in Jerusalem. In each case their wives are made pregnant by a king and give birth to a son, who has to die because he is the fruit of sin. However, the Genesis account is told without comments and it was Pharaoh himself who sent Sarah away on discovering that she was already married. In contrast, in the Book of Samuel we have later concepts of morality forcing judgments on the characters involved. The relationship between David and Bathsheba is regarded as adultery, with Uriah sent to his death to remove him from the scene, and, while Isaac's life is spared and a lamb is sacrificed in his stead, here the child had to die. The king is threatened with some future troubles as a punishment: it is only the woman who escapes punishment – and the line of descendants from the sinful relationship is promised the throne.

Hermann Gunkel, the great German biblical scholar, dismissed the whole story of Uriah and his wife as having no historical basis. The basis lies, however, in the Abraham-Sarah-Pharaoh story in the Book of Genesis. If we examine the name of Uriah, who is listed in II Samuel, 23:39, we find that it is composed of two elements – Ur, a Hurrian (northern Mesopotamian) word meaning 'city' or 'light', and Yah (iah), which is the short form of Jehovah, the Israelite God. The meaning of the name could therefore be 'Jehovah's light'. Yet he is described as being a Hittite. How can we expect a Hittite, a traditional enemy of Egypt and the Israelites, to be one of the heroes of David's army? We have no information to explain the sudden appearance of this foreigner and his wife in Jerusalem, where they appear to have had their home.

To look at the matter from another point of view, these fictional names usually give some indication of the original character who inspired them. Ur, the first part of Uriah's name, relates him to the birthplace of Abraham. The first reference to this in the Bible describes how Abraham and Sarah 'went forth . . . from Ur of the Chaldees, to go into the land of Canaan' (Genesis, 11:31). This could mean either 'a city of the Chaldees' or if the word Ur was used as a proper noun, 'Ur of the Chaldees'. Whatever the situation regarding this early reference, later on Ur certainly became a proper noun indicating the birthplace of Abraham. Thus the name Ur-iah relates the invented character both to Abraham's God and his city of origin.

We have a similar situation with the name Bathsheba. Originally it was to be read Beth-Sheba. The 'a' was introduced later by scribes striving to achieve unified pronunciation, but the insertion has served to obscure the original sense of the word. Here again we have two elements – Beth, meaning 'a girl' or 'a daughter', and Sheba, an area to the south of Canaan that takes its name from the local well, Beer-Sheba. The name Beth-Sheba can therefore be interpreted as 'a girl (or daughter) of Sheba', which was the area in which Sarah and Abraham settled after their return from Egypt.

Although the tradition of Uriah-David-Bathsheba was a legendary composition based on the memory of Abraham-Pharaoh-Sarah, it is possible that Abraham did meet King David in Jerusalem as well. The story of Abraham describes two incidents that would make this feasible.

The first was when Abraham was blessed by Melchizedek, the priest and king of Salem: 'Blessed be Abram of the most high God, possessor of heaven and earth' (Genesis, 14:19). This blessing must have taken place on the holy ground of Mount Moriah, later the site of the Temple Mount, which I identified earlier in this book as Zion. The second incident refers to the same location. Abraham, being tested by God, was instructed to 'Take now thy son, thine only son Isaac, whom thou lovest, and get thee into the land of Moriah; and offer him there for a burnt offering upon one of the mountains which I will tell thee of' (Genesis 22:2).

The purpose of Abraham's visit to Jerusalem, which does not fit in with the general development of the story being told, is not clear, but John Gray is one scholar who has suggested that it was connected with David: 'The significance of the incident (the threatened sacrifice of Isaac), which is probably out of context, is uncertain, and it probably served a particular purpose of the compiler of the time of David and Solomon. This has been thought to be the authentication of David's adoption of the local cult of El Elyon (God Most High).'[1] A possible sequence of historical events that lie behind the visit of Abraham to Jerusalem would be as follows:

After leaving Egypt, Abraham and Sarah settled in Canaan, where Isaac was born. Later, in the course of his first Asiatic campaign, Tuthmosis III set up residence in the fortress of Jerusalem.

On learning this, Abraham took Isaac to Jerusalem, presented him to the king and threatened to kill the child. However, the king, while warning Isaac not to go down to Egypt, persuaded Abraham to abandon this course of action by a promise of some land in Canaan if he would agree to bring up Isaac as his own son. This sequence of events would point to Isaac having been the unnamed son of Bathsheba by King David in the Uriah-David-Bathsheba version of the story. It does not ring true because it was normal at the time for Hebrew children, and other children, to be named as soon as they were delivered. The narrator, eager to conceal the true facts about the parenthood of Isaac, and aware that Isaac had not been put to death, therefore invented the story of the child of sin who died and left him unnamed.

Solomon is said by the Old Testament to have followed David on the throne at Jerusalem. Working on the theory that David was the tribal chief who ruled in the tenth century B.C., scholars have assigned c. 965–925 B.C. as the dates of Solomon's forty-year reign, his accession coinciding with the Egyptian rule of King Siamun (c. 976–956 B.C.) of the weak Twenty-first Dynasty. However, if, as I have argued here, King David was actually Tuthmosis III, we have to go back some four centuries, to the middle of the Eighteenth Dynasty of Egypt, to try to establish the identity of the ruler known from the Bible as Solomon. The task is complicated by the fact that we have no historical record of a ruler named Solomon at any time, and that both the Old Testament and the Talmud agree that this was not the king's original name. According to II Samuel, 12:25, at the time of his birth the prophet Nathan gave Solomon the name of Jedidiah, meaning 'because of the Lord' or 'by the word of the Lord'. However, the evidence points to Amenhotep III, not the immediate successor to King David (Tuthmosis III) but his great-grandson, as being the historical figure identified in the Old Testament as Solomon.

As this evidence simply gives further support to the arguments already advanced about the real identity of King David, it can be found in Appendices F–J, along with the source of Solomon's enduring reputation for wisdom.

Book Three

CHRIST THE KING

28

THE LIVING IMAGE OF THE LORD

ALL the evidence points to the identification of Tutankhamun as the historical Jesus. This, I realize, is a challenging – and will, for many people, be a disturbing – statement. Yet it seems the only logical conclusion to draw from the evidence.

We have two names of successors to Moses, whom I have identified as the Pharaoh Akhenaten. One is the biblical Joshua, the prophet: the other is Tutankhamun, the anointed king who succeeded Akhenaten on the throne after his abdication. We have already identified Joshua as Jesus. Can the same be said of Tutankhamun?

Luke describes the forthcoming birth of Jesus in the following terms: 'He shall be great, and shall be called the Son of the Highest: and the Lord God shall give unto him the throne of his father David: And he shall reign over the house of Jacob for ever; and of his kingdom there shall be no end' (1:32–3). There is nobody apart from Tutankhamun of whom it can be said that these conditions – Son of the Highest, seated upon the throne of his father (the sense here is ancestor) David – were fulfilled.

Tutankhamun was born in the city of Amarna. A linen shirt found in his tomb and dated to Year 7 of Akhenaten, indicates that this was the year of his birth. There cannot be any doubt that he belonged to the Tuthmosside royal family of which Tuthmosis III (King David) had been the head four generations earlier. A text on a lion of red granite in the British Museum states that 'He restored the monuments of his father (again ancestor is meant) Amenhotep III.'[1]

Professor R. G. Harrison, the late Professor of Anatomy at the University of Liverpool, who examined the king's mummy in 1963, found a striking similarity with artistic impressions of

Akhenaten, suggesting that they were close relations. Howard Carter, who discovered the tomb of Tutankhamun, was equally struck by the matching appearance of his mask and mummy both to Akhenaten and to his mother, Queen Tiye: '. . . certain aspects of the face here recall . . . Akhenaten, in others, especially in profile, perhaps an even stronger likeness to the great Queen Tiye, Akhenaten's mother, or, in other words, as those features gazed on you there was an incipient gleam of affinity to both of those predecessors.'[2] In the young king's tomb inscribed objects were found bearing the names of many members of the royal family – Akhenaten, Queen Tiye, Amenhotep III, Tuthmosis III, as well as two of Akhenaten's brothers, Tuthmosis and Semenkhkare.

Some scholarly debate has been devoted to the question of whether Tutankhamun was the son or brother of Akhenaten, and the identity of his mother. These matters are not difficult to resolve. Akhenaten had a co-regency with his father, Amenhotep III, for twelve years, then ruled alone for five. The birth of Tutankhamun in – according to the shirt found in his tomb – his father's Year 7 would make him ten years of age when he came to the throne and nineteen when he died. These dates are confirmed by anatomical examination of his body as well as by dated objects found in his tomb.

Year 7 of Akhenaten corresponds to Year 33 of his father. At this time, Queen Tiye was about forty-one. Two years earlier she had given birth to a daughter, Baketaten, and from a purely physical point of view she would have been able to give birth to a son, Tutankhamun, two years later. However, had she been the mother of Tutankhamun:
1) The date of his birth would have been related to Amenhotep III, not to Akhenaten;
2) Tiye's first visit to Amarna, as can be shown from the Amarna tomb of her steward Huya, did not take place earlier than Akhenaten's Year 10, so she could not have given birth to Tutankhamun at Amarna in Akhenaten's Year 7.

The only reasonable conclusion is that Akhenaten was the father of Tutankhamun. What of his mother? Without any evidence to support their argument, some scholars have suggested a different mother from Queen Nefertiti for the young king. However, there is strong archaeological evidence confirming that, both before and after Tutankhamun came to the throne, he lived with Nefertiti at the northern palace of Amarna.[3] This can only confirm the maternal relationship.

Some scholars have also been confused about the relationship between Tutankhamun and the royal family because, although he had to marry the heiress in order to ascend to the throne, his bride was Ankhsenpa-aten, the third daughter of Akhenaten. This, too, is simply explained. As their eldest daughter had already been married to Semenkhkare, who died a few days before the coronation of Tutankhamun, and their second daughter had herself died, Ankhsenpa-aten was the heiress at the time.

The young king-to-be was given the name Tut-ankh-aten when he was born. As I have shown elsewhere, Aten in Egyptian is the equivalent of Adonai – the Lord – in Hebrew.[4] His birthname therefore means 'the living image of the Lord'. Thus he was recognized from the time of his birth – or perhaps even before it, as it was the custom of Egyptian kings to choose names for their children before they were born – as the Son of God, 'the eldest Son of Aten (the Lord) in heaven'[5] as well as the successor to Akhenaten (Moses).

Messianic beliefs originated in Egypt. The English word 'Christ' comes from the Greek 'Kristos', which is the equivalent of the Hebrew and Aramaic *Mashih*. This word is derived from the root *MeSHeH*, a verb meaning to anoint. Thus 'the Christ' indicated originally 'the anointed one', who is 'the king'.

The basis of Messianic beliefs was the divine nature that Egyptians attributed to their kings, whose authority came from God. From the start of their history, even earlier than thirty centuries B.C., they identified their king as being the same person as Horus, the falcon god. Then he developed into an incarnate version of the god, who appeared 'on the throne of Horus'. This concept placed the king between god and man.

Another important development took place from the time of the Fourth Dynasty (the twenty-seventh century B.C.), the era of the builders of the pyramids, when the king ceased to be identified with Horus and became the human Son of Ra, the cosmic god. The king's actions were seen as merely fulfilment of his father's commands. This special relationship between the god, Ra, and the king was manifested in the three principal events in the ruler's life – his holy birth, his anointment at the time of his coronation, and his resurrection after his death.

The holy birth of the king is documented in scenes as well as texts found on the north wall of the central colonnade of Queen Hatshepsut's mortuary temple at Deir el Bahari and in the hall built by Amenhotep III in the Luxor Temple. 'In both cases the procreation and birth of the king concerned are depicted as proceeding from the union between the national god (Amun-Ra) and the consort of the ruling Pharaoh: God, in the guise of the Pharaoh, is shown approaching the woman thus blessed. The images and text depict the scene with a fine delicacy, yet dwell frankly upon the act of sexual union. There is nothing here of that ascetic spiritual treatment so characteristic of the late Hellenistic age, which led to the Christian idea of the miraculous birth of Jesus.'6

At the time of his coronation the ruler became the bearer of the divine kingly office. The coronation ceremony included purification by water, anointment, putting on royal attire, holding the sceptre of office, having the two crowns (of Upper and Lower Egypt) placed on his head, and declaration of his fixed royal names and titles. The king was not anointed with oil, but with the fat of the holy crocodile. This is the original source of the word 'Messiah'. MeSSeH was the word for crocodile in Ancient Egypt,7 and the image of two crocodiles was used for the title of sovereign, bestowed on the king at the time of his coronation. This could be read in two ways – messhee and messeeh – because the long ee used in the dual form could be inserted either at the end or in the middle of the word.8 As an Egyptian s becomes sh in Hebrew and Aramaic, it is clear that the biblical word Messiah derives initially from mesheeh, the ancient Egyptian word indicating a specific kind of ritual anointing of the king.

The final decisive event in the ruler's life was his death and resurrection: '. . . just as coronation enabled a man to enter the world of the divine, so upon his death he ceased to belong to the human world.'9 From then onward the king was believed to have been united with the gods with whom he shared eternal spiritual existence: 'Evidence of this belief is afforded by "becoming Osiris" whereby the king entered the eternal nature of this god and, instead of just acting analogously as at first, acquired an identity of existence with him.'[10]

Thus, when we read in the Old Testament about the Israelites waiting for their 'anointed Messiah', this could mean only that they were waiting for a king to rule them, unite them and defeat their enemies. The Messiah, like Osiris, had to die before he could be a Redeemer, and it is the hope that the king, Son of God, met his death but was resurrected that can give his followers the prospect of eternal life with him. This Egyptian idea, alien to the early Israelites, could not have been accepted by them before their kingly Messiah had lived and met his death. It was the prophet Isaiah who first introduced the idea of the Messiah as a Redeemer in the character of the Servant, who thus became a Saviour of the world – the precise concept used in the Gospels for the role of Jesus. The very idea of Christ being the Redeemer confirms that he had already lived his historical life and died.

29

THE VIRGIN BIRTH

THE Virgin Birth is a theological matter. Here we are concerned only with the historical facts. However, it is worth considering some of the points of discussion involved in what has become a dogma of the Roman Catholic Church.

In Ancient Egypt, divine birth was looked upon as an aspect of royal birth, and, although the child was regarded as the son of the deity, this did not exclude the human father or the sexual relationship between the parents. The spirit of the deity used the physical body of the king to produce the child. In Christian belief, however, no human father is involved: the mother is a virgin, the child is conceived by the Holy Spirit without any sexual relationship.

The Church seems, in declaring that Mary, the mother of Jesus, was 'ever a virgin', to have ignored the Gospel evidence that she had other children as well (Matthew, 12:46, Mark, 3:31 and 6:3, Luke, 8:19, John, 2:12), and also the testimony that Joseph 'knew her not till she had brought forth her firstborn son . . .' (Matthew, 1:25).

No mention of the birth of Jesus is to be found in New Testament writings of the first century A.D.; only the later Gospel-writers refer to it. His death and resurrection were the main focus of interest: hence we find no account of the events surrounding his birth in Acts or any of the Epistles. Ignatius, the Bishop of Antioch at the beginning of the second century A.D., was the first of the Church Fathers to refer to the birth of Jesus: 'For our God, Jesus the Christ, was conceived by Mary, in God's plan being sprung both from the seed of David and from the Holy Spirit.'[1] Despite the fact that reference to 'the seed of David' would require a human descendant of David, Ignatius also described Mary as a virgin: 'Mary's virginity and her giving birth escaped from the prince of this world, as did the Lord's death.'[2]

The comments of another Church Father, Justin Martyr, in the middle of the second century A.D., make it clear that the idea of a virgin birth can be looked upon as the fulfilment of an Old Testament prophecy: 'Therefore the Lord himself shall give you a sign; Behold a virgin shall conceive, and bear a son, and shall call his name Immanuel' (Isaiah, 7:14).

Although the Hebrew word *alma* indicates a damsel or an unmarried woman, Christians took it to mean a virgin. It has been suggested that this proclamation of the Virgin Birth of Jesus was part of an attempt to popularize Christianity among the Gentiles. The Greeks believed that Semele, a human being, was impregnated directly by their chief god, Zeus, which resulted in the birth of Dionysos. Thus Justin Martyr addresses them: 'In saying that the word . . . was born for us without sexual union, as Jesus Christ our Teacher . . . we introduce nothing new beyond [what you say of] those whom you call sons of Zeus.'[3]

Two of the Gospels that appeared in the second century A.D. – Matthew in the first half, Luke in the second – give accounts of the Nativity. Matthew relates it in this manner: '. . . When as his mother Mary was espoused to Joseph, before they came together, she was found with child of the Holy Ghost . . . Now all this was done, that it might be fulfilled which was spoken of the Lord by the prophet (Isaiah), saying, Behold a virgin shall be with child, and shall bring forth a son, and they shall call his name Emmanuel, which being interpreted is, God with us' (Matthew, 1:18, 22–3).

For his part, Luke describes how news of the child to be born to Mary was revealed to her by an angel: '. . . the angel Gabriel was sent from God . . . To a virgin espoused to a man whose name was Joseph, of the house of David; and the virgin's name was Mary . . . And the angel said unto her . . . behold, thou shalt conceive in thy womb, and bring forth a son, and shalt call his name Jesus . . . Then said Mary unto the angel, How shall this be, seeing I know not a man? And the angel answered and said unto her, The Holy Ghost shall come upon thee, and the power of the Highest shall overshadow thee: therefore also that holy thing which shall be born of thee shall be called the Son of God' (1:26–7, 30–31, 34–5).

By the year 200 A.D., Christianity had become an institution headed by a three-rank hierarchy of bishops, priests and deacons.

It had also become known as Catholic, meaning universal, and the label 'orthodox', meaning straight-thinking, had been attached to its members in contrast to the Gnostic sects, which were looked upon as heretical. The Church established the Creed, a list of beliefs that had to be accepted by all its members and included the statement that Jesus Christ was 'conceived by the Holy Ghost' and 'born of the Virgin Mary'.

This belief developed until it reached its climax when Mary, the mother of Jesus, became regarded as 'ever-virgin', a concept established at the Council of Trullo in 692 A.D.: 'As the Catholic Church has always taught the Virgin-birth as well as the Virgin-conception of our Blessed Lord, and has affirmed that Mary was ever-virgin, even after she had brought forth the incarnate Son, so it follows necessarily that there could be no child bed nor puerperal flux.'[4] By the thirteenth century these ideas reached their culmination in the writings of St Thomas Aquinas and had become part of the unchallenged traditions of the Church: 'Because she conceived Christ without the defilement of sin, and without the stain of sexual mingling, therefore did she bring him forth without pain, without violation of her virginal integrity, without detriment to the purity of her maidenhood.'[5]

The separated Gnostic sects, scattered all over Egypt and the Levant, had varied and different views in this matter. The Gnostics sought knowledge through meditation and the monastic life and believed that, as man is created from the spirit of God, knowledge of the Supreme Being can be achieved through inner channels, enabling the human spirit to reach out to the godly spirit. It was this union that they regarded as 'light' while those who lacked it lived in darkness. Monastic life, with its emphasis on the spirit rather than the flesh, was believed to bring the spirit closer to its salvation, but complete salvation would be achieved only in the after-life when the human spirit rid itself of its physical body and was united with the spirit of God.

Christianity became politically stronger once the Roman Catholic Church was able to unite Christians all over the world under one priestly authority following one canonic tradition. The Gnostics, who had already been persecuted by the Jews and Romans, then found themselves persecuted by the Church, which looked upon their teachings as heretical. These pre-Catholic sects had their own Gospels and other writings that were excluded from the New

Testament canon. Moreover, the Church tried to make sure that none of these writings survived, with the result that until the end of the Second World War our knowledge of them was based almost entirely on the criticisms voiced by opponents of Gnosticism.

However, in December 1945 Mahammad Ali el-Samman, an Egyptian peasant, uncovered accidentally a large earthenware jar, just over three feet high, on el-Tarif mountain, near the Upper Egyptian town of Nag Hammadi. On breaking open the jar, he did not find the golden treasure he expected, but thirteen papyrus books, which he gave to his mother to burn in the oven. It was only when the local history teacher recognized the possible importance of the manuscripts that those which had escaped the flames were saved for posterity. On examination, the surviving documents proved to be a Gnostic library of fifty-two texts, including the Gospel of Thomas, consisting of 114 sayings attributed to Jesus but not found in the New Testament. The texts, written in Coptic, the liturgical language of Egyptian Christians – but clearly having been copied from earlier texts, thought to have been Greek or possibly Demotic, the ancient form of Egyptian writing – belonged to the fourth century A.D.

These texts made it clear that the Gnostics had varying views about the Virgin Birth. One group dismissed the Virgin Birth as not being a historical fact because no child can be conceived without two human parents: at the same time, they identified the mother of Jesus as the third person of the Trinity, which consisted of God the Father, God the Son and the feminine, maternal, Holy Ghost. The Gospel of Philip, one of the Nag Hammadi texts, explains: 'Christ . . . was born from a virgin' (that is, from the Spirit). But the author ridicules those literal-minded Christians who mistakenly refer the Virgin Birth to Mary, Jesus's mother 'without a human father'.[6]

Other Gnostics identified the mystical Silence, an aspect of God's nature, as the virgin mother of Jesus, while a third group suggested Wisdom (the Greek Sophia), a feminine aspect of the Supreme Being. For their part, the Dead Sea Scrolls, while identifying God as the father of the Messiah, have no mention of a virgin mother: 'In the order of the Messianic Banquet (Passover meal) it is said that God would "beget" the Davidic Messiah, and a Qumran document dealing with the re-establishment of the kingdom of David in the last Days, the prophecy of II Samuel, 7:13–14:

"I will stablish the throne of his kingdom for ever. I will be his father, and he shall be my son", is referred to the same figure as it is in the New Testament (Hebrews, 1:5). We appear then to have in Qumran thought already the idea of the lay Messiah as the Son of God, "begotten" of the Father.[7]

There are, however, indications that the idea of the birth of the Messiah without sexual intercourse originated not in Rome but in Ancient Egypt. Isis is said to have conceived her son Horus by using the phallus of Osiris, her brother and husband, after his death and dismemberment. This posthumous sequence of events is illustrated on the walls of the Osiris temple at Abydos in Upper Egypt.

A later development of the legend rid it of its physical connotations and related the pregnancy of Isis to a cosmic force. Spell 148 of the Coffin texts, which is concerned with the announcement to Isis that she is pregnant with Horus, has been interpreted as: 'The crocodile star (MeSSeH) strikes . . . Isis wakes pregnant with the seed of her brother Osiris.'[8]

30

THE HOLY FAMILY

THE name Mary is given to many women in the New Testament, two of whom are placed in a close relationship with Jesus – his mother and Mary Magdalene. The Greek version of the name is Maria, the Hebrew is Miriam, but its origins lie in Ancient Egypt where the word *mery* means 'the beloved'.

This epithet is also applied to many members of the Egyptian royal family, including Nefertiti, the mother of Tutankhamun, and to Ankhsenpa-aten, his wife. I have already identified Queen Nefertiti, the half-sister and wife of Akhenaten, as being the Old Testament Miriam, the sister of Moses.[1] Her name, Nefertiti, means 'the beautiful one has come'. From her celebrated bust in the Berlin Museum it is clear that she was indeed a beautiful woman. It is also known that she had a beautiful voice: she used to sing the evening prayers at the Aten temple in Amarna. There are, in addition, Talmudic and Christian traditions that describe the mother of Jesus as having been of royal descent, for example: 'She was the descendant of princes and rulers' (b. Sanh., 106a).

Before the birth of Tutankhamun, she had three daughters, and another three afterwards. No evidence of other sons has been found. From the archaeological remains of Amarna's northern palace it can be concluded that she remained there with her son, Tutankhamun, and did not accompany her husband into exile in Sinai although she seems to have joined Akhenaten there after the death of Tutankhamun.

After Nefertiti's death, she assumed many qualities of Isis, the ancient Egyptian mother figure of the god Horus. Akhenaten had abolished the worship of Isis and, after her death, Nefertiti's image was used in place of that of the mother goddess on Amarna funerary objects. For instance, it is to be found instead of the image of Isis in the sarcophagus of Akhenaten. Furthermore, there are statues in Rome, originally made to represent Isis and her son, which were used by the Church to represent Mary and her son.

The other Mary, who seems to have been emotionally related to Jesus, appears to be a younger woman – Mary Magdalene. Her first appearance is as an unnamed sinner: 'And being in Bethany in the house of Simon the leper, as he sat at meat, there came a woman having an alabaster box of ointment of spikenard very precious; and she brake the box, and poured it on his head' (Mark, 14:3). For his part, Luke makes her anoint the feet of Jesus: 'And [she] stood at his feet behind him weeping, and began to wash his feet with tears, and did wipe them with the hairs of her head, and kissed his feet, and anointed them with the ointment' (7:38).

Subsequently, the name of Mary Magdalene appears among those who followed Jesus and remained close to him until after his death. Although no satisfactory explanation is given, she was clearly very attached to the person of Jesus, emotionally as well as physically. She remained by the temporary burial place where he was placed after his death and is described as having encountered Jesus after the Resurrection: 'Jesus saith unto her, Mary. She turned herself, and saith unto him, Rabboni; which is to say, Master. Jesus saith unto her, Touch me not; for I am not yet ascended to my Father: but go to my brethren, and say unto them, I ascend unto my Father, and your Father; and to my God, and your God' (John, 20:16–17).

This Mary can only have been Ankhsenpa-aten, Tutankhamun's queen. Alabaster ointment jars were found in the king's tomb and she is represented at the back of the royal throne anointing him with perfume exactly as the evangelists say. In four other scenes found on objects in the tomb, the couple are represented together, always in relaxed, romantic scenes.[2] We can see how much she was attached to his person in the same manner that Mary Magdalene is described in the Gospels.

The epithet 'Magdalene' has been explained by saying that she belonged to the city of Magdala, an unidentified location on the western shore of the Sea of Galilee. On the other hand we know both from biblical and Egyptian sources of such named locations at the time of Tutankhamun. The Hebrew word *migdol* means a watchtower and indicates a fortified city. Such a city is recorded

as having been the second military post to the east of Zarw on
the Road of Horus, leading from Egypt to Gaza. This location is
shown on Seti I's roadmap in his Hypostyle Hall at Karnak and
mentioned in many Egyptian texts. Its remote location in the
Eastern Delta can also be seen from the biblical reference: '. . .
I will make the land of Egypt utterly waste and desolate, from
the tower (*migdol*) of Syene (in the Eastern Delta) even unto the
border of Ethiopia' (Ezekiel, 29:10).

Apart from a visit to Jerusalem when he was twelve (Luke,
2:42–3), the Gospels do not tell us anything about the childhood
of Jesus. Two of them, as we saw, do not even mention his birth.
However, there is no reason to suggest that he could not have
married during this time. The evangelists were mainly concerned
to convey his teachings and message rather than give details of
his personal life. Even details of his mother's life are absent from
the New Testament: this does not mean that she had no life to
be reported, but simply indicates that it was outside the scope of
the Gospels. In fact, John's account of Mary Magdalene and the
Resurrection is right. Ankhsenpa-aten, being both the wife and
queen of Tutankhamun, was the only person who could attend his
funerary rites, see him as he was declared risen from the dead by
the priests during their mummification ritual and bear the news
to the disciples. The fact that Jesus's disciples at the time of John
the Baptist are the ones mentioned in the Gospels does not mean
that the historical Jesus did not have disciples during his lifetime.
In every generation from the time he lived there was a group of
followers and disciples who kept his memory and teachings alive
until they were brought into the open through John the Baptist's
death. The first twelve could have been his ministers.

Did Tutankhamun have any children? The fact that Ankhsenpa-
aten lost two children is indicated by the fact that two foetuses,
both thought to be female, were found in his tomb. A slab of stone
found at Ashmunen, across the river from Amarna, mentions a
small daughter, who could only be his, bearing her mother's name.
We know from evidence of diplomatic communications with the
Hittite kingdom of Asia Minor that Tutankhamun died without
an heir: 'Tutankhamun died without [male] issue, which accords
with the claim' made by his widow 'that she had no son to succeed
to the throne'.[3]

*   *   *

The name Joseph is used in the Gospels for two persons. One is described as a carpenter, descended from the House of David, and the stepfather of Jesus. Of the four Gospel authors, only Matthew and Luke mention this Joseph, who disappears from the scene before the ministry of Christ. Nothing is said about his fate. The second person bearing the name is Joseph of Arimathaea, who is said to have been rich, a man of authority, a disciple of Jesus, and to have appeared suddenly after the Crucifixion to demand the body of Jesus for burial. I believe they are to be identified as the same person – Aye, Tutankhamun's great-uncle, vizier and successor, whom I have identified as being Ephraim, the son of Joseph the Patriarch.

The disappearance of the first Joseph, completely unexplained, is matched only by the sudden appearance of the second Joseph: 'When the even was come, there came a rich man of Arimathaea, named Joseph, who also himself was Jesus' disciple: He went to Pilate, and begged the body of Jesus . . . And when Joseph had taken the body, he wrapped it in a clean linen cloth, And laid it in his own new tomb, which he had hewn out in the rock . . .' (Matthew, 27:57–60). Mark gives us a little more information about him: 'Joseph of Arimathaea, an honourable counsellor, which also waited for the kingdom of God . . . went in boldly unto Pilate, and craved the body of Jesus . . . And he bought fine linen, and took him down, and wrapped him in the linen, and laid him in a sepulchre which was hewn out of a rock' (15:43, 46). From these passages we know that Joseph arrived on the scene on the evening of Christ's death . . . he was a follower of Jesus . . . he was also a member of the Israelite leadership . . . he had sufficient authority to demand the body and have his wish granted . . . he waited for – that is, was near – the kingdom.

This mysterious character has much in common with Aye, who also had authority and was near to the kingdom. In addition, these passages, if taken in conjunction with the statement in Isaiah that the Suffering Servant 'made his grave with the wicked, and with the rich', indicate that Aye took the body of Tutankhamun after his death at the foot of Mount Sinai and buried him in a tomb – the first tomb, not the one later usurped by Horemheb – that was not originally his but was meant for Aye himself, hewn out of the rock in the Valley of the Kings. The archaeological evidence supports this view. Certainly there is no argument that Aye supervised the young king's burial: 'It was King Aye,

Tutankhamun's successor, who buried our monarch, for there, on the inner walls of Tutankhamun's tomb-chamber, Aye, as king, has caused himself to be represented among the religious scenes, officiating before Tutankhamun, a scene unprecedented in the royal tombs of this necropolis.'[4]

31

THE HIDDEN ONE

THE worship of the Aten – a supreme monotheistic God who would not manifest himself visually to his people – was a highly intellectual concept, completely remote from both the Egyptian and Israelite masses in the fourteenth century B.C. The closing of the temples of the ancient gods of Egypt also caused wide-spread resentment. It was Aye – his uncle, vizier, Commander of the Chariots, Master of the King's Horses and Chief of the Bowmen – who warned Akhenaten (Moses) of a plot against his life and the threat of an army rebellion unless he allowed the old gods to be worshipped alongside the Aten.

When Akhenaten refused, Aye advised him to flee to the safety of Sinai while Aye himself – the most powerful man in Egypt – remained as the strong military force behind the throne of his successor, Tutankhaten. The young king was ten years of age when he started his rule in 1361 B.C., and he took as his wife his sister, Ankhsenpa-aten, two years his senior and the third of Akhenaten's daughters. The nine years he sat on the throne of Egypt can be divided into four stages.

For the first four years he continued to live at Amarna, the capital city built by his father. However, he stopped all attempts to force worship of the Aten on his subjects. Nefertiti, who did not join her husband in his Sinai exile, at least at this stage, but continued to live with her children in the northern palace at Amarna, was still referred to as the 'Great King's Wife', confirming that Akhenaten was still alive and regarded, at least by some of his followers, as king. During this period the young king began building activities at Thebes with 'additions . . . to the older temples [of the Aten] Akhenaten had constructed . . . and mentions made of Akhenaten'. That Akhenaten was still alive at this time is confirmed by the fact that 'the rigours of the old monotheism' were maintained.[1] None of the ancient gods of Egypt feature in these constructional changes at Thebes, only the name of the Aten.

The second stage of his reign, starting at some point in his Year 4, saw the young king, now about fifteen years of age, move his residence from Amarna to Memphis, south-west of modern Cairo. It was then that he allowed the temples of the ancient gods of Egypt to reopen and the gods to be worshipped alongside the Aten. The popular response brought home to him the fact that the majority of his people did not share his own beliefs. He therefore, in this third stage of his reign, changed his name – in recognition of the State god, Amun – from Tutankhaten to Tutankhamun, while his queen became Ankhsenpa-amun. The priesthood was given formal recognition, temple income was restored and work was begun on making good the ravages wrought by years of neglect. A stele of the king at Karnak includes the official edict of these reforms: 'Now His Majesty appeared as king at a time when the temples of the gods and goddesses from Elephantine as far as the Delta marshes had fallen into ruin, and their shrines become dilapidated. They had turned into mounds overgrown [with] weeds, and it seemed that their sanctuaries had never existed.'[2] We find here a similar complaint to the one that Jesus is said to have made about the state of the temple at Jerusalem.

As sovereign over the whole of Egypt, Tutankhamun was looked upon as the representative of Amun of Thebes, Ra of Heliopolis, Ptah of Memphis and all the other deities. Nevertheless, the king himself remained an Atenist until the very end. This can be seen clearly from the scene on the back panel of the throne found in his tomb. The panel – wood, overlaid with gesso and gold and silver foil, and inlaid with coloured glass and faience – shows the king and queen in an intimate scene. Both are wearing coronation crowns and garments of silver. The standing queen is anointing the seated king with perfume from a vessel held in her left hand.

Although it is clear from one of the cartouches placed behind his crown that the king used the throne after he had changed his name, it is obvious that he still adhered completely to the Aten faith for, top centre, we see the symbol of the Aten with its extending rays that give the *ankh*, Egyptian key of life, to the royal pair. The

Aten is here represented as the sole God, with his two cartouches of a ruling king of the universe dominating the scene. Howard Carter was struck by this fact: 'It is curious, to say the least of it, that an object which bore such manifest signs . . . should be publicly buried in this, the stronghold of the Amun faith . . . It would appear that Tutankhamun's return to the ancient faith was not entirely a matter of conviction.'[3] This is confirmed from a text found on other objects in the tomb furniture which, after mentioning some of the important Egyptian deities, ends with the statement that Tutankhamun was the 'eldest son of the Aten in Heaven'.[4]

Tutankhamun's change of name is also attested in biblical sources concerning Christ. In the Book of Isaiah we find three references to Immanuel: 'Therefore the Lord himself shall give you a sign; Behold, a virgin shall conceive, and bear a son, and shall call his name Immanuel' (7:14). Opinions differ about the significance of the name. The Jewish interpretation is that the reference does not indicate the Messiah and is not even a proper noun. However, the evidence of the Dead Sea Scrolls shows that the Qumran Essenes looked upon it as a name.[5] The evangelist Matthew also considered it a name, a synonym for Jesus: 'Now all this was done, that it might be fulfilled which was spoken of the Lord by the prophet, saying, Behold, a virgin shall be with child, and shall bring forth a son, and they shall call his name Emmanuel, which being interpreted is, God with us' (1: 22–3).

This interpretation is arrived at by dividing the word into two elements – Imma-nu (with us) and El (Elohim, God). While this reading is possible, another is here intended: Imman-u (his Amun) El (is God). This, too, is possible as Abraham Yahuda, the American biblical scholar, has shown that the Hebrew *ayain*, the first letter of Immanuel, does transliterate into the Egyptian *aleph*, the first letter of Amun.[6]

We find confirmation of this meaning when we examine the original Hebrew text of Isaiah where we find play on the double meaning of a word. The Egyptian word *amun*, as well as being the name of the State god, means 'hidden' or 'unseen': the Hebrew word *alam* also means 'to hide' or 'conceal'. Isaiah used *alma*, the feminine form of *alam*, in his verse about the birth of Immanuel. While *alma* can be translated as either 'a young girl' or 'virgin' it is also a feminine form of 'the hidden one'. The reason why both the Essenes and the early Christians insisted on relating the verse to the Messiah is that they interpreted correctly the sense in which Isaiah was using the word – to indicate a feminine aspect of the hidden power of God. This, too, is why the Church insisted on the virginity of the mother, for this is not a human mother but God presented as God the Father and God the Mother as well as God the Son. To make this clear, a literal translation of the Hebrew text reads: 'Therefore Adonai (the Aten) gives himself to you as a sign. Behold, Alma (the hidden one) conceives, a Son is born, and she (the hidden one) called his name Amun-u-el (his hidden one is God).'[7] Thus the word Amun was used here to indicate an aspect of the 'hidden' Adonai. The words used by Isaiah also make it clear that the birth had already taken place at the time he was writing.

Although Matthew, as well as other Christian writers, has taken the view that Immanuel is a synonym for Jesus, no clear explanation has hitherto been given, and it is only when we examine the events in the life of Tutankhamun, the historical Christ, that the meaning becomes clear, as does the source of the word 'Amen' to be found at the end of Jewish and Muslim as well as Christian prayers.

The fourth and final stage of Tutankhamun's reign occurred in his Year 9 when he undertook his mission to Sinai to try to persuade Akhenaten and his followers to return to Egypt where they could live in peace if they accepted the religious changes he had made and that other people could have their own form of worship. In his attempts to persuade Moses and his priests, while the Israelites were still in Goshen, to return to Egypt and live in harmony with people of different belief whom they regarded as enemies, we find a reflection of the Gospel account in Matthew, chapter 5, of the Sermon on the Mount given by Jesus: 'Blessed are the peacemakers: for they shall be called the children of God . . . Think not that I am come to destroy the law, or the prophets: I am not come to destroy, but to fulfil . . . Agree with thine adversary quickly . . . Ye have heard that it hath been said, An eye for an eye, and a tooth for a tooth: But I say unto you, that ye resist not evil: but whosoever shall smite thee on thy right cheek, turn to him the other also . . . Ye have heard that it hath been said, Thou shalt love thy neighbour, and hate thine enemy. But I say unto you, Love your enemies, bless them that curse you, do good to them that hate you . . . That ye may be the children of your Father which is in Heaven.' One can also sense the supplication of Tutankhamun, ruling over two peoples divided by race and religion, in the words of the Lord's Prayer that follows. However, instead of his pleas being accepted, he was accused of betraying his faith – and killed.

32

EVIDENCE FROM THE TOMB

THE violent nature of Tutankhamun's death is attested by the state of his mummy. It was first examined by Douglas E. Derry, a pathologist, in 1925. However, it was only a visual inspection and he was unable to make a pronouncement about the cause of death: '. . . visible signs upon the external parts of the body which are the result of the causative factor of death [were] remarkably few.'[1]

A more thorough examination, including the use of X-rays, was carried out in 1968 by R. G. Harrison, Professor of Anatomy at the University of Liverpool, and A. B. Abdalla, Professor of Anatomy at Cairo University. They reported: 'When the bandages around the remains were removed, it was immediately obvious that the mummy was not in one piece. The head and neck were separated from the rest of the body, and the limbs had been detached from the torso . . . The resin exuded a sweet smell which soon pervaded all through the tomb and became a noticeable feature of the remainder of the examination. Further investigation showed that the limbs were broken in many places as well as being detached from the body. The right arm had been broken at the elbow, the upper arm being separated from the forearm and hand . . . The left arm was broken at the elbow, and in addition at the wrist . . . The left leg was broken at the knee. The right leg was intact . . . The heads of the right humerus [bone of the upper arm] and both femora [thigh bones] had been broken off the remains of the bone . . . The head and neck had been distracted from the torso at the joint between the seventh cervical and first thoracic vertebrae.'[2]

Their account goes on: 'The tissues of the face are contracted on the skull so that the cheekbones appear very prominent'[3] . . . 'The teeth are tightly clenched together'[4] . . . The radiographs of the thorax confirmed the fact that the sternum and most of the ribs on the front of the chest had been removed.'[5] The age at the time of death is thought to have been about eighteen and the height of the body 5ft 6½in: 'It is of interest that the heights of the two statues of the young king, which stood on either side of the sealed door leading to the burial chamber, are within a few millimetres of the height estimated above.'[6] The examination also confirmed the refined looks reflected in his golden mask: 'All present at the exposure of the king's remains agreed with Howard Carter's description of a "refined and cultured face" and a "serene and placid countenance".'[7]

The examination failed to find any evidence of disease as the cause of death, and it is clear from the state of his remains that Tutankhamun did not die of natural causes but must have been exposed to severe physical torture before he was hanged.

The main charge against the historical Jesus was his claim to be 'the Son of Ra' – an Egyptian rather than Israelite deity. This title was found inscribed on the king's stele that was discovered in the Karnak Temple in 1905.[8] This throws light on the views expressed by the Talmudic rabbis, who regarded Jesus, the son of Mary, as being also the son of someone named Pandira. As Pandira is not a Hebrew word, various explanations of its origin have been put forward. While the Gospels relate Jesus to a divine father who was not the husband of his mother, the Talmud stories assert that he had no father because of an irregular union between his mother and Pandira. It has even been suggested that Pandira could have been a Roman soldier who had a love affair with Mary.

In fact, the word Pandira is simply a Hebrew form of an ancient Egyptian royal epithet. That the rabbis kept the word without knowing what it meant supports its authenticity. The word in Hebrew is Pa–ndi–ra. In Egyptian, its original form, this becomes Pa–ntr–ra – that is, Pa–neter–ra, the god Ra. Son of Ra was an essential title for all Egyptian kings from the time of the builders of the pyramids during the Fourth Dynasty, twenty-seven centuries before the Christian era. Thus this ancient Egyptian tradition identified Jesus as an Egyptian king.

The cover-up over the Day of Atonement, which we examined earlier, also indicates that the victim of the assassination at the foot of Mount Sinai on the day that Jesus died was an

Egyptian king – and, what is more, a king whose father was still alive. After the Day of Atonement was separated from the feast of the Passover, not only did it become an occasion for general repentance for sin: in place of the Messiah as the victim, we find an enemy of the Israelites, and the Lord as the agent of death rather than the one who died: 'the Lord smote . . . the firstborn of Pharaoh that sat on his throne . . .' (Exodus, 12:29).

The meaning of this passage has been misinterpreted. If it was simply the firstborn of a ruling Pharaoh who was smitten, it would not be necessary to add the words 'that sat on his throne'. Pharaohs sat on their throne as a matter of course: therefore there was no need to use the expression unless there was another Pharaoh who was not sitting on his throne. While the narrator was reporting a historical event, the way he presented it was meant to conceal the real identity of the victim, the ruling Pharaoh of the time. In order further to confuse the issue, the biblical editor in the next passage of the Book of Exodus introduces yet a third Pharaoh – the Pharaoh of the Oppression. However, he cannot have had an heir who met a sudden death at this time because there is no historical record of such an event.

Howard Carter reported that he found a great deal of evidence in Tutankhamun's tomb that linked the contents to later Christian beliefs and practices.

Among them were some personal ritual objects – two gala robes and a pair of gloves – similar to those later used by the Roman Catholic Church: 'The two garments, which I have chosen to call gala robes, recall official vestments of the character of priestly apparel, such as the dalmatic worn by deacons and bishops of the Christian Church, or by kings and emperors at coronations . . . They take the form of a long, loose vestment, having richly ornamented tapestry-woven decoration with fringes on both sides. In addition to this ornamentation, one of them has needlework of palmette pattern, desert flora and animals over the broad hem at the bottom. The openings of the neck and at the chest are also adorned with woven pattern. One of the vestments, with field quite plain, has narrow sleeves like the tunicle; the other, with the whole field woven with coloured rosettes as well as figures of flowers and cartouches across the chest, has its collar woven in the design of a falcon

with outspread wings, and it also has the titulary of the king
woven down the front . . .

'Perhaps they were worn on special occasions . . . and . . .
they were a symbol of joy, very much in the manner of the
dalmatic placed upon a deacon when the holy order was
conferred, whereby the following words are repeated: "May
the Lord clothe thee in the Tunic of Joy and the Garment
of Rejoicing." Moreover, these robes may well have had the
same origin as the Roman garment, whence the liturgical
vestment – the dalmatic – of the Christian Church derives.'9

The pair of gloves, according to Carter, were in a much better
state of preservation, 'neatly folded, also of tapestry-woven linen.
They were possibly intended to go with the robes (a Roman
Catholic bishop wears gloves when pontificating – also buskings,
tunic and dalmatic under his chasuble) and are similarly woven
with a brilliant scale-pattern and have a border at the wrist of
alternate lotus buds and flowers.'10

Other objects were also found that related to later Christian
beliefs and practices: 'There were also a number of ostrich-feathers,
recalling the flabella still used at a papal procession in Rome, such
as was witnessed in the Eucharistic procession of His Holiness the
Pope in July 1929. These fans, like the pontifical flabella, were
carried by grooms-in-waiting in Pharaonic processions, or were
held beside the throne, and appear always on either side of the
king or immediately behind him.'11

The shining face familiar from the biblical accounts of the
Transfiguration of Jesus on the Mount shortly before his death
and again when Moses descended from Mount Sinai for the
second time with the Ten Commandments is also ascribed to
Tutankhamun on one of the objects found in his tomb. A royal
sceptre, used in connection with offerings, bears this text: 'The
Beautiful God, beloved, dazzling of face like the Aten when it
shines . . . Tutankhamun.'12 There was a wooden gold-plated
statuette 'representing the king as the Youthful Warrior Horus
upon a reed-float in the act of killing the Typhonical Animal,
probably the ancient Egyptian prototype of St George and the
Dragon of the Christian era. It is one of a pair of statuettes
found in a black shrine-shaped chest and was carefully draped
in linen.'13

A triple lamp, symbol of the Trinity, was also found: 'an

exquisite triple lamp of floral form, carved out of a single block of translucent calcite. In design it comprises three lotiform oil cups with stems and lotus leaves springing from a circular base.'14 The tomb also contained fruits and seeds of Christ-thorn, a tree like a hawthorn, native to Ancient Egypt, used for food, medicine and timber, and also said to have had religious significance. It is said to have been used for Christ's crown of thorns: 'And the soldiers plaited a crown of thorns, and put it on his head . . .' (John, 19:2).

It was wrongly assumed by Howard Carter that Tutankhamun was buried in the spring.[15] As the mummification process took seventy days, this would have meant that he died in the winter. The botanical evidence found in the tomb, however, shows that he must have died in the spring and been buried in the summer. Most of it consists of spring blossoms and fruits – small Picris flowers, cornflowers, mandrake fruits, woody nightshade berries – found in wreaths covering the second and third coffins. The mandrake fruits and nightshade berries could not have been used without being first dried. This is quite clear from the collarette on the third coffin where the mandrake fruits, sliced in half, obviously had to be dried out before, together with blue sequin beads, they were sewn on to the collarette. Furthermore, the blue water-lily used in these wreaths does not bloom until the summer. Tutankhamun most probably died in April, the same time as Christ's death.

Evidence found elsewhere in the Valley of the Kings throws light on the story found in Matthew about the three wise men who came from foreign countries to offer presents as well as pay homage to the new-born king. This is a story of Egyptian origin. During the time of the Empire, when Egypt had control over most of western Asia as well as Nubia and part of northern Sudan, such visits and gifts were common.

A box was found in a room to the north of the tomb of Horemheb in the Valley of the Kings. The box contained several pieces of gold leaf bearing the names of Tutankhamun and Aye, clues which eventually contributed to the discovery of the young king's tomb as well as pointing to the source of the story of the three wise men. One of these pieces of gold leaf had the two royal cartouches of Aye on the left side, faced on the right side by three foreigners whose arms are raised in a position of adoration towards the king's names.

'The first has a large beard and thick hair falling on the neck; his garment is ornamented with dotted designs forming circles above and squares below; the cape and broad girdle are also decorated. This is the typical type of the Syrian from the Mediterranean coasts.

'The second has the hair arranged in tiers and surmounted by a feather, the collar fits closely to the neck, the scarf crosses the breast, and the robe falls in straight folds. He is undoubtedly a negro of the Sudan.

'The third wears a pointed beard; in his flowing hair are fixed two plumes; a large cloak envelops the body, leaving the limbs bare. It is in this way that, in the tombs of the kings and other ethnological pictures, are represented the . . . white-skinned races of the North, Libyans of Marmarica and inhabitants of the Mediterranean islands. Here, then, is a representation of the three biblical races, Shem, Ham and Japhet.'[16]

This, therefore, is the original idea of the three wise men, who represented the different peoples of the ancient known world.

Whichever method was used for the execution of Jesus, from a theological point of view he suffered on the Cross. The Roman cross was simply an instrument of punishment. However, it is a known fact that ancient Egyptians regarded the cross (*ankh*) as a symbol of life. In his monotheistic beliefs, Akhenaten made the cross an essential element of the Aten, his god. Descending rays of light end in hands that hold the cross to the nostrils of the king, giving him life as he stands before the altar at prayer. The *ankh*, of course, formed part of his name, and we find many examples of the *ankh* in his tomb, including the scene on the back of his throne chair – indicating the belief of his followers that, whereas he may have suffered and died in the Tabernacle at the foot of Mount Sinai, at the site of today's St Catherine's monastery, he had simply made the transition from one form of life (physical) to another (spiritual).

33

THE LOST SHEEP

SOME of the ideas put forward in this book – and certainly the conclusion to be drawn from them – will undoubtedly prove startling for readers who have not encountered them before. However, the purpose has been to try to identify the historical figure of Christ, not to argue about theological interpretations of his life and teachings that developed subsequently. All of the criteria in the Old and New Testaments attributed to the Messiah – being the son of David, who sat on his throne; the son of Aten, the God who became identified with the Hebrew Jehovah – the Lord – as Adonai, and who met a violent end and was believed to have risen from the dead; and a prophet like Moses, as well as his successor – are found in the life of Tutankhamun.

His great quality, frustrated by his early death, was as a unifying force. He himself never abandoned belief in the God of Moses, but he wanted to include Gentiles in the faith. Unlike Moses, he accepted that not everyone had the same perception of God and not everyone worshipped him in the same way, but these were the lost sheep. Part of his plan for converting them embraced even the ancient gods of Egypt, who are shown in paintings as having been converted to worship of the Aten and are the source of the later Christian concept of angels and saints. For example, a fragment of the Song of Moses in Deuteronomy 32, found in a cave at Qumran, includes a text of verse 43 which mentions the word 'gods' in the plural: 'Rejoice, O heavens, with him; and do obeisance to him, ye gods.' 'When the passage is quoted in the New Testament (Hebrews, 1:6), the phrase is appropriately rendered "angels of God".'[1]

In contrast to Akhenaten (Moses), Tutankhamun (Jesus) also introduced belief in resurrection and life after death, the main message of the New Covenant. On the wall of his tomb, he himself is shown resurrected and alive, facing Aye, in complete contrast to the beliefs of Akhenaten (Moses), as can be shown from *his* tomb.

The paths trodden in this book are not by any means new paths. Other scholars have been down them, only to turn back because they were leading to disturbing territory that challenged accepted wisdom or clashed with their own beliefs. The arguments I have put forward here can be summarized fairly simply.

There is not a shred of contemporary evidence to support the New Testament story that Jesus was born during the reign of Herod the Great and was condemned to death in the first century A.D. when Pontius Pilate (26–36 A.D.) was the procurator of Judaea, which had become a Roman province. On the other hand, there is a mass of evidence that points to the fact that Jesus lived many centuries earlier. For instance, the Dead Sea Scrolls, which pre-date the Gospels, contain an account of the Annunciation couched in almost the same words we find in St Luke and make it clear that the Essenes believed that the Messiah (their Teacher of Righteousness) had already lived and died at the hands of the Wicked Priest, and they were awaiting his Second Coming, not the first. The same view is expressed in the Book of Isaiah, dating from the eighth to sixth centuries B.C., where the Messiah is named as the Suffering Servant, who was conceived by the Lord and met a violent death – sacrificed like a lamb – at the hands of his people.

Some Talmudic traditions, dating from the third century A.D., make it clear that the Talmudic rabbis knew of Jesus, who is described as 'a deceiver', but they do not relate him to the time of Herod or Pontius Pilate. Instead they say that he was slain by a priest named Pinhas. Pinhas is to be identified as Phinehas, the biblical priest who was a contemporary of Moses, and also Panahesy, the Chief Servitor and Second Priest of the Aten (the Lord), the monotheistic God Akhenaten (Moses) introduced in Egypt and forced on his people during the five years he was sole ruler.

The Old Testament describes Joshua as the successor of Moses. However, the early Church Fathers looked upon Joshua and Jesus as the same person, a belief still echoed in the King James Bible where references to Joshua have an accompanying marginal note identifying him as Jesus, and vice versa. If, as I have argued elsewhere, Moses and Akhenaten are the same person, and if Joshua and Jesus are the same person, then Joshua (Jesus) must be a descendant of Moses (Akhenaten). This identification throws a new light on the account of how, shortly before his death, Jesus, accompanied by three disciples, met Moses and Elijah on Mount Sinai and was transfigured before them. The seeming discrepancy in dates has resulted in the presence of Moses and Elijah being interpreted as symbolic, but, if Jesus and Moses were contemporaries, it can be looked upon as a real meeting witnessed by three disciples.

As we have seen, the religion of Jesus differed from the religion of Moses. Although keeping the Aten (Adonai) as the one true God, he accepted the old gods of Egypt as angels through whom Egyptians could reach the true God; he asked the Egyptians and Israelites to accept each other, and, unlike Moses, he believed in life after death. However, Phinehas looked upon these teachings as blasphemy and, on the eve of the Passover, killed him in the Tabernacle at the foot of Mount Sinai. The killing was avenged by the slaughter of thousands of Israelites, including Phinehas, at the hands of Ephraim (Aye), the second son of Joseph the Patriarch.

It was the death of John the Baptist many centuries later that persuaded the Essene leaders, who had been awaiting the Second Coming of Christ as a judge at the end of the world, to claim that they had witnessed Jesus, allowing the evangelists to retell the story of Christ adapted to the time of Herod the Great and Pontius Pilate.

The true course of events has been obscured largely for two reasons. Jesus, we are told, would be a descendant of King David and sit on his throne. Confusion has arisen because the Old Testament provides us with two Davids – one who spent much of his time in conflict with the Philistines, the other the founder of an empire that stretched from the Nile to the Euphrates. The David who fought the Philistines was simply a tribal chief who lived in the tenth century B.C.: the David from whose House the Messiah was to come was Tuthmosis III (c. 1490–1436 B.C.), the great-great-grandfather of Akhenaten and the mightiest warrior of his age, who forged the first link between the Israelites and Egyptian royalty as the father of Isaac. Between the reign of Tuthmosis and conquest of the territory by the Persians in the sixth century B.C., nobody else can be said to have founded an empire stretching from the Nile to the Euphrates. It was also Tuthmosis who made Jerusalem a holy city when he resided there for a time in the course of his military campaign and brought up the Ark of his god.

The other obscuring factor has been an elaborate cover-up. This has included the 'resurrection' of Joshua and Phinehas for an account in the Book of Joshua of how the Promised Land was conquered in a swift military campaign more than a century after they were both dead. This is a total invention that cannot be supported by modern archaeological excavation and has also been dismissed on literary grounds by biblical scholars. We also find in the Book of Numbers a garbled account of the events that took place in the Tabernacle at the foot of Mount Sinai. Even the Day of Atonement, which used to be observed at the same time as the Passover in the spring, is now observed in the autumn. The secrecy surrounding the hidden contents of the Dead Sea Scrolls makes it clear that this cover-up is still continuing.

As a final word, I hope that establishing the identity of the historical figure of Jesus will strengthen rather than weaken people's faith in him – and that we may perhaps at last be allowed to learn the unpublished secrets of the Dead Sea Scrolls.

APPENDICES

APPENDIX A

Testaments Old and New

The French scholar P. L. Couchoud listed the following Old Testament verses that also mirror some of the major events to be found in the later Gospels:

THE VIRGIN BIRTH

'. . . Behold, a virgin shall conceive, and bear a son, and shall call his name Immanuel' (Isaiah, 7:14).

BIRTH OF JESUS AT BETHLEHEM

'But thou, Bethlehem Ephratah, though thou be little among the thousands of Judah, yet out of thee shall he come forth unto me that is to be ruler in Israel . . .' (Micah, 5:2).

THE STAR IN THE EAST

'. . . there shall come a Star out of Jacob, and a sceptre shall rise out of Israel . . .' (Numbers, 24:17).

THE MAGI

'. . . all they from Sheba shall come: they shall bring gold and incense; and they shall shew forth the praises of the Lord' (Isaiah, 60:6).

THE FLIGHT INTO EGYPT

'When Israel was a child, then I loved him, and called my son out of Egypt' (Hosea, 11:1).

MASSACRE OF THE INNOCENTS

'. . . A voice was heard in Ramah, lamentation, and bitter weeping; Rahel weeping for her children refused to be comforted for her children, because they were not' (Jeremiah, 31:15).

RESIDENCE AT NAZARETH

'And he came and dwelt in a city called Nazareth: that it might be fulfilled which was spoken by the prophets, He shall be called a Nazarene' (Matthew, 2:23, quoting from an unknown book of prophecy).

THE TRIUMPHAL ENTRY INTO JERUSALEM

'Rejoice greatly, O daughter of Zion; shout, O daughter of Jerusalem: behold, thy king cometh unto thee: he is just, and having salvation; lowly, and riding upon an ass, and upon a colt the foal of an ass' (Zechariah, 9:9).
'Blessed be he that cometh in the name of the Lord . . .' (Psalms, 118:26).

CLEANSING OF THE TEMPLE

'. . . and in that day there shall be no more the Canaanite in the house of the Lord of hosts' (Zechariah, 14:21).

BETRAYAL BY JUDAS

'Yea, mine own familiar friend, in whom I trusted, which did eat of my bread, hath lifted up his heel against me' (Psalms, 41:9).

THIRTY PIECES OF SILVER USED TO BUY A POTTER'S FIELD

'. . . So they weighed for my price thirty pieces of silver . . . And I took the thirty pieces of silver, and cast them to the potter . . .' (Zechariah, 11:12–13).

THE AGONY IN THE GARDEN OF GETHSEMANE

'O my God, my soul is cast down within me . . .' (Psalms, 42:6).

FLIGHT OF THE DISCIPLES

'. . . smite the shepherd, and the sheep shall be scattered . . .' (Zechariah, 13:7).

THE PASSION

'But he was wounded for our transgressions, he was bruised for our iniquities . . .' (Isaiah, 53:5).

CRUCIFIXION BETWEEN TWO THIEVES

'. . . he was numberèd with the transgressors; and he bare the sin of many, and made intercession for the transgressors' (Isaiah, 53:12).

THE SCOURGING

'I gave my back to the smiters, and my cheeks to them that plucked off the hair; I hid not my face from shame and spitting' (Isaiah, 50:6).

JESUS'S LAST CRY

'My God, my God, why hast thou forsaken me . . . ?' (Psalms, 22:1).

THE CRUCIFIXION

'. . . they pierced my hands and my feet' (Psalms, 22:16).

CASTING OF LOTS FOR HIS GARMENTS

'They part my garments among them, and cast lots upon my vesture' (Psalms, 22:18).

THE SCENE AT THE CROSS

'All they that see me laugh me to scorn: they shoot out the lip, they shake the head, saying, He trusted on the Lord that he would deliver him: let him deliver him, seeing he delighted in him' (Psalms, 22:7–8).

BURIAL IN THE TOMB OF A RICH MAN, JOSEPH OF ARIMATHAEA

'And he made his grave with the wicked, and with the rich in his death . . .' (Isaiah, 53:9).[1]

APPENDIX B

The Destruction of Hazor

After defeating the kings of the south, we are told that Joshua turned north where he defeated Jabin, the king of Hazor and head of a coalition against the Israelites, and burned his city – and his city alone (Joshua, 11:10–13). Before considering supposed evidence put forward by Yigael Yadin, it is worth pointing out that the Old Testament itself gives a contradictory account of these events. The Book of Judges, dealing with occurrences that took place generations after Joshua's death, describes Jabin as still being the king of Hazor and the head of all the northern Canaanite kingdoms (Judges, 4:17 and 23).

Hazor (modern Tell el-Qidah) was a large Canaanite city in Upper Galilee, nearly nine miles north of the Sea of Galilee and strategically situated to dominate the main branches of the Way of the Sea, the road leading from Egypt to Syria, Mesopotamia and Anatolia. We find many references to it in Egyptian sources. It was one of the cities conquered by Tuthmosis III in the early fifteenth century B.C. The Amarna letters, dating from the fourteenth century B.C. and giving accounts of Egypt's relations with foreign countries, include many mentions of Hazor where Abdi-Hirshi, its king, proclaims his loyalty to Egypt. We find Hazor listed again among the cities conquered by Seti I (c. 1333–1304 B.C.), the second ruler of the Nineteenth Dynasty, and, in his Temple of Amun at Karnak, by Ramses III (c.1200–1168 B.C.).[1]

The site of Hazor consists of two separate areas, the older (and upper) of two cities on a tell (hill), 130 feet above the plain and covering thirty acres, and, to the north, the lower city, occupying a large rectangular plateau of about 175 acres. Yadin, one of those scholars who is at pains to try to demonstrate that *everything* in the Bible is to be taken literally, established that the lower city on the plateau was a settlement that dated back to the eighteenth century B.C. while the upper city on the hill was even more ancient, having been occupied since the twenty-seventh century B.C. and right up to Hellenistic times, the first century B.C. Yet Yadin placed the time of the destruction of Hazor as 'most probably . . . some time in the second third of the thirteenth century B.C. (i.e. during the reign of Ramses II).'[2] This was an encouraging theory for those who believe, wrongly, that the Israelites entered the Promised Land under Joshua in the latter part of the thirteenth century B.C., immediately after their Exodus in the reign of Ramses II or that of his son Merenptah. On what evidence, however, does Yadin base a theory that is at odds with all historical records, which show that Palestine was completely under Egyptian control at the period in question, with a number of military posts in the area?

He sums up his basic reasons as follows: 'The striking similarity between the size of Hazor as revealed by the excavations and its description in the Bible as "the head of all those kingdoms", plus the insistence of the biblical narrator that Hazor – and only Hazor – had been destroyed by Joshua and burned, leave little doubt, it seems, that we found the Canaanite city of Jabin that was destroyed by Joshua. In this case, the excavations at Hazor provided, for the first time, decisive archaeological data for fixing both Joshua's dates and, indirectly, the date of the Exodus from Egypt'[3] (which the author must have assigned to the reign of Ramses II).

In order to agree with the biblical evidence, Yadin goes to some lengths to demonstrate that Hazor was destroyed by fire. Yet the evidence he produces in support of this view does not stand up to close analysis. This, for example, is what he has to say about an Area C of the lower city on the plateau: 'The end of Stratum IA (which is the upper level of the final city, the last one built on the site) came about as a result of violent fire, as indicated by ashes found in the less exposed areas excavated in Areas H and K.'[4] Here he is not putting forward any hard evidence that Area C was destroyed by fire, but suggests – on the basis of evidence found elsewhere (in areas H and K) – that similar evidence cannot be found in Area C because this part of the site was 'exposed'.

However, the evidence he uses from Area H, too, does not withstand close scrutiny: 'The temple of Stratum IA – the latest in Area H – . . . it was found just below the modern surface, with a thick layer of brick-wash from the rampart, covering in many places fallen *white* (my italics) plaster of the ceiling. The latter layer actually sealed off the remains of the temple as they had been left, after the temple was destroyed and set on fire. This course of events saved for us a unique assembly of cult-vessels and furniture, practically in their original place.'[5]

Yadin is still talking about fire having occurred in this area, although it seems to have provided the strongest evidence that it was never exposed to fire. The fallen ceiling is still white: no walls, furniture or other objects found in this area or, indeed, in any other area of Hazor, showed any evidence of burning, except for some ashes – and their source is not difficult to establish. Yadin concedes that here, in the temple: 'Right in front of the niche we found, lying on its side, a basalt incense-altar . . . On the top flat side remains of burning were still visible.'[6] What else did he expect – an incense-altar without any evidence, in the form of ashes, of anything having been burned? Furthermore, how can an altar fire be advanced as evidence that the whole city was burned down?

Yadin dealt also with the evidence provided by Mycenaean pottery. The fact that there are various types, and that the approximate date of each type has been fixed, has resulted in the pottery being used to date different archaeological strata. Yadin found quantities of Mycenaean pottery 'of the Myc. IIIB type (typical of the thirteenth century B.C.) on the floors of the top level . . . These finds made it quite clear that the large (lower) city of Hazor in the enclosure . . . was destroyed during the thirteenth century B.C. while Mycenaean pottery was still in use. According to Furumark (Arne Furumark, the Swedish archaeologist) Mycenaean pottery went out of fashion around 1230 B.C., so the evidence in hand shows . . . that the city was destroyed around 1230 at the latest.'[7]

What Yadin is saying is that, as the upper layer of the lower city provided examples of Myc. IIIB pottery, which is dated to the era 1300–1230 B.C., and no examples of subsequent types of Mycenaean pottery, such as type Myc. IIIC, were found, the destruction of Hazor must be dated to the thirteenth century. This is a false argument. One cannot say that a jug made in 1230 B.C. was broken in the year it was made: plenty of families today have china dating from the period of their great-grandparents or even earlier. Furthermore, as is the case here, the absence of any later Mycenaean pottery from the site of Hazor may have another explanation – that none was imported.

This is what Arne Furumark has to say in this matter: 'Myc. IIIB was the period of the greatest Mycenaean expansion. (The Mycenaean city) Argolis was – more than ever – the political and cultural centre of the Aegean world, and the king of Mycenae was doubtless the overlord of a great realm. The Mycenaean pottery obtained its widest distribution, and the Levanto-Mycenaean centres stood in an intimate connection with Argolis . . . In the eastern Mediterranean this period was a golden era, characterized by cultural and commercial exchange and peaceful intercourse . . . This flourishing epoch was followed by the Myc. IIIC/I period, which brought the decline and fall of Mycenaean power and glory. The external cause of this is well known: the western parallel of those great migrations which crushed the Hittite empire and destroyed the old political system of the Near East. The archaeological evidence gives us some glimpses of the long and bitter struggle of the Mycenaean kings to ward off the repeated attacks known as the Dorian invasion . . . Flourishing Myc. IIIB settlements . . . were not inhabited in this period, probably because they were no longer safe. Disaster was inevitable, and Mycenae fell . . . In the time of unrest following Myc. IIIB, the overseas connections of mainland Greece became less regular and of a different nature.'[8] Therefore, no Myc. IIIC pottery was found at Hazor, not because the city had been destroyed in the thirteenth century B.C., but because no such type reached the area of Upper Galilee at all.

As we said before, the remains at Hazor consist of two different locations, the older (upper) city on the tell (hill) itself and the lower city on the plateau. While the latter was not occupied again after the destruction of the last Canaanite city to occupy the site, the city on the hill went on until the Hellenistic period during the first century B.C. Yadin explains: 'In all the excavated areas of the Upper City (on the tell) the remains of this stratum are found above the ruined Canaanite city and below the later Iron Age strata . . . the pottery associated with the structures, pits and installations of Stratum XII (the one above the destroyed city) is basically different from that of the earliest phase of the Iron Age (i.e. Philistine).'[9]

This means that, after the Myc. IIIB pottery city was destroyed, the settlement that followed used Philistine pottery belonging to the Iron Age of the twelfth, not the thirteenth, century B.C., indicating that the city was destroyed during this period.

Yadin has not produced a shred of evidence to prove that Hazor was conquered by Joshua during the second half of the thirteenth century B.C. The fact that Hazor was mentioned by Ramses III (c. 1200–1168 B.C.) in his Karnak Temple of Amun indicates that the city was still in existence and under his control during his reign as well as the possibility that Hazor, like so many other sites in Syria/Palestine, was actually destroyed by the 'Peoples of the Sea', the Philistines, against whom Ramses III fought a war in the same area.

APPENDIX C

David and Goliath

The way that the Bible has come down to us has contributed to the confusion that surrounds the stories of the two Davids.

The second of them, the tribal chief, is said to have ruled Judaea and Israel in Canaan during the first forty years of the tenth century B.C. However, the Hebrew text of Samuel, which was originally one book, did not receive its finished form until more than four centuries later, at the time of the Exile. This occurred around 587 B.C. with the Babylonian invasion of Judaea and subsequent destruction of the Jerusalem Temple. The Judaean king as well as a large number of the Israelite upper class, including the priesthood, were taken into exile in Babylon. Their exile lasted seventy years until Cyrus, the Persian king, defeated Babylonia and allowed the Israelites to return to Jerusalem and rebuild the Temple.

When the Israelite priests and scribes were forced to leave Jerusalem, they took with them a collection of their sacred writings, and, on reflection in Babylon, decided to reconsider their past history and set down a new account of it for future generations. It was then that the text of Samuel was produced, based on a number of separate traditions, out of which the scribes tried to make a cohesive whole. The editor responsible had in his possession a number of sources, each covering a different part of the story, such as:

- The boyhood of Samuel;

- The Ark, and its movement from one place to another;

- Two separate stories of Samuel and Saul and the unification of the twelve tribes, one associated with Mezpah and Ramah, which ended when Saul failed to destroy the Amalekites and their booty and was rejected by God, the other associated with Gilgal, which ended when he was again rejected by God for offering sacrifices to initiate a war with the Philistines;

- The story of David's rise to power, from the time he was introduced to Saul until he was accepted as king of all Israel;

- The court history, or succession, story of David, including his relations with his sons;

- The Egyptian story of the slaying of 'a mighty Canaanite man' in *The Autobiography of Sinuhe*;

- The taking of Jerusalem;

- The story of Tuthmosis III's marriage to Sarah, the wife of Abraham;

- The war annals of Tuthmosis III.

The biblical editor, faced with this mass of material in the sixth century B.C., but lacking any explanation of its origins, settled down to try to form it into one story. The fact that the war annals of Tuthmosis III found a place in it shows that the Israelites never forgot their great ancestor, the real father of Isaac, and, from a semantic point of view, this Pharaoh's name posed no problem. It consists of two elements, *Tut* or *Twt*. In hieroglyphic writing, the first part takes the form of an ibis bird, representing Thoth, the Egyptian god of wisdom and learning, and in transliteration into Hebrew becomes *Dwd*, which is the Hebrew name of David: the second element, *mos*, simply means 'child' or 'son'. In fact, there is evidence suggesting that it may have been the biblical editor who gave the tribal chief the name *Dwd*. Some scholars believe that this was not his original name: 'Elhanan was David's original name, which was later changed to David.'[1] This idea is reinforced by the fact that the Targum, the early translation of the Hebrew Bible into Aramaic, substitutes 'Elhanan' for 'David' in II Samuel, 21:19 where we find the account of how 'Elhanan slew the brother of Goliath the Gittite' (see Note[1] in Chapter 20).

The tale of the slaying of Goliath does not belong to the story of either David.

David, the youngest son of Jesse, is introduced to Saul as a shepherd and harpist in I Samuel, 16, and Saul appoints him as his armourbearer. Yet in the very next chapter we find this David transformed into a mighty warrior at the head of Saul's army, encamped on a mountain on one side of the valley of Elah, midway between Bethlehem and the Philistine Mediterranean coast. From the Philistine camp on an opposite mountain emerged Goliath with an offer to settle the whole conflict by man-to-man combat.

Goliath is said to have been an impressive figure, 'whose height was six cubits and a span. And he had an helmet of brass upon his head, and he was armed with a coat of mail; and the weight of the coat was five thousand shekels of brass. And he had greaves of brass upon his legs, and a target of brass between his shoulders. And the staff of his spear was like a weaver's beam; and his spear's head weighed six hundred shekels of iron: and one bearing a shield went before him' (I Samuel, 17:4–7). Goliath asked the Israelites to choose a champion and promised: 'If he be able to fight with me, and to kill me, then we will be your servants . . .'

At this point the story of the confrontation is interrupted by an account of events not to be found in the Septuagint, the Greek version of the Bible, where the story of Goliath is based on one of the early Hebrew texts. Here we are again informed that David was the youngest of the eight sons of Jesse of Bethlehem-judah. His three eldest brothers had already joined Saul's forces for the forthcoming campaign against the Philistines and Jesse called him in from the field where he was tending sheep and told him to take some food to his brothers and their commander.

David was in the camp when Goliath appeared again and repeated his threat. David also heard that Saul was willing to shower riches on anyone who killed the Philistine, and was prepared to give him his daughter's hand in marriage. He therefore volunteered to challenge Goliath. David's eldest brother was distressed by this news and Saul also sent for David and tried to dissuade him from taking up the challenge. At this point the story resumes as in the Greek text.

Saul tried to persuade David not to enter the lists on behalf of the Israelites because 'thou art but a youth'. However, David replied: 'Thy servant kept his father's sheep, and there came a lion, and a bear, and took a lamb out of the flock: And I went out after him, and smote him, and delivered it out of his mouth: and when he arose against me, I caught him by his beard, and smote him, and slew him. Thy servant slew both the lion and the bear: and this uncircumcised Philistine shall be as one of them, seeing he hath defied the armies of the living God. David said moreover, The Lord that delivered me out of the paw of the lion, and out of the paw of the bear, he will deliver me out of the hand of this Philistine' (I Samuel, 17: 34–7).

This oration convinced Saul, who said to David: 'Go, and the Lord be with thee.'

David refused to wear armour or carry a sword into the conflict that lay ahead of him. Instead, he went out to face Goliath with his staff, a sling and five smooth stones. An affronted Goliath demanded: 'Am I a dog, that thou comest to me with staves? . . . Come to me, and I will give thy flesh unto the fowls of the air, and to the beasts of the field.'

David replied: 'Thou comest to me with a sword, and with a spear, and with a shield: but I come to thee in the name of the Lord of hosts, the God of the armies of Israel, whom thou hast defied. This day will the Lord deliver thee into mine hand . . .'

In the familiar story of the short conflict that followed, David felled Goliath with a stone from his sling, took the Philistine's sword and cut off his head. On seeing this, the Philistine forces fled, pursued by the Israelites, who subsequently returned to plunder the Philistine camp. We are then told in I Samuel, 17:54 that 'David took the head of the Philistine, and brought it to Jerusalem; but he put his armour in his tent.'

In the Greek text, the story of David's slaying of Goliath ends here. However, the Masoretic text – a more 'sophisticated' version of early Hebrew texts and the source of our English versions of the Bible – contains an additional four verses. These provide another account of the first meeting between Saul and David, suggesting that they did not know each other at all until *after* the slaying of Goliath: 'And when Saul saw David go forth against the Philistine, he said unto Abner, the captain of the host, Abner, whose son is this youth? And Abner said, As thy soul liveth, O king, I cannot tell. And the king said, Inquire thou whose son the stripling is. And as David returned from the slaughter of the Philistine, Abner took him, and brought him before Saul with the head of the Philistine in his hand. And Saul said to him, Whose son art thou, thou young man? And David answered, I am the son of thy servant Jesse the Bethlehemite' (I Samuel, 17:55–8).

The Goliath tale, as I said earlier, does not belong to the stories of either biblical David. It was borrowed from an ancient Egyptian literary work known as *The Autobiography of Sinuhe*. Once he was committed to including the great victories of Tuthmosis III, it seems that the biblical editor, in order to present a convincing story, felt the need to build up the warrior-like qualities of David the tribal chief. He therefore incorporated the Sinuhe legend although there is nothing in its contents that relates them to David or his time. This is simple to demonstrate.

● A number of differences exist between various versions of I Samuel. Portions of the Book of Samuel in Hebrew were among biblical scripts found in the caves of Qumran, near the north-western end of the Dead Sea, after the Second World War. On examination, the text of this early Hebrew version proved to correspond more closely to the text of the Greek Septuagint Bible, which seems to have relied on a more accurate Hebrew text tradition in relating the story of Goliath than we find in the Masoretic version. The main points that become clear are:

1 The Goliath story in the Septuagint came from an earlier Hebrew text, when it was still treated as a separate story, with little effort to weave it into the general account of the lives of Saul and David;

2 After the initial challenge by Goliath, the editor of the Masoretic text inserted twenty additional verses, explaining David's origins and giving a reason – bringing food – for his presence at the battlefront in the valley of Elah;

3 He inserted two other verses (41 and 50) that we do not find in the Greek, although they are unimportant in the sense that they simply repeat facts that we know already;

4 He inserted the final four verses of Chapter 17, another account of David's first introduction to Saul – as a mighty warrior this time, not the shepherd who could play the harp – *after* the slaying of Goliath;

5 And finally, at the start of Chapter 18, he inserted a further five verses about the love Saul had for David, the covenant between them and Saul's appointment of David as the head of his army.

● Although Jerusalem was still a Jebusite city during the reign of Saul, we are told that 'David brought the Philistine's head to Jerusalem'. This would not have been possible if the story had originally formed an integral part of the Book of Samuel. At the relevant time, according to the Book of Samuel text, Jerusalem was not yet under Israelite control. Why should David take Goliath's head to a foreign city?

● In complete contradiction to the story of the slaying of Goliath by David in I Samuel, we find a different version of events in II Samuel: '. . . Elhanan the son of Jaareoregim, a Bethlehemite, slew the brother of Goliath the Gittite, the staff of whose spear was like a weaver's beam' (II Samuel, 21:19). The introduction of 'the brother', as we saw in Chapter 20, was an interpolation by the editor of the King James biblical text in order to overcome the problem of the previous account of David's slaying of Goliath in I Samuel. The same contradiction was noticed by the author of the Book of Chronicles, who attempted to resolve it by representing Elhanan as having killed 'Lahmi the brother of Goliath the Gittite' (I Chronicles, 20:5).[2]

● As we have seen, the Philistines arrived in Canaan from the islands of the Mediterranean *before* the Israelites in the twelfth century B.C., and it was their subsequent efforts to expand their territory from the coastal plain which they had made their home that led to the continuous conflict with the Israelites, who had by then arrived and were also trying to settle in Canaan. In adapting the ancient Egyptian story of Sinuhe, which dealt with events a thousand years earlier when there were no Philistines in Canaan, but only different Syrian and Canaanite tribes, the biblical editor therefore chose for historical reasons to identify Goliath as a Philistine. However, II Samuel, 21:2 speaks of him as having been 'born to the giants (Rapha in Hebrew)'. The English translation used the word 'giant' for the Hebrew 'Rapha', which occurs again in I Chronicles, 8:20. Yet the Rephaim were not Philistines, but the giant people who are said to have lived in Canaan in ancient times, and, unlike the Philistines, had no knowledge of iron.

These various contradictions point to the Goliath story as not having been initially an integral part of the accounts in I and II Samuel, a fact that becomes even clearer when we examine *The Autobiography of Sinuhe*.

APPENDIX D

The Autobiography of Sinuhe

Sinuhe was a courtier in the service of Nefru, daughter of Amenemhat I, the founder of the Twelfth Egyptian Dynasty in the twentieth century B.C. The form in which his autobiography is cast – the story of his sudden flight from Egypt, his wanderings, his battle with a 'mighty Canaanite man' like Goliath, and his eventual return to be buried in the land of his birth – makes it clear that it was written originally in his actual tomb. Many copies of the story, which is recognized as being based on fact, were found subsequently, dating from the twentieth century B.C., when the events actually occurred, until as late as the Twenty-first Dynasty in the eleventh century B.C. It was a popular tale in ancient Egypt, taught as a literary example to students, and there can be no doubt that all educated persons in Egypt, no matter what their ethnic background, would have been familiar with its contents.

The story begins around 1960 B.C., Year 30 and the last of Amenemhat I's reign. Sinuhe was at the time absent from the capital with the Egyptian army, led by the king's eldest son, heir and co-regent, Sesostris. While the army was making its way back from campaigns against Libyan tribes in the Western Delta, a messenger arrived from the palace during the night with news that caused Sesostris to leave his troops immediately and set out for the palace. Messages had also been sent to younger sons of the king serving with the army, and Sinuhe overheard one of them being read aloud. It said there had been a palace conspiracy and an unsuccessful attempt had been made on the life of Amenemhat I while he slept.

On hearing this, Sinuhe became so afraid that he decided to run away. He does not say why he was afraid. In fact, at one point in his story he is at some pains to make it clear that there was no apparent reason for him to run away at all, although, as one of the palace courtiers himself, he could well have been indirectly involved, or, at least, there could have been grounds for suspecting his involvement.

In reporting a conversation with Nenshi, the son of Amu and the ruler of Upper Retenu (northern Palestine), he says that Nenshi asked: 'Why have you come here? Has anything happened at the residence?' and he replied: 'The King of Upper and Lower Egypt, Sehetepibre (Amenemhat I), has departed to the horizon (died) and no one knows what may happen because of it . . . When I returned from an expedition in the land of the Libyans, someone announced it to me. My mind reeled. My heart was not in my body, and it brought me to the path of flight. Yet no one had spoken about me; no one spat in my face. No reviling word was heard, nor was my name heard in the mouth of the herald. I do not know what brought me to this land. It was like the plan of a god.'[1]

Whatever the reason, Sinuhe fled. From the Western Delta, he headed south until he reached a spot where the Nile was a single stream, somewhere near modern Cairo, and crossed to the east bank. He then turned north, following the edge of cultivated land until he came to the entrance of the Wadi Tumilat, the valley that connects the Eastern Delta with Lake Timsah, near modern Ismailia, and was the starting point of a Sinai road leading to Edom, south of the Dead Sea, and the Negeb, the vast desert in southern Palestine, now part of modern Israel. Here Amenemhat I had built a fortress, known as 'The Walls of the Prince', as a barrier to infiltration by bedouins, and Sinuhe was forced to hide in a bush so that the guard on the wall of the fortress would not see him. Once darkness had fallen, he continued his journey into Sinai where the chief of a bedouin tribe gave him food and drink and helped him to reach southern Palestine. From there he continued his journey northward along the road known in the Bible as the Way of the Sea where he was ultimately befriended by the prince Nenshi.

It is not easy to locate the precise area where Sinuhe spent his exile years. His account of this stage of his wanderings contains the statement: 'I set out for Byblos (an ancient port in northern Phoenicia) and turned to Kedem (which generally means the east). I spent half a year there. Then Nenshi, son of Amu, the ruler of Upper Retenu, brought me (to him, Nenshi).' The mention of Byblos has been interpreted as meaning that the area where Sinuhe eventually settled is to be found somewhere to the east of that city in northern Syria, but this is completely wrong, and Sinuhe's words have to be examined in the light of the sketchy geographical knowledge of western Asia possessed by Egyptians of that time.

It was only from the beginning of the Eighteenth Dynasty in the sixteenth century B.C. that the Egyptians gained detailed information about this area. Until then, they applied the term Retenu generally to Palestine–Syria. However, they knew the port Byblos because they had regular trade contact with it by sea. As the biblical Way of the Land of the Philistines joins the Way of the Sea at Gaza, linking Egypt with western Asia, leading to northern Syria and by-passing Byblos, the only location in western Asia well known to the Egyptians, the statement that Sinuhe 'set out for Byblos' is simply a means of signifying the geographical direction of his journey and indicates: 'I took the road that leads to Byblos.' He never states that he actually reached this city. Instead, he abandoned the Way of the Sea and 'turned to Kedem (east)' at some point in Upper Retenu.

During this period (the Middle Bronze Age, 2200–1550 B.C.), the Way of the Sea was crossed, at a point level with the northern section of the Dead Sea, by an east–west road connecting Jerusalem on the River Jordan with Jaffa (Joppa) on the Mediterranean.[2] It was most probably here, near the area which was the reported scene of the combat between David and Goliath, that Sinuhe turned east, as it kept him near the road leading to Egypt, the land of his birth. Certainly, Upper Retenu, where he chose to settle, can have been only the central area of northern

Palestine rather than the city states of northern Syria, as has been suggested. The city states were fortified, surrounded by strong walls, with villages and cultivated land outside the walls. However, the life Sinuhe describes was among a people who were semi-nomadic, lived in tents and were shepherds and hunters.

As we saw earlier, after he had lived in Upper Retenu for six months, his presence came to the notice of Nenshi, the ruler of the territory, who saw in this exiled Egyptian and former courtier a useful ally, took him under his protection and gave him favoured treatment: 'He placed me before his children. He married me to his eldest daughter. He made me choose from his country the choicest part of what he owned on the border with another country. It was a good land called Yaa. Figs were there as well as grapes, and more wine than water. Its honey was abundant and its olive trees numerous. On its trees were all kinds of fruit. Barley and emmer (corn), and there was all kinds of cattle without limit . . . Men hunted for me and laid (food) before me in addition to the catch of my hunting dogs . . . I spent many years while my children grew into mighty men, each managing his own tribe.'

Nenshi also appointed Sinuhe as commander of his army. This favouritism towards a foreigner would appear to have made local men jealous, for Sinuhe tells us: 'There came a mighty man of Retenu to challenge me at my tent. He was a champion without equal, and he had defeated all of Retenu. He said that he would fight with me, for he thought to beat me. He plotted to plunder my cattle through the counsel of his tribe. That ruler talked with me. I said: I do not know him. I am not his friend that I might walk about freely in his camp . . . He is jealous because he sees me carrying out your affairs . . . If he wishes to fight let him say so. Does God not know what is predicted for him, knowing how it is?

'I spent the night stretching my bow. I shot my arrows. I took out my dagger. I fixed up my weapons. When dawn broke, Retenu had come. It had incited its tribes, and had assembled the lands of half of it. It had planned this combat. He came to me where I was standing, and I placed myself near him. Every heart burned for me, men and women yelled. Every heart ached for me, saying: "Is there another strong man who could fight him?" He (took up) his shield, his axe and his armful of javelins. But after I had come away from his weapons, I made his remaining arrows pass me by, as one was close to the other. Then he made out a yell, for he intended to strike me, and he approached me. I shot him. My arrow struck in his neck. He cried out and fell on his nose. I felled him with his own axe. I yelled my war cry over his back. Every Asiatic roared . . . and his people mourned for him. This ruler, Nenshi, son of Amu, took me in his embrace.'

The period of Sinuhe's exile began, as we saw earlier, around 1960 B.C., the last year of Amenemhat's reign. After his father's death, his eldest son, Sesostris, married his sister, Nefru, in order to inherit the throne – as was the Egyptian custom – and ruled alone for a further thirty-five years. Throughout this time, his period in exile, Sinuhe continued to long for the land of his birth and sent repeated messages to the palace asking that he might be allowed to return to Egypt so that he could die and be buried there. Eventually his plea was granted and he spent his last years at court. His tomb has not yet been found although its location is known to have been in the area of Lisht in Middle Egypt where the pyramids of Amenemhet I and his son, Sesostris, have been discovered.

Sinuhe is actually a much more important figure in biblical history than this account reveals. His story is told here merely to make the point about the story of his combat with the 'mighty Canaanite man' that took place in the twentieth century B.C. and finds its echo in the confrontation between David and the 'giant' Goliath a thousand years later. The similarities between the two accounts have been noted by many scholars, such as William Kelly Simpson: 'The . . . account of the fight with the champion of Retenu has frequently been compared to the David and Goliath duel, for which it may have served as a literary prototype.'3

There are many indications to support the idea that the biblical scribe who incorporated the Goliath story into the Samuel text used as his source *The Autobiography of Sinuhe*:

1   The Sinuhe account existed in many texts from the twentieth century B.C. and was popular during the fifteenth century B.C., the time of the Israelite Sojourn in Egypt.

2   It has been shown earlier in this book that the story of the slaying of Goliath in I Samuel, 17, could not have been an original part of the Saul and David story, related in verses 16 to 31, but was a later insertion, putting forward a different version of the first meeting between the two characters.

3   While the enemies of Saul were the Philistines, who arrived in the land during the twelfth century B.C., Goliath is said to have been descended from the Rephaim, people who lived in Canaan in ancient times, including the time of Sinuhe.

4   Sinuhe was given the post of commander over Nenshi's fighting men: similarly, David is given an identical position in the inserted Goliath account where we learn: 'Saul set him (David) over the men of war' (I Samuel, 18:5).

    Yet this is contradicted in those parts of the story of the David-Saul relationship that do not depend on the interpolated Goliath story. Here we find that it was Abner who was 'the commander of the army' of Saul (I Samuel, 17:55 and other verses), that David was initially appointed as Saul's armourbearer and later that he was not actually placed in command of the entire army but became 'captain over a thousand' (I Samuel, 18:13).

5   As we have seen, later biblical editors, faced with three versions of the Goliath story, have felt it necessary to introduce 'the brother of Goliath' into the second and third of these accounts in order to overcome the difficulty that Goliath was ostensibly already dead when these encounters took place. All three accounts also find an echo in yet another combat in which we learn that a man named Benaiah slew an Egyptian who 'had a spear in his hand; but he went down to him with a staff, and plucked the spear out of the Egyptian's hand, and slew him with his own spear' (II Samuel, 23:21).

The conclusion must be that *The Autobiography of Sinuhe*, highly popular during the time of the Israelite Sojourn in Egypt and taught in schools as an example of literary excellence, survived in the memories of the Israelites when they left for the Promised Land. Later, the Hebrew scribes in Babylonia, anxious to enhance the image of the tribal David in order to make it possible for readers to accept that it was he who established the great empire stretching from the Nile to the Euphrates, included Sinuhe's encounter with a 'mighty Canaanite man' as an element of the First Book of Samuel.

APPENDIX E

The Virgin Fountain

Jerusalem was built on a plateau and limited in size by two valleys, Kidron (modern Silwan) to the east and Hinnomm (modern Gehenna) to the west. The two valleys join to the south of the city. The plateau itself is divided into two ridges by a north–south valley, the Tyropoen. The site of the ancient fortress city was the southern part of the eastern ridge, which is no more than a hundred or a hundred and fifty metres wide. The northern part of the ridge, Mount Moriah, the ancient sacred high ground where Solomon built his Temple and where the al-Aqsa mosque stands now, is higher and flatter. To the north of the plateau the ridges merge into the line of mountains that form the backbone of Palestine.

The earliest settlement in Jerusalem was situated on the eastern ridge because of its proximity to a spring of water known as the Gihon, the Christian Virgin Fountain, which lies in the Kidron valley at the foot of the ridge, some 325 metres from its southern extremity. The area was like an elongated triangle, with Mount Moriah, the Temple Mount, to the north and the Kidron and Tyropoen valleys on either side. In archaeological terms, this area, with the exception of the Temple Mount, is called the City of David, the location of the ancient fortress.

Investigation of the surface remains began nearly two hundred years ago and, from the middle of the nineteenth century, Jerusalem became increasingly the focus of attention for archaeologists. The first systematic excavations were carried out between 1867 and 1870 by Sir Charles Warren for the newly-founded Palestine Exploration Fund. A line of walls along the eastern crest of the eastern ridge was discovered by Warren. Further south, another portion of this defensive wall was cleared by R. A. S. Macalister in the course of excavations carried out with J. G. Duncan between 1923 and 1925. Macalister also found an imposing tower which he related to David and Solomon, his son and successor according to the Bible, and considered it to be an addition to the original Jebusite defences.

As we saw before, Tuthmosis III obtained control over Jerusalem without the need for battle. However, as I Kings, 11:27 states that 'Solomon built Millo, and repaired the breaches of the city of David his father', Macalister and Duncan were persuaded to believe that this tower was the point at which David broke into the city. They claimed to have found evidence of the breach of the wall and a subsequent building, which they regarded as a fortress, to strengthen the wall at this point.

The biblical account of David and his followers and their construction work at Jerusalem influenced Macalister's expectations about what he could expect to find at the site – a breached city wall, a structure of some kind built inward therefrom and a tower or other structure filling the breach[1] – and he seems to have believed that this was exactly what he had been able to discover in a site two hundred metres south of the present mosque and above the spring of Gihon down in the Kidron valley: 'All these things are just what we have found. The outer wall on the scarp was practically thrown flat. The stones were cast down inward toward the city in wild confusion, but not so completely confused but that they preserved some relics of their original courses in their fall. These large stones were difficult to move, and were allowed to lie where they fell by the ancient inhabitants, and, as we considered that anything that could be identified with a breach made by David was an important national monument, we did not disturb them either, except so far as it was absolutely necessary to settle one or two points about the underlying scarp . . .

'Inward of this breach and closing it, there was a long straight wall running almost entirely across the field from east to west. It was about 3ft.6ins. thick, and some 80ft. of it remained standing. At its present eastern end it had been destroyed by the intrusion of later structures. This wall showed a peculiarity of construction not noticed elsewhere in the walls uncovered. It consists of alternate courses of large stones and small spalls (chips). This is just what we should naturally expect in the circumstances. The builders of this wall had the great breach in the Jebusite rampart to draw upon as a quarry. But the large stones of the rampart were unwieldy to manipulate: the builders therefore trimmed them down to a more manageable size. They then found themselves with a large number of spalls on their hands, which they worked into the wall in the way described. At each end of the wall there is a strong tower. This wall we connected with the work attributed to David . . .

'A rectangular tower was erected upon it (the wall); and a small fragment of wall remained to suggest that it was one of the towers with a passage-way between them. This structure, filling the breach ['Millo' = 'a filling'] we venture to identify with the long-lost Millo.'[2]

Macalister's report seemed to imply that at last solid archaeological evidence had been found to confirm the biblical account of David's capture of Jerusalem in the early years of the tenth century B.C. However, the problems Macalister's conclusions solved were countered by new problems they created about the method suggested in the First Book of Samuel by which David took the city – by means of a 'gutter'. On the east ridge, Macalister located a water shaft giving access to the Gihon spring almost directly beneath it in the Kidron valley. Unfortunately, the top of this shaft emerged from the earth about twenty-five metres outside the line of the wall Macalister found. This would clearly have been an unsatisfactory arrangement for the inhabitants to obtain water at a time of siege.

Kathleen Kenyon, the British archaeologist, addressed herself to this problem when she began work at the site in 1961. She decided to start by the water shaft to the east of Macalister's site and found that the ancient inhabitants of the city had dug a tunnel to ensure their water supply. At first they tried to dig a shaft straight down to the water level, but failed because of the hardness of the rock. They then dug an angular tunnel with stairs and, at its end, a shaft that descended to the level of the spring. Through this shaft water could be drawn without the knowledge of any enemy besieging the fortress city. It is believed that this system is what is meant by the word 'gutter' used in the II Samuel account of the conquest of Jerusalem by David.

A trench was dug from the shaft on the ridge down the slope to the spring. Already at an early stage of the excavations it became clear that the wall assumed to have belonged to the Jebusite city could not be so: 'A trench . . . was laid out from the foot of Macalister's "Tower of David" to a level 27.25 metres lower down. It did not take long to establish the negative point that the tower did not belong to the time of David.'[3] The tower considered to have been built by David to strengthen the Jebusite defences was found to have been erected over the debris of buildings dating from the seventh century B.C. and the tower itself dated from no earlier than the third or second century B.C. In addition, the finds in the trench dug by the shaft in the slope showed that the 'earliest wall was built on the edge of the scarp in the natural rock at the beginning of the Middle Bronze Age-IIA (about 1800 B.C.). It is 2.5 metres wide and built of very large boulders. On the strength of the finds discovered in the foundation trench of the wall, it is definitely dated to Middle Bronze Age II . . . This was the wall which protected the city until the period of the Israelite monarchy.'[4]

No signs of repair were found: 'From the topographical standpoint, it is quite clear why the wall had been built on this line. It was erected on the slope so that the entrance to the early shaft leading to the spring would be brought within the walled area.'[5]

In fact, although archaeological work of one kind and another has been going on in Jerusalem for a century and a quarter, no shred of evidence has been found to support the idea that the city was taken by force during the time of the tribal David in the early part of the tenth century B.C. or that a construction of any kind was made in the city during this period. Thus the tribal David has left neither historical nor archaeological evidence.

Although evidence of the Millo mentioned in the Bible was found, it does not date from the time of the tribal David or his successor, but from the successors of Tuthmosis III. In I Kings, 9:27 we are told that Solomon, who came after David, built Millo. It has been accepted that this Millo was a kind of filling to extend the size of the city and strengthen its defences. Kathleen Kenyon was also able to resolve this problem. It was found that, as a result of the steepness of the eastern slope, a series of graduated terraces had been established, filled in with stones and supported by stone walls that rose upward from the base of the city: 'The earliest walled town of Jerusalem, therefore, on the present evidence extended well down the eastern ridge, with buildings climbing up in conformity with the steep slope of the ridge. The evolutionary stage in the lay-out of Jerusalem came apparently in the fourteenth century B.C. . . . In 1961, it was established that on the upper part of the crest an elaborate system of platforms had been constructed with the object of extending the very restricted level area of the summit of the hill. This year these platforms were examined in detail. The part of this complex that formed such an impressive termination of the work in 1961 proved to have been in use down to the seventh century B.C., and probably to the Babylonian constructions . . .

'It consisted essentially of retaining walls parallel to the line of the ridge supporting a fill that was stabilized and compartmentalized by a number of rib-walls at right angles to the slope. These rib-walls were not substantial in themselves, being for the most part only one stone thick, but were set at close intervals, usually about a metre. The part uncovered seemed to have been constructed outwards from a central spine, against which additional fills had been added on either side, each faced by a rib-wall built on a batter leaning back against the central spine . . . and most of the area cleared was to the south of the spine. Presumably there was a series of such sections, each built outwards from a similar spine. The fill of the compartments varied: in some cases it was completely of loose rubble, in some of earth, and in some of a striated fill that looks in section like turves or mud bricks (except that the striations are much too extensive and have firm terminations like mud bricks) and which is difficult to interpret.

'There was not a great deal in the way of finds in the fill, but there was enough pottery, including a few shreds of Mycenaean ware and White Slip II milkbowls, to show that the date is c. fourteenth century B.C. . . .'[6] This was the time when Amenhotep III, great-grandson of David/Tuthmosis III and the father of Moses/Akhenaten, ruled Egypt and had control over Jerusalem about three decades after Tuthmosis III's death.

'The structure was elaborate and was obviously a major town-planning operation, extending in the first instance the width of the level area suitable for proper buildings by about 18.5 metres on this (eastern) side of the wall. It was, however, vulnerable to disaster, for the platform so created depended on the ability of the retaining walls to support the thrust of the considerable weight of the fill behind them. These retaining walls were of roughly-fitted dry stone masonry, excellent while intact, but, once disturbed, liable to crumble rapidly. Either enemy action or natural agencies such as earthquakes or torrential rains could cause such disturbances . . .'[7]

Thus, although the biblical account of King David's entry to Jerusalem and his use of the holy high ground of Mount Moriah includes accurate historical statements, all the evidence indicates that these events did not take place during the time of the tribal David in the early part of the tenth century B.C., but five centuries earlier when David (Tuthmosis III) used the city as his residence during the siege of Megiddo. From this time on, the fortress was known by its new name, Urusalim, and was linked with King David and his descendants.

APPENDIX F

King of Peace

Solomon inherited a vast empire. He 'reigned over all the kingdoms from the river (Euphrates) unto the land of the Philistines, and unto the border of Egypt' (I Kings, 4:21). This empire, as we have seen, existed from the fifteenth century to the thirteenth century, after which northern Syria as far as the Euphrates no longer formed part of it, and the whole Asiatic empire had been lost by the middle of the twelfth century. From then until the second half of the sixth century, when the Persians conquered Egypt, no king could claim to rule from the Nile to the Euphrates. Solomon cannot therefore have been the successor of the tribal chief David because there was no empire for him to inherit in the tenth century B.C.

That empire was the original creation of Tuthmosis III. He was succeeded on the throne by Amenhotep II (c. 1436–1414 B.C.), another warrior king said to have been so strong that he could shoot at a metal target the thickness of a palm and his arrow would stick out on the other side. Early in his reign he marched into northern Syria to crush a rebellion. On returning to Thebes, the king brought with him seven rebel chiefs, imprisoned head downward in his ships, and eventually hanged them from the walls of Napata in northern Sudan. Subsequently, he tried to extend the frontiers of his empire even further into Asia Minor. Amenhotep II was followed in turn by his short-lived son, Tuthmosis IV (c. 1413–1405 B.C.), 'when attempt was made of dubious intent and extent to involve Egypt in further military action in Syria'.[1]

Then, thirty-two years after the death of the great conqueror, Tuthmosis III, 'his great-grandson sat upon the throne of Egypt. Three generations had sufficed to bring to fruition the dream of the early potentates of the Eighteenth Dynasty: Egypt was the universal leader of the known world. Her messengers ranged unimpeded over the Middle East to Babylon, the Hittite kingdom, Mitanni (northern Mesopotamia) and Cyprus; her merchant fleet sailed unmolested by pirates to Byblos, Tyre, Ugarit (in Syria), Crete and Aegean Greece. Untold wealth poured in from the gold mines of the Sudan and the far-flung lands of central Africa; tribute came annually from the north, borne on the backs of cowed Canaanites and Hurrians.'[2] Ruling this vast empire between the Nile and Euphrates, Amenhotep III occupied a unique place in the ancient history of the Orient. Later he became known as 'the great Hor, king of kings, ruler of rulers

. . . Amenhotep III and the Egypt he ruled over never had been, nor would be again, in a position of such absolute power in the world.'[3]

Why should he be remembered as Solomon? The answer lies in the fact that the name means 'safety' or 'peace'. Other than a minor military operation in northern Sudan during his Year 5, Amenhotep III's reign was almost entirely peaceful. He was the first ruler of the Egyptian empire who did not launch any war campaigns in western Asia. Instead, he relied on alliances and exchanges of gifts and diplomatic letters between himself and other leaders of the then-known world to create a climate of international friendship. He also furthered the cause of peace by a series of judicious marriages to foreign princesses – two from Syria, two from Mitanni, two from Babylonia as well as a princess from Arzawa in south-western Asia Minor. The prosperity and extravagance of the age is indicated by the fact that Gilukhepa, one of his Mitannian wives, is said to have arrived in Egypt with a caravan that included 317 ladies-in-waiting.

His reputation as the wise descendant of King David was further enhanced by the fact that he united the two branches of Tuthmosis III's family. On the death of his father, Amenhotep III, who was about twelve years of age at the time, married his baby sister, Sitamun, in order to inherit the throne, as was the Egyptian custom. Shortly afterwards, however, he married Tiye, the daughter of Joseph the Patriarch and the great-great-granddaughter of Tuthmosis III and Sarah, and made her rather than Sitamun his Great Royal Wife (queen).

Coronation

We find similarities between Amenhotep III and Solomon in the biblical account of the latter's coronation. It was, according to the Bible, David who ordered Solomon to be anointed 'king over Israel' (I Kings, 1:34). Anointing the king at the time of his coronation was an Egyptian, not a Canaanite custom, although it is referred to in the preceding Book of I Samuel as having been adopted in the case of both Saul and the tribal David. However, the very Hebrew word used, *MeSHeH* is borrowed from the Egyptian *MeSeH*.

Then David is reported as saying that, having been anointed, Solomon should come and 'sit upon my throne' (I Kings, 1:35). No mention is made in the Bible of either Saul or the tribal David having had a throne, and in two earlier Old Testament references – the appointment to high office of Joseph the Patriarch ('only in the throne will I be greater than thou' [Genesis, 41:40]) and in the account of the smiting of the firstborn 'of Pharaoh that sat on his throne' (Exodus, 12:29) – the word is used to signify the seat of pharaonic power. The German biblical scholar Otto Eissfeldt has made the point: 'It is comparatively easy to visualize the throne of gold and ivory with its six steps which stood in the audience chamber as it is described in I Kings, (10:18–20) . . . The lavish use of gold can be compared without hesitation with the wonderfully-preserved chair of Tutankhamun.'[4] Other aspects of the account of Solomon's coronation in I Kings – trumpet blowing, the acclamation 'God save king Solomon', and following the king in procession – accord with Egyptian custom but are absent from the coronation stories of Saul and the tribal David.

The idea of kingship, originally foreign to the Hebrews, was accorded a place in Israelite theology similar to that of Egypt in the biblical books relating to the time of the tribal David onward: 'Some scholars argue that, in adopting the institution of kingship, Israel also adopted a pagan theory of kingship and a ritual pattern for expressing it, allegedly common to all her neighbours. In this view the king was regarded as a divine or semi-divine being.'[5] This situation has nothing to do with either Saul or the tribal David because they were merely heads of the tribal coalition, but applied mainly to King David and his dynasty. In their case, as in Egyptian tradition, the king is regarded as the son of the deity. 'Thou art my son; this day have I begotten thee,' Jehovah tells King David in Psalms, 2:7. He also says of Solomon: 'I will be his father, and he shall be my son' (II Samuel, 7:14). The Israelite Lord now also refers to his kingly son as his 'anointed' (Psalms, 2:2, 18:50, 20:6).

The ancient idea of kingship was built on a kind of holy right of the king and his descendants to rule and be obeyed. This was because ancient kings were regarded as semi-gods descended from the gods. The Israelite idea of a chosen people did not imply this kingly view. Israel (Jacob) and his descendants had a covenant with God to follow him with the promise that he would make them victorious. No single man or dynasty in this tribal society was regarded as having the right to rule. So for the Israelites to accept David's becoming the son of God and having a right to rule was a new departure for them.

Marriages

Solomon, according to the Bible, 'made affinity with Pharaoh king of Egypt, and took Pharaoh's daughter, and brought her into the city of David' (I Kings, 3:1). He must therefore have been a member of the royal house of Egypt, not the tribal David, as we know from the Amarna letters that Egyptian Pharaohs never gave their daughters in marriage to foreign rulers. However, Amenhotep III's first marriage was to his baby sister, Sitamun. The attempt of the biblical narrator to place Solomon's marriage to Pharaoh's daughter in the tenth century B.C. is misplaced, but the tradition of the marriage itself fits the historical evidence of Amenhotep III.

The reason for the survival of this tradition is to contrast this event with the fact that, although Solomon is said to have had seven hundred wives and three hundred concubines (I Kings, 11:3), they were all foreigners: 'But King Solomon loved many strange women, together with the daughter of Pharaoh, women of the Moabites, Ammonites, Edomites, Zidonians and Hittites' (I Kings, 11:1). This love of foreign women is also attested in the case of Amenhotep III who, after marrying Sitamun to inherit the throne, married Tiye, the daughter of Yuya (Joseph), an Israelite, and the seven princesses listed above.

The mention of Pharaoh's daughter being Solomon's first and principal wife indicates that, as in the case of Amenhotep III, she was the wife of his own nationality. Had Solomon been King of Israel you would expect to find biblical mention of an Israelite wife to bear his successor, especially as, according to Israelite tradition, the line of descent is from the mother. Yet all we find in the Solomon story is foreign wives, beginning with Pharaoh's daughter. Even his crown prince, Rehoboam, is said to have been the son of an Ammonite (I Kings, 14:21).

The basis of the story lies in Amenhotep III making Tiye, an Israelite, his queen, with the result that her son was subsequently rejected because his mother was a foreigner.

The Burning of Gezer

The name of the king whose daughter was married by Solomon is not mentioned, but the Pharaoh in question is said to have 'gone up, and taken Gezer, and burnt it with fire, and slain the Canaanites that dwelt in the city, and given it for a present unto his daughter, Solomon's wife' (I Kings, 9:16). When exactly this event took place, and the name of the Pharaoh who led the campaign, are not known but it cannot have been at the time (c. 965–925 B.C.) assigned conventionally to the rule of Solomon. None of the kings of the weak Twenty-first Dynasty, which, according to the accepted evidence, came to an end in 945 B.C., is known to have been involved in military campaigns in western Asia. Then again, Gezer, in the Judaean upland some 30 kilometres west of Jerusalem, is known to have formed part of Philistine territory in the tenth century B.C. Why would the Pharaoh concerned find himself doing battle with Canaanites rather than Philistines? In fact, no mention of the Philistines is to be found anywhere in the story of Solomon, which again points to his having reigned *before* the mass invasion by the 'Peoples of the Sea' led to Egyptian loss of control over Palestine in the second half of the twelfth century B.C.

Having a large and secure Empire, and not having to fight any wars, enabled Solomon to embark on a large number of projects and changes in the way Egypt was administered.

APPENDIX G

Rebellion

According to Otto Eissfeldt there were five characteristic features of Solomon's reign, all of which can be related to the life and times of Amenhotep III rather than those four centuries later of the tribal David:

1. Change in Israel's military organization, introducing chariotry as an essential arm of war;
2. The creation of new administrative districts;
3. Building activity on a large scale, including the royal palace and its adjoining temple, and fortified barracks for his garrisons in the north;
4. Changes in the taxation system;
5. The refinement of court procedure and the maintenance of diplomatic relations with foreign courts.[1]

To deal firstly with the question of military organization . . .

In all periods of human history, those in possession of the more technically-developed military equipment have been able to defeat their enemies in battle unless overwhelmed by sheer numbers. Only in the case of the biblical story of David are we asked to believe that he, with his modest force of six hundred warriors, plus some untrained tribal elements, using primitive armaments at a time when the Philistines had knowledge of iron, was able to defeat all the powerful kingdoms of western Asia with their fortified cities and fast chariots. This, of course, was not the real situation, but is the result of the biblical narrator's attempt to marry the war achievements of the mighty Tuthmosis III to the exploits of the tribal Israelite leader.

King David (Tuthmosis III) did have a strong, well-trained, well-organized army equipped with the best chariots of his age, otherwise he would not have been able to establish his extended Empire. However, the American philologist Alan Richard Schulman has shown[2] that the chariot simply formed part of the army at this time. It was only in the early part of the reign of Amenhotep III that the chariotry became identified as a separate entity from the infantry.

Thus it was, as the Bible says, Solomon in the guise of Amenhotep III who organized the chariotry as a separate unit of warfare. How many chariots did he have? One figure given in the Old Testament is 'a thousand and four hundred' (I Kings, 1:26). We know from historical sources that the chariot force in some of the Canaanite garrisons at the time of the Empire constituted around thirty chariots while the excavated stable area in the location of the ancient fortified city of Megiddo – the largest in the land of Palestine and, as we saw earlier, wrongly dated to the tenth century B.C. – would suffice for the accommodation of about a hundred and fifty. A chariot force on this scale could not have been created in a short time since special training over a period of years was necessary to master this developed weapon: 'The charioteer had to be given a long and thorough training, and remained in the service while fit, or at least for several years; that is, he had to become a professional soldier.'³

Although Egyptian records confirm the development of a professional army from the time of Tuthmosis III, there is no evidence, even in the Bible itself, that such an organization existed in Israel at the time of the tribal David or his successor. Nor, had a king of the tenth century B.C. had such a powerful and independent organization, would it have vanished completely as soon as the king died, which is the case with the biblical Solomon.

According to the Bible, the empire inherited by Solomon became to some extent weakened during the course of his reign: 'Solomon left it somewhat smaller than he found it. First, there was trouble in Edom (in southern Palestine) . . . Hadad made trouble over a period of time, (but) we do not know what success he had or what measures Solomon took against him. Solomon certainly never lost his grip on Edom . . . Troubles in Syria were more serious. Solomon had inherited control of Aramean (Syrian) lands . . . (his control) was seriously damaged when Rezon, a one-time retainer of Hadadezer, with a band of men, seized Damascus and made himself king there. We neither know what action Solomon took, nor with what success, nor at what period in his reign this occurred. But the language implies that Rezon was never brought to terms. The extent of Solomon's loss in Syria is unknown. Although he probably retained at least nominal control in his Aramean (Syrian) holdings, save Damascus, his influence throughout Syria was certainly weakened.'⁴

These rebellions find their echo in the Amarna diplomatic archives relating to the reign of Amenhotep III. Letters sent by Palestinian kings, especially Abdi-Kheba of Jerusalem, speak of continuous trouble in the area of Edom and southern Palestine: 'All the king's land is rebellious.'⁵ Some nomadic elements, identified as the Khabiri, attacked city states in southern Palestine during the early part of the fourteenth century B.C., the time of Amenhotep III's rule and the short sole reign of his successor, Akhenaten. In another letter to Pharaoh, Abdi-khiba identified the source of the rebels: 'They have fought against me as far as Seeri (Mount Seir in Edom).'⁶

These problems in southern Palestine were not so serious that they led to any weakening of the king's control in the area. The situation in northern Syria was far more critical. Even before Amenhotep III came to the throne, the northern Mesopotamian kingdom of Mitanni, to the east of the Euphrates, defeated by Tuthmosis III, had begun to reassert its influence over city states in northern

Syria. Amenhotep III responded to this threat by a peace treaty with the King of Mitanni and marriage to two Mitannian princesses. He also sent the King of Mitanni thirty units of gold each year in return for his protecting the north Syrian section of the empire: 'We know that a definite agreement existed with Mitanni, which was concerned to a greater or lesser extent with frontier problems . . . It is quite possible that at this period the limit of definite Egyptian control was a line to the north of Gubla (Byblos on the northern Phoenician coast) . . . and passing inland to the south of the city of Qadesh on the Orontes (in northern Syria).'7 To put this another way, the area of empire lost to Egypt at this stage lay between Qadesh on the Orontes, north of Damascus, to the borders of the Hittite kingdom of Asia Minor to the north and the borders of Mitanni in the east.

However, Amenhotep III's problems in the region were not yet over. Towards the end of his reign, the king's authority over the northern part of the empire, including Damascus, was endangered by the powerful Hittite king, Suppululiuma. He also posed a threat to Mitanni, Egypt's ally in the area. Akizzi, ruler of the northern Syrian city of Qatna, a few miles north of Qadesh, spoke of these dangers in letters to Amenhotep III: 'To King Annumuria (Amenhotep III), Son of the Sun, my Lord, thus (says) this thy servant Akizzi. Seven times at the feet of my Lord I bow. My Lord in these my lands I am afraid. Mayest thou protect one who is thy servant under the yoke of my Lord. From the yoke of my Lord I do not rebel. Lo, there is fear of my foes . . . this country is among thy lands: the city of Qatna is thy city . . . the soldiers and chariots of my Lord's government have received corn and drink, oxen and beasts . . . now the king of the land of the Hittites . . . and men who are destroyers serve the king of the land of the Hittites: he sends them forth. My Lord, my servants, the men of the city of Qatna, Aziru expels (Aziru was the king of the north Syrian land of Amurru, on the coast north of Phoenicia, and was encouraged by the Hittites to conquer Egyptian positions in Syria) . . . out of the land of the dominion of my Lord; and behold (he takes) the northern lands of my Lord.'8

In a following letter, Akizzi informed the king that the land of Ubi, west of Damascus, is under threat: 'Just as Damascus . . . is terror-stricken at the league of the enemy, and is lifting up its hands in supplication at the feet of the king, so likewise does the city of Qatna lift up its hands.'9

To summarize the matter, Frederick J. Giles, the Canadian Egyptologist who made a study of the Amarna letters, came to the conclusion that 'most of the letters which deal with the alleged collapse of the Egyptian empire during the Amarna period come from the reign of Amenhotep III'.10 He later goes on to say: 'At the time of the death of Tuthmosis III it (the empire) was, to be sure, of somewhat greater extent than that at the death of Amenhotep III. Yet the apparent decrease may have been due to policy rather than military defeat.'11 Thus the biblical account of changes in King David's empire during the time of Solomon can be seen to agree with historical records relating to events during the reign of Amenhotep III.

The Amarna letters also throw some light on the biblical account which states: 'King Solomon gave Hiram (the king of Tyre) twenty cities in the land of Galilee' (I Kings, 9:11). The name of Tyre's king in these letters is not Hiram, but

Abimilichi. From his letters we know that: 'The king, my Lord, hath appointed me the guardian of the city of Tyre, the "royal handmaid" . . . I am an officer of the king.'[12] In another letter, No. 99, in the Berlin Museum, Abimilichi asked the king to give him another city: 'Let the king, my Lord, give his countenance to his servant and let him give the city of Huzu to his servant.'[13] In yet another letter, No. 29, which is to be found in the British Museum, the King of Tyre indicated that another of the Egyptian cities had been placed under his control: 'And now the city Zarbitu is to be guarded by the city of Tyre for the king, my Lord.'[14]

In this same letter we have an indication that more of Amenhotep III's cities had been placed under Abimilichi's guardianship: 'I heard the gracious messenger from my Lord . . . behold he said, O king, my Lord, that the region (is) to be established by the presence of many soldiers; and the servant says for his Lord that my plain is my land over against my highlands, over against the plain of my cities . . . Thou art the sun God whom he has proclaimed before him; and the decision which shall set at rest is lasting for one. And because she judges that the king, my Lord, is just, our land obeys the land that I am given. This Abimilichi says to the Sun god.'[15]

It seems that Abimilichi was probably given some authority over Galilee, about which he reported to Pharaoh: 'The king of the city of Khazura (Hazor, the Galilean fortress city) is leaving his city, and goes out with men of blood.'[16]

APPENDIX H

District Commissioners

The structure of the political system up to the time of Solomon was, according to the Bible, a tribal one. Then Solomon did away with tribal divisions and united Israel, together with other parts of the empire, in one political entity: 'And Solomon had twelve officers over all Israel, which provided victuals for the king and his household: each man his month in a year made provision' (I Kings, 4:7). Yet, if we examine the matter closely, we find that this administrative system does not belong to the Palestinian Israel, but to the period of the Egyptian empire.

'According to the Old Testament traditions, the tribes of Israel sprang up from one family, having descended directly from the sons of a common ancestor. Those sons of a common father in turn are presented as the ancestors of the clans which made up the tribe . . . The human families which rest on a natural blood bond are family, extended family and clan. The clan is the largest group within which blood relationships can still be recognized, while the tribe represents a community of clans which has arisen under the influence of historical events.'[1]

At the head of the extended family is a chief, while the clan is led by an assembly of elders, who are usually the heads of extended families. Although we have an extensive list of the Israelite tribes and their clans in the Book of Numbers (26: 5–51), they became established only after they entered Canaan and settled in their new lands. This was especially true in the time of the Judges, between the entry into Canaan in the thirteenth century B.C. and the era of Saul towards the end of the eleventh century B.C.: 'In this period, Israel existed in the form of a sacred confederation of twelve tribes with a common sanctuary as a centre.'[2] Therefore, at this time each tribe was living separately in its own land, governed by its elders, yet sharing a common spiritual centre.

However, once they found themselves vulnerable to the assaults of the Philistines, organized in their city states, competing for occupation of the same territory and unified in their action, the Israelites felt the need for a common leader to unify *them* against their enemies: 'Then all the elders of Israel gathered themselves together, and came to Samuel unto Ramah, And said unto him,

Behold, thou art old, and thy sons walk not in thy ways: now make us a king to judge us like all the nations' (I Samuel, 8: 4–5). So Samuel chose Saul, a son of Kish, a wealthy Benjaminite, and declared him king. He was accepted by all the tribes, but this did not change the political system overnight: each tribe continued to govern its own affairs as before, including Saul himself, who went on managing his field until the day when Nahash, the Ammonite, went up to Jabesh, besieged some Israelites and threatened to disgrace them and make them serve him. 'And, behold, Saul came after the herd out of the field; and Saul said, What aileth the people that they weep? And they told him the tidings of the men of Jabesh. And the Spirit of God came upon Saul when he heard those tidings, and his anger was kindled greatly. And he took a yoke of oxen, and hewed them in pieces, and sent them throughout all the coasts of Israel by the hands of messengers, saying, Whosoever cometh not forth after Saul and after Samuel, so shall it be done unto his oxen. And the fear of the Lord fell on the people, and they came out with one consent' (I Samuel, 11:5–7).

Therefore, although in his conflict with the Philistines Saul used warriors from all the twelve tribes of Israel, the tribes themselves preserved their day-to-day independence, unified only in the fact that Saul was their common leader in the face of adversity. The very fact that David was accepted as king over Judah after Saul's death, then over Israel – the rest of the tribes living in central Palestine and Galilee – after the death of Ishbosheth, Saul's son, indicates two separate tribal units under his personal control. During the time of the tribal David, there was no one state, with fixed boundaries and a unified system of government. It is the inclusion of the annals of Tuthmosis III in the biblical story of David that has created, as we have seen, the false belief of David ruling over a vast empire. Yet we have no evidence of a political system for administering such an empire, including hundreds of separate kingdoms, at this time; no taxation system; no organized army to guard its boundaries. The biblical story of Solomon implies, in fact, that a sophisticated political system – signifying the end of the tribal society and the integration of the population in one political entity, under the control of the king and his central government – sprang up suddenly during his forty-year reign, only to vanish again as soon as he died.

When analysed, the story is found to rely heavily on Egyptian experience. From as early as 3000 B.C., the Egyptian administration controlled the activities of the Two Lands of Egypt. It organized the royal court as well as the economy in the name of the king, the official owner of all the land. Palace officials were responsible for each administrative region, where there was another high official with a local bureaucracy under his control. During the empire period – and particularly during the time of Tuthmosis III – the political system was reorganized to suit the needs of the age, and later further developed by Amenhotep III. It was then that, for the purposes of taxation, the empire was arranged in the twelve administrative sections, an arrangement that the biblical narrator drew on for his account of the same king the world now knows as Solomon.

The Great Builder

Solomon is said to have been a master builder who created buildings of royal proportions. He built 'the house of the Lord, and his own house, and Millo (the filling at Jerusalem), and the wall of Jerusalem, and Hazor, and Megiddo, and Gezer' (I Kings, 9:15) and 'Beth-horon the nether, And Baalath and Tadmor in the wilderness . . . And all the cities of store that Solomon had, and cities for his chariots, and cities for his horsemen, and that which Solomon desired to build in Jerusalem, and in Lebanon, and in all the land of his dominion' (I Kings, 9:17–19). Further reference to this mass of building work, including 'store cities, which he built in Hamath', is to be found in II Chronicles, 8:4–6. From these biblical accounts we can conclude that Solomon built 1) garrisons and fortifications, 2) the Millo, 3) a royal palace, 4) a temple.

Garrisons

We have archaeological evidence in the case of only three of the places listed – Hazor, Megiddo and Gezer. Hazor was a large Canaanite city state in Upper Galilee and has been identified as modern Tell el-Qedah, fourteen kilometres north of the Sea of Galilee. It was one of the major commercial centres in the Fertile Crescent and we find references to it in both Egyptian and Mesopotamian texts going back as far as the eighteenth century B.C. Megiddo, which has been identified as modern Tell el-Mutesellim, was the largest of the ancient fortified city states in Canaan, overlooking the Jezreel Valley of central Palestine, while Gezer, located in the foothills of the Judaean Range east of Jerusalem, was another important fortified city. All three of these city states are listed in the western Asiatic cities conquered by Tuthmosis III in the middle of the fifteenth century B.C. This has been confirmed by archaeological digging, which has produced evidence of the cities' destruction in the right strata for this period.

In addition, in all three cases evidence has been found of large-scale reconstruction work half a century later during the reign of Amenhotep III. New royal palaces, temples, ordinary houses and fortifying walls were established. In each case a local ruler was appointed, paying tribute to Pharaoh and enjoying the support of an Egyptian garrison. Egyptian objects, including a cartouche of Amenhotep III, were found in the strata belonging to this period, as was also the case in other excavated cities of Canaan such as Beth-shean, between the Jezreel Valley and the Jordan, and Lachish, about thirty kilometres south-east of Ashkelon in southern Canaan. Evidence of the cities' wealth and trade was found. It was clearly in this period in the fourteenth century B.C. that these cities prospered.

However, the picture is completely different when we come to the tenth century B.C. Although we again have evidence of destruction of all three cities, it is to be dated – as we saw earlier – to the time in the twelfth century B.C. when the 'Peoples of the Sea' attacked the whole eastern Mediterranean coast from Anatolia in the north to Egypt in the south. This wave of destruction was followed by rebuilding operations two centuries later in the mid-tenth century B.C. Yet this chronology, supported by archaeological evidence, carried no weight with Yigael Yadin, who came to the conclusion as a result of his work at Hazor: 'On the basis of the stratigraphy, pottery and biblical references, these fortifications (at Hazor) are to be attributed to Solomon.'³ What evidence did he produce to support this view?

At Hazor, following the twelfth-century B.C. destruction of the city by the 'Peoples of the Sea', the appropriate stratum (XII) led him to the view that after 'a certain gap, a small settlement rose at the beginning of the Iron Age . . . This settlement, which can hardly be called a city, consisted mostly of . . . foundations for tents and huts.' This was followed by a layer which he attributed to the time of the tribal David and in which he found 'no definite structures'. Then, of stratum X he says: 'This stratum represents Hazor rebuilt as a fortified city. Its main features are a casemate wall and a large gate with six chambers, three on either side, and two towers flanking the passage way.'⁴ Yadin found similar construction both at Gezer and Megiddo.

This is slender evidence on which to attribute building to a king for whose existence at any time we have no evidence outside the Bible. Not surprisingly, Yadin found no inscription – unlike the case of Amenhotep III – that identified a king named Solomon, nor anything testifying to a Solomonite kingdom. Nor is there any evidence in the Old Testament to support the view that Solomon's constructions included a fortified city with 'a casemate wall and a large gate with six chambers, three on either side, and two towers flanking the passage way'. On the other hand, in all three locations we have evidence of the existence of the Philistines, a section of the invading 'Peoples of the Sea', in the form of their special pottery and iron objects. How, then, can we be sure that the construction work attributed to Solomon by Yadin on evidence that does not stand up to analysis was not, in fact, an attempt by the 'Peoples of the Sea' to rebuild Hazor after their initial destruction of the city in the twelfth century B.C.?

The Millo

As we saw earlier, the British archaeologist Kathleen Kenyon succeeded in uncovering the remains of the Millo (filling), inserted to widen the upper surface of the rock on which the ancient fortress of Jerusalem was built by extending its limits towards the sloping ground to the east. She was able to date the first construction of the Millo to the fourteenth century B.C., the time of Amenhotep III. No evidence was found to relate the Millo to the tenth century B.C., when Solomon is supposed to have succeeded David on the throne.

APPENDIX I

The Queen of Sheba and the Glass Lake

One of the major building achievements attributed to Solomon was the new royal house, reputed to have taken thirteen years to complete. This great palace is said to have been constructed to the north of the ancient city of Jerusalem and south of the temple area, yet no further mention of it is made during the period that followed Solomon's death. Moreover, although Jerusalem has been extensively excavated, no remains of such a palace have been found. However, when we compare the biblical description of Solomon's royal palace with the great palace of Amenhotep III at Thebes, it becomes clear that it was this royal residence that the biblical narrator was describing.

From the account in I Kings, 7:2–12 we can see that Solomon's palace consisted of five elements: 1) The king's palace, 2) The house of Pharaoh's daughter, 'whom he had taken to wife', 3) The throne room, 4) A hall of columns, 5) The house of the forest of Lebanon. The foundations were of costly stones while pillars of Lebanon cedarwood supported the roofs.

Up to the time of Amenhotep III, although Thebes was the religious and administrative capital of Egypt, the main royal residence was at Memphis, on the west bank of the Nile a few miles to the south of the Great Pyramid of Giza. With the great wealth of his empire at his disposal and no wars to fight, Amenhotep III embarked on the construction of a great royal complex at Thebes. His own palace was ready by Year 8 of his reign, but the whole complex was not completed until towards the end of his third decade. The area of the palace was excavated between 1910 and 1920 by the Egyptian Expedition of the Metropolitan Museum of Art of New York. From the result of these excavations we can see that the sections mentioned in the Bible formed only part of the large complex.

The King's Palace

'The oldest and most important building, the palace of the king, occupies the south-east quarter of the great complex and is adjoined on the east by its kitchens, offices and storerooms.'[1] This palace has also a section for the king's harem and is connected with a smaller palace, the residence of Queen Tiye, daughter of the king's high official Yuya.

The House of Pharaoh's Daughter

As we saw before, Amenhotep III married his sister Sitamun, the daughter of Tuthmosis IV, in order to gain his right to the throne, which was the Egyptian custom: '. . . the great North Palace . . . appears to have been the residence of an extremely important royal lady, quite possibly Queen Sitamun. The western end of this building is given over to magazines and workshops, and farther to the west are the remains of a workmen's village.'2

The Throne Room

'The reception quarters consist of a large squarish hall with many rows of columns in wood and a throne dais set along the axis of the entrance corridor, a second, smaller hypostyle hall with a throne dais near it, a throne room and a bedroom.'3

The Hall of Columns

North of the workmen's section 'is the royal Audience Pavilion, its floor elevated above the surrounding terrain, its northern facade provided with a balcony-like projection jutting out into a deep, colonnaded courtyard'.4 ('And he made a porch of pillars . . . and the other pillars and the thick beam were before them' (I Kings, 7:6).)

The House of the Forest of Lebanon

This was a 'Festival Hall, prepared for the celebration of Amenhotep III's second Sed-festival',5 a big colonnaded building that extended at the very north of the palace complex. The complex also included houses for other members of the royal family as well as court officials and servants. Exactly as the Bible says, all the pillars were of wood imported from the Lebanon.

'Ceilings were of timber rafters, covered beneath with lath and plaster and painted with a series of protecting Nekhebet vultures in the official halls and in the bedroom of Pharaoh, or with vines within a frame of rosettes and chequered pattern, spirals and bulls' heads, similar to Aegean ornament. Floors were decorated in the same technique to represent a pool with papyrus, lotus and fowl.'[6]

Badawy's description of the floor of the smaller hypostyle hall with a throne dais near it suggests that an incident described in the Koran during a visit by the Queen of Sheba to King Solomon can only have taken place in this room where 'the floor resembles a water basin filled with fish, aquatic plants, swimming ducks, geese and land birds, and bordered by papyrus and plants shown in rabattement'. In describing the Queen of Sheba's visit, the Koran tells how:

> She was asked to enter
> That lofty Palace: but
> When she saw it, she
> Thought it was a lake
> Of water, and she (tucked up
> Her skirts), uncovering her legs.
> He said: 'This is
> But a palace paved
> Smooth with slab of glass.'
> She said: 'O my Lord!
> I have indeed wronged
> My soul: I do (now)
> Submit (in Islam), with Solomon,
> To the Lord of the Worlds.'
>
> The Ants Sura, v.44[7]

The Temple

The Bible describes how Solomon built a temple on the ancient holy high place of Mount Moriah, to the north of Jerusalem. It was on a rock altar there that Abraham is said to have attempted the sacrifice of Isaac. David brought the holy Ark to this same area, where the rock became the Holy of Holies of Solomon's temple. It has not been possible to carry out excavation in search of the Solomonic shrine because the site is now occupied by the Islamic Dome of the Rock. What evidence is there, however, that points to Amenhotep III as the king who actually built Solomon's temple?

The account of the building of the temple is found in the sixth chapter of I Kings. From this we know that it was a rectangular structure, facing east, with a vestibule or forecourt. In the forecourt were two free-standing pillars, the one to the south called Jachin, the one to the north called Boaz. Then came the main hall of the sanctuary, lit by small windows under the roof and surrounded by a three-storeyed walking place divided into cells. Finally, at the rear of the temple came the Holy of Holies, a cubical, windowless room where the Ark was placed. Solomon is said to have set the construction work under way in his Year 4 and completed it in his Year 11.

Amenhotep III is known to have built many temples, both in Egypt and in

Canaan. He began his building programme in his Year 2. The sites of his temples for different deities, including himself, were at Hermopolis, opposite Amarna, two temples at Karnak, the great Luxor temple, three temples in Nubia, his mortuary temple north of his palace complex in western Thebes and in almost all the Canaanite cities that had Egyptian garrisons. Although no remains of the mortuary temple in western Thebes have been found, two colossal statues of the seated king, just under seventy feet tall, stood at the front of the temple and still exist in western Thebes. Like the two pillars of Solomon's temple, these two statues have names. The northern one has come to be known as Memnon, after Greek visitors of antiquity, who identified him with their own character of that name. To the left of this statue is a smaller image of the king's mother, Queen Mutemuya, while on the right stands his wife, Queen Tiye. The upper part of this statue used to emit a musical sound as it was warmed by the rays of the rising sun until it fell as a result of an earthquake in 27 A.D. The southern statue was known as the Ruler of Rulers and had its own priests.

On the other side of the stele known as the Israel Stele, which came from this temple and was used later by Merenptah to give an account of the Libyan war in his Year 5, we find the original inscription of Amenhotep III in which he describes the temple as 'an everlasting fortress of sandstone, embellished with gold throughout, its floor shining with silver and all its doorways with electrum (alloy of silver and gold). It is wide and very long, adorned for eternity, and made festive with this exceptionally large stele. It is extended with royal statues of granite, of quartzite and precious stones, fashioned to last for ever. They are higher than the rising of the heavens: their rays are in men's faces like the rising sun . . . Its workshops are filled with male and female slaves, the children of chieftains of all the countries which my majesty conquered. Its magazines have stored up uncountable riches. It is surrounded by villages of Syrians, peopled with children of chieftains; its cattle are like the sands of the shore, totalling millions.'[8]

Like Solomon's temple, in whose construction, according to the Bible, much precious material was used, Amenhotep III's temples used a wide range of precious metals in addition to cedarwood from the Lebanon: 'The recorded figures of metals and precious stones that went into the Montu temple (one of the Karnak temples) is quite staggering: 3.25 tons of electrum, 2.5 tons of gold, 924 tons of copper, 1,250 pounds of lapis lazuli, 215 pounds of turquoise, 1.5 tons of bronze and over 10 tons of beaten (?) copper. Such was the return on Egypt's investment in an empire!'[9]

It is possible to see some similarity when one compares the general plan of Solomon's temple, as it is described in the Bible, with some types of Egyptian temple: 'This plan recalls vividly the basic tripartite plan of the cult temple in Egypt during the New Kingdom. The elements, including interior wood panelling, a front porch flanked by towers, and the cherubs seem to have been of an Egyptianizing style.'[10] The cherubs were looked upon as a protective image, usually found in Egyptian temples, and are said to have been placed over the Ark in Solomon's temple at Jerusalem.

Nevertheless, although the main elements of Solomon's temple at Jerusalem are similar to those of Egyptian temples, there are also some non-Egyptian elements.

Eissfeldt suggests: 'The hypothesis that perhaps Egyptian or Assyrian temples had served as models for the Phoenicians, and so through them for the Solomonic building, seemed thoroughly justified.' He goes on to say, however: 'An Egyptian temple of Beth-shean of the fourteenth century B.C. (the time of Amenhotep III) corresponds to the Solomon temple.'[11]

The evidence that Amenhotep III built a temple in almost all Canaanite cities that had Egyptian garrisons can be seen from the result of excavation work at Hazor, Beth-shean, Lachish, Megiddo and Gezer. Yadin gave this account of the fourteenth century B.C. temple at Hazor: 'The temple comprised three main elements built in succession from north to south, with the doorways on a single axis leading into each chamber.

The Porch: Situated on the southern side of the temple, this constituted the main innovation in the (plan of) previous (temples on the same site). It is somewhat narrower than the hall and served as a sort of entrance hall to the temple proper, but, unlike that of stratum 2, it was attached directly to the main structure. (On either side of the entrance to the porch stood a basalt orthostat [standing structure] with a lion in relief);

The Hall: This chamber was identical in its basic features with the porch of the previous temple;

The Holy of Holies: This was a broad room, similar to that of the previous temples, with a rectangular niche in its northern wall. In the centre of the room were two bases of columns which supported the roof. In its general plan, this temple resembles . . . Solomon's temple.'[12]

Thus archaeological evidence confirms that more than one example of the biblical Solomonic temple was built in Canaan during the time of Amenhotep III. The practice of carrying the deity on an Ark that is placed in the Holy of Holies of the temple is purely Egyptian. Protection of the Ark by two cherubs holding their wings over it corresponds to the protective role of Horus with his wings, found everywhere in Egyptian temples, protecting the holy being. The two pillars, or representations, at the entrance of the temple indicate the purely Egyptian idea of the split of the spiritual element into two, through which you have to pass in order to reach the inner element.

The Amarna letters, six of which were sent to Amenhotep III by Abdi-Kheba, ruler of Jerusalem, make it clear that a Nubian garrison was stationed there, located in the south-eastern corner of the holy high area of Mount Moriah where the remains of what have been called 'Solomon's stables' have been found. They belonged, in fact, to the cavalry of Amenhotep III. The inescapable conclusion is that, as in the case of other garrisoned cities, a temple was built at Jerusalem where the only possible location would have been Mount Moriah, the same location as the present-day Dome of the Rock, where local people worshipped at the time and Amenhotep III's great-grandfather, Tuthmosis III, kept the Ark of the Egyptian god.

To summarize, we have historical and archaeological evidence of building during the reign of Amenhotep III that matches the building attributed to Solomon, but nothing to match it during the tenth century B.C., the supposed time when Solomon ruled.

APPENDIX J

The Wisdom of Solomon

Running an empire that reached out from Egypt to the distant Euphrates required a complex system of taxation and bureaucracy.

Taxation

Almost all scholars agree that the taxation system which the Bible says was introduced by Solomon matches precisely the system that was used in Egypt at the time of its Empire. It had been the custom from its earliest history for all producing units in Egypt to render part of their annual output in the form of tax. As Pharaoh was looked upon as the owner of the land, it was he who apportioned this tax to different institutions of the State such as temples, palaces, garrisons.

After Tuthmosis III had established the new Egyptian empire, foreigners within its borders were obliged to pay the same tax. For this purpose, as we have seen, the empire, including the Two Lands of Egypt, was divided into twelve areas. Each area was the responsibility of a high official and was expected to contribute sufficient tax to cover the country's needs for one month of the year. The similarity between this arrangement and the system said to have been introduced by Solomon is striking: 'Solomon, too, divided a specific territory into twelve districts, requiring each to furnish victuals and materials for one month of the year. As in the case of Egyptian *htr* (tax), the levy on the Israelites was for the purpose of provisioning: "And Solomon had twelve officers over all Israel, which provided victuals for the king and his household: each man his month in a year made provision" (I Kings, 4:7) . . . "And those officers provided victual for king Solomon, and for all that came unto king Solomon's table, every man in his month" (I Kings, 4:27) . . . Again, like the Egyptians, Solomon employed the levy to stock his garrison posts with supplies . . . The stocking of garrison posts by means of the annual *htr* (levy) was well known in Palestine under the Egyptian empire . . . It is highly likely that Solomon was consciously using this common

Egyptian means of taxation for supplying the organs of a central government with sustenance.'[1]

In fact, the biblical statements regarding taxation during the time of Solomon come directly from Egyptian sources relating to the time of the Empire and Amenhotep III.

Bureaucracy

A leader of the combined tribes of Israel would not have needed a large bureaucracy to manage his affairs. Saul is said simply to have had Abner as the commander of his army. However, to cope with the administrative burdens of a vast empire, both King David and Solomon needed a highly-developed administration. The sudden appearance of such an administration in Israelite society, with no roots in previous Israelite history, has led scholars to seek a foreign origin for such a system: 'The suggestion has often been made that the court functions . . . of David and Solomon were in part modelled on officers of the royal administration in Egypt.'[2]

The names of David's court officials are to be found in II Samuel, 8:16–18 and 20:23–6, those of Solomon in I Kings, 4:2–6. In the case of Solomon we find among the list of officials the priest, the scribes, the commander-in-chief of the army, the official in charge of the palace and another in charge of the tribute. All of these new offices are similar to appointments made by Tuthmosis III and Amenhotep III. Even the forced labour pressed into service in Egypt for the king's building projects is said to have been imposed for the first time by Solomon on native Israelites as well as foreigners: 'And king Solomon raised a levy out of all Israel; and the levy was thirty thousand men' (I Kings, 5:13). The number of senior officials argues for a large number of minor ones. I Kings, 9:23 gives a figure of five hundred and fifty simply to supervise labour. The relationship between Solomon's court offices and the ancient Egyptian system is obvious: David, followed by Solomon, is described as having patterned it at least in part on Egyptian models. Indeed, one author has pointed out: 'One of his officials (Shisha, I Kings, 4:3) bore an Egyptian name and possibly was an Egyptian.'[3]

As in all the other cases we have seen, the similarity between King David's and Solomon's organization of the State with that of Egypt was not a result of their borrowing a foreign system, but a consequence of mixing the original sources of these Israelite ancestors with the later traditions of tribal unification.

The Mystery of Zadok

Zadok, the priest, is a mysterious character who appears as a strong supporter of Solomon from the early days and then replaces Abiathar as the high priest of the new temple at Jerusalem: 'The figure of Zadok has always commanded the interest of Old Testament students, and the problem of his antecedents has found no certain solution. He appears suddenly beside Abiathar in the Jerusalem priesthood in the time of David, but the Old Testament gives us no reliable information as to whence he came.'[4]

The situation becomes more complicated because of the doubts and obscurity about Zadok's lineage: 'He is provided, indeed, with two different genealogies, but of these one is almost certainly due to textual corruption and the other to the pious fabrication of a later age. For whereas II Samuel, 8:17 declares him to be the son of Ahitub and so apparently of the family of Eli, I Chronicles, 24:23 represents him as belonging to the house of Eliazar . . . while I Chronicles, 5:30–34 (and) 6:35–8 . . . provides him with a full genealogy back to Aaron.'[5]

Zadok was appointed high priest during the reign of Solomon, and the office was held by his successors down to the time of the Babylonian exile. Suspicions have been expressed, however, that he may not have been of Israelite origin: 'I believe . . . we should recognize in Zadok the pre-Davidic priest of the Jebusite shrine in Jerusalem,' wrote the influential Harold Henry Rowley.[6] Many biblical scholars have followed Rowley's lead as a means of identifying Zadok: 'Zadok . . . is thought to have been a foreigner . . . admitted to the priesthood of Yahweh (Jehovah) by David.'[7]

We therefore have the situation where, although the family of Aaron is said in the Book of Leviticus to have been appointed by Moses to the priestly office, now Solomon is said to have given it to a complete foreigner and his family. A more possible explanation suggests itself once we accept the identification of Solomon as Amenhotep III. One of the most important of the king's officials was Yuya, Deputy of His Majesty in the Chariotry, who also became the king's father-in-law on his marriage to Queen Tiye. Elsewhere[8] I have identified Yuya as Joseph the Patriarch, who brought the Israelites to Egypt.

Now the Babylonian Talmud refers to Joseph in one instance as Zadok (the righteous) and the same reference, in which the equivalent word *siddiq* is used, is to be found in the Koranic account of Pharaoh asking him to interpret his dream about the seven good years that would be followed by seven lean years (Sura XII, v.46). Elsewhere again,[9] I have argued in favour of the two following genealogies:

Joseph the Patriarch	Joseph the Patriarch
Tiye	Aye
Moses (Akhenaten)	Aaron

I have further made the point that Moses and Aaron were not actually brothers, as the Old Testament suggests, but 'feeding brothers', a bedouin concept still recognized, in the sense that Aye's wife, Queen Tiy (not to be confused with Queen Tiye), nursed Moses as well as her own son. Thus Zadok at the time of Solomon could be identified with Joseph the Patriarch, the great ancestor of the Aaronites, who were thus identified as correctly holding the priestly office.

The Wisdom of Solomon

Solomon is depicted in the Bible as being exceedingly wise. 'So king Solomon exceeded all the kings of the earth for riches and for wisdom' (I Kings, 10:23). Even this attribute, as we shall see, can only strengthen the argument in favour of identifying him as Amenhotep III.

Undoubtedly the best-known story about the wisdom of Solomon is the dispute between two mothers over the parenthood of a child, to be found in I Kings, 3:16–28. Each of the women, who lived in the same house, gave birth to a baby boy. One of the babies died, however, and both women claimed the surviving child as her own and eventually came before the king with their dispute. Thereupon Solomon ordered the child to be cut in half with a sword, and one half to be given to each woman. This immediately helped to identify the real mother, who tried to save the boy's life by asking for the child to be given to the other woman.

It is hardly to be believed that the king, who had professional judges and officials, would involve himself personally in such a dispute between two women who are described in the Bible as harlots. In fact, the inspiration for this story lies, I believe, in the events that are said to have surrounded the birth of Moses, who, according to my previous arguments, was the son of Amenhotep III. Both the Bible and the Koran make it clear that the child's life was threatened by Pharaoh from the time of his birth. The Koran indicates that, when Moses was placed in the water in a basket, the basket was intercepted by Pharaoh's guards, and, not revealing that she was the child's mother, Pharaoh's wife appealed for him not to be killed. It was only when the king ordered his death that she revealed her true relationship and handed the child to his nurse for concealment and safekeeping. The fact that the king sat in judgment personally in such a case also points to the fact that we are dealing with two women – his wife, Queen Tiye, the mother of Moses (Akhenaten), and Tiy, his nursing mother, who was already nursing Nefertiti, his sister – who were both living in the royal palace.

Solomon is also believed to have been the author of the books of Hebrew wisdom and poetry: 'It is quite out of the question that the king was, in fact, the composer of the whole books of Proverbs, of Ecclesiastes and Wisdom, of Psalms: . . . how then did his name come to be attached to them? How is this picture of Solomon's wisdom as intellectual brilliance and literary productivity to be related to the quite different interpretation of it – as discernment to render justice – in the famous story of the dream at Gibean?'[10]

In his attempt to trace the possible historical origin for the attribution of wisdom literature to Solomon or his court, this author, R. B. Y. Scott, goes on to say: 'The reasons may well be the known connections of the king with the Egyptian court, where wisdom literature had flourished since the days of the Middle Kingdom or before . . . Certainly it must be acknowledged that the assertions . . . that Solomon (or his court) was famous for developing wisdom on the Egyptian model are not, on general historical grounds, improbable.'[11] John Bright also confirms: "That parts of the Proverbs . . . are based on the Egyptian Maxims of Amenemope (Amenhotep III) . . . is well known".[12]

Foreign Wives and Foreign Gods

But 'king Solomon loved many strange women, together with the daughter of Pharaoh, women of the Moabites, Ammonites, Edomites, Zidonians, and Hittites; Of the nations concerning which the Lord said unto the children of Israel, Ye shall not go in to them, neither shall they come in unto you; for surely they will turn away your heart after their gods: Solomon clave unto these in love' (I Kings, 11:1–2).

'For it came to pass, when Solomon was old, that his wives turned away his heart after other gods: and his heart was not perfect with the Lord his God, as was the heart of David his father. For Solomon went after Ashtoreth the goddess of the Zidonians, and after Milcom the abomination of the Ammonites' (I Kings, 11:4–5).

This sequence of events can hardly ask for greater confirmation than we find in the historical evidence relating to the reign of Amenhotep III. Although there are many indications that he became converted to the worship of the Aten, the monotheistic God of the Amarna kings, he also worshipped other gods. Towards the end of his life he suffered severe dental problems, as shown by his mummy, where his teeth were found to be badly worn and his gums riddled with abscesses. This could be the reason why Tushratta of Mitanni, his brother-in-law, sent him an image of his goddess, Astareth, in Amenhotep III's Year 35.

Thus both Tuthmosis III, the historical King David, and his great-grandson Amenhotep III, who became known in the Bible as King Solomon, belonged to the Egyptian kings of the Eighteenth Dynasty, who ruled four to five centuries earlier than the present composition of the Old Testament would have us believe. At the same time, the chronology has been confused, presenting them as having belonged to the period following not only the Exodus but settlement in the Promised Land.

Now we can see why, despite the diligent efforts of biblical scholars, historians and archaeologists, no single piece of evidence has been found to support what has become known as the period of the United Monarchy of David and Solomon. The absence of such evidence does not mean that they are not historical characters, but that scholars have been confused by the present forms in which biblical traditions are related and have been seeking their evidence in the wrong period of time.

CHRONOLOGY

c. 1480 B.C.   Abraham and his wife, Sarah, made their way from Canaan to Egypt where he introduced her as his sister. The Pharaoh Tuthmosis III (David) (c. 1490–1436 B.C.) married her. On learning that Sarah was another man's wife, he sent her and Abraham back to Canaan, where she gave birth to Isaac, Pharaoh's son.

c. 1413 B.C.   Joseph the Patriarch (Yuya) – the grandson of Isaac and the son of Jacob – was sold into slavery in Egypt by his jealous half-brothers during the last days of the reign of Amenhotep II (c. 1436–1413 B.C.).

He was later appointed as a minister to Tuthmosis IV (c. 1413–1405 B.C.) and his son and successor, Amenhotep III (Solomon) (c. 1405–1367 B.C.).

c. 1405 B.C.   Amenhotep III married his infant sister, Sitamun, in order to inherit the throne, as was the Egyptian custom, but shortly afterwards married Tiye, the daughter of Joseph, and made her rather than Sitamun his Great Royal Wife (queen).

Early in the reign of Amenhotep III, Joseph was given permission to bring his father, Jacob, his half-brothers and the rest of the tribe of Israel down from Canaan to join him, and they were settled at Goshen in the Eastern Delta.

c. 1394 B.C.   Akhenaten (Moses) was born at the frontier fortress city of Zarw. As he was of mixed Egyptian-Israelite descent, being the son of an Egyptian King, Amenhotep III, and Queen Tiye, the daughter of Joseph, he posed a threat to the Eighteenth Dynasty. His father had therefore given the midwives orders to kill the child if it was a boy. On learning of this, Tiye sent her son to the safe guardianship of her Israelite relations at nearby Goshen, which was connected with Zarw by water.

c. 1382 B.C.   Akhenaten, aged about twelve or thirteen, made his first appearance at Thebes, the capital in Upper Egypt.

c. 1379 B.C.   Akhenaten became co-regent with his father. In order further to secure his right to the throne, Tiye arranged for him to marry his half-sister, Nefertiti, the daughter of Sitamun, the real heiress.

c. 1375 B.C.   The building of temples to Akhenaten's monotheistic God, the Aten, at Karnak and Luxor aroused such hostility that his mother, Queen

Tiye, suggested he built a new capital for himself at Tell el-Amarna, roughly halfway between Thebes and modern Cairo.

c. 1367 B.C. On the death of his father, Akhenaten became sole ruler and shut down the temples of the ancient gods of Egypt. This provoked such increased hostility that, in 1363 B.C., he was forced to proclaim his brother, Semenkhkare, as co-regent.

c. 1361 B.C. Warned by his uncle, Aye (Ephraim and Joseph of Arimathaea), that his life was in danger, Akhenaten abdicated and fled to Sinai with a handful of followers, among them Panehesy (Phinehas, Pinhas), one of the priests of the Aten at Amarna. Semenkhkare survived this abdication by at most a few months, possibly only a few days. Akhenaten was succeeded on the throne by his son, Tutankhamun.

c. 1361 B.C. Tutankhamun (Jesus), aged ten, came to the throne as Tutankhaten. He attempted to create a compromise between the Aten and the ancient gods of Egypt, and in his Year 4 changed his name from Tutankhaten to Tutankhamun.

c. 1352 B.C. Tutankhamun made his way to Sinai to try to persuade Akhenaten's followers that they could return to Egypt and live there in peace if they accepted that different people had different perceptions of God and how He should be worshipped. He was tortured and hanged by the priest Panehesy, on the eve of the Passover in April, for what was seen as a betrayal of his religious beliefs.

Aye, the second son of Joseph and the most powerful man in Egypt at the time, claimed the body of Tutankhamun and buried his remains in the Valley of the Kings.

c. 1352 B.C. Aye ruled for four years before disappearing mysteriously.

c. 1348 B.C. Aye was succeeded by Horemheb, the biblical Pharaoh of the Oppression, who was an army general and obtained his right to the throne by marrying Queen Nefertiti's sister, Mutnedjemet.

c. 1335 B.C. The death of Horemheb saw the start of a new dynasty, the Nineteenth, when he was succeeded by his elderly vizier, Ramses I, the king 'who knew not Joseph'. On hearing the news, Akhenaten returned to Egypt from Sinai to try to reclaim his throne, but failed because of Ramses I's control of the army. He then led the Israelites into the wilderness (the Exodus).

c. 1333 B.C. On coming to the throne in succession to his father, Seti I set out in pursuit of the Israelites and their bedouin allies, the Shasu, almost certainly because – either through his authority or by force – Akhenaten had tried to obtain water for his followers from Egypt's guarded Sinai settlements. Akhenaten was among those who died in the heavy slaughter that ensued.

NOTES

Biblical quotations are from the Authorized Version. Further details of the works cited below will be found in the Bibliography, pp. 233–5.

Book 1: The Scarlet Thread

1 SCANDAL OF THE DEAD SEA SCROLLS
1 Dupont-Sommer, *The Jewish Sect of Qumran and the Essenes*, p. 150.
2 *The Journal of Jewish Studies II*, No. 2, pp. 67–99.
3 Burrows, *The Dead Sea Scrolls*, p. 330.
4 Allegro, *The Sacred Mushroom and the Cross*.
5 Mowry, *The Dead Sea Scrolls and the Early Church*, p. 1.
6 Baigent and Leigh, *The Dead Sea Scrolls Deception*, p. 101.

3 SILENT WITNESS
1 Smith, *Jesus Not a Myth*, p. 15.
2 Whiston (trans.), *The Works of Flavius Josephus*, pp. 491–2.
3 *Ibid.*, p. 491.
4 *Ibid.*, p. 487.
5 Smith, *Jesus Not a Myth*, pp. 16–17.
6 Bruce, *Jesus and Christian Origins Outside the New Testament*, p. 42.
7 Whiston (trans.), *The Works of Flavius Josephus*, p. 545.

4 A MISCHIEVOUS SUPERSTITION
1 Couchod, *The Enigma of Jesus*, p. 27.

2 *Ibid.*, p. 26.

5 THE NAZARENE
1 Baigent and Leigh, *The Dead Sea Scrolls Deception*, p. 174.
2 Black, *The Scrolls and Christian Origins*, p. 69.

6 ANOTHER TIME, ANOTHER PLACE
1 b. Gitt., 56b, for instance.
2 Ali (trans.), *The Meaning of the Glorious Quran*, p. 421.

7 THE MAN SENT FROM GOD
1 Whiston (trans.), *The Works of Flavius Josephus*, p. 616.
2 *Ibid.*, p. 491.
3 Herford, *Christianity in Talmud and Midrash*, p. 347.
4 Whiston (trans.), *The Works of Flavius Josephus*, pp. 543–4.
5 *Ibid.*, p. 484.
6 Baigent and Leigh, *The Dead Sea Scrolls Deception*, p. 132.

8 THE SUFFERING SERVANT
1 North, *The Suffering Servant in Deutero-Isaiah*, p. 24.
2 *Ibid.*, p. 25.

9   THE AFTER-LIFE

1   North, *The Suffering Servant in Deutero-Isaiah*, p. 54.

2   Freud, *Moses and Monotheism*, pp. 138–9.

3   Wells, *Did Jesus Exist?*, p. 66.

4   Brandon, *Myth, Ritual and Kingship*, p. 275.

5   Apuleius, *The Golden Ass*, p. 70.

6   North, *The Suffering Servant in Deutero-Isaiah*, p. 70.

7   Dupont-Sommer, *The Essene Writings from Qumran*, p. 131.

8   *Ibid.*, p. 33.

9   *Ibid.*, p. 126.

10   *Ibid.*, p. 131.

10   ECHOES FROM THE PAST

1   Hanson, A. T., *Jesus in the Old Testament*, p. 7.

2   Hanson, R. P. C., *Allegory and Event*, p. 79.

3   *Jesus in the Old Testament*, p. 6.

4   *Ibid.*, p. 27.

5   *Ibid.*, p. 58.

6   Migne, *Origenis Op. Omn., Selecta in Genesim, PG*, vol. 2.

11   DEATH IN THE WILDERNESS

1   Rot and Wigoder, *The New Standard Jewish Encyclopaedia*, p. 191.

2   Osman, *Stranger in the Valley of the Kings*.

3   Osman, *Moses: Pharaoh of Egypt*.

12   THE SCARLET THREAD

1   Dupont-Sommer, *The Essene Writings from Qumran*, p. 266.

2   *Ibid.*, p. 226.

3   In September 1991 I was invited to address the Sixth International Congress of Egyptologists in Turin on the subject of the similarity between the war annals of Tuthmosis III and the biblical account of the campaigns fought by King David, which are the subject of chapters 22 and 23 of this book. During the course of the Congress, Professor Manfred Bietak, the distinguished Viennese archaeologist who is leading the Austrian team currently excavating in the Eastern Delta, agreed in a private conversation that Egyptian historical references to the Shasu should be interpreted as relating to the alliance between these bedouin tribes and the Israelites.

4   Osman, *Moses: Pharaoh of Egypt*.

5   Osman, *Stranger in the Valley of the Kings*.

13   COVER-UP

1   Allegro, *The Dead Sea Scrolls*, pp. 130–31.

2   Scholars have recognized that the verse in Leviticus – '. . . on the tenth day of this seventh month there shall be a day of atonement . . .' (23:27) – contains a date that cannot be attributed to Moses: 'The order of procedure, as given in Leviticus 16, is a very late addition to the Pentateuch.' *The Jewish Encyclopaedia*, vol. 5, p. 378.

14   AND THE WALLS CAME TUMBLING DOWN

1   Kenyon, *The Bible and Recent Archaeology*, p. 75.

2   *Encyclopaedia Judaica*, vol. 2, p. 471.

3   Kenyon, *The Bible and Recent Archaeology*, pp. 75–6.

4   Yadin, *Hazor* (1975), p. 145.

5   *Encyclopaedia Judaica*, vol. 10, p. 271.

6   Romer, *Testament*, p. 69.

15   THE GOSPELS

1   Allegro, *The Dead Sea Scrolls*, p. 155.

2   Robertson, *Jesus and Judas*, p. 51.

3   Dupont-Sommer, *The Essene Writings from Qumran*, p. 90.

4   Wells, *Did Jesus Exist?*, p. 145.

5   Wells, *The Early Christians*, p. 255.

6   Dupont-Sommer, *The Essene Writings from Qumran*, p. 91.

Book 2: The House of the Messiah

16   CHILD OF SIN

1   Osman, *Stranger in the Valley of the Kings*.

2   Conder, *The Tell Amarna Tablets*.

3   Polano (trans.), *Selections from the Talmud*, p. 72.

17   HIDING THE SINFUL TRUTH

1   An account of how Jacob's name was changed by the Lord to Israel is given later in this chapter.

18   PEOPLES OF THE SEA

1   Pritchard, *Ancient Near Eastern Texts*, p. 262.

2   Gardiner, *Egypt of the Pharaohs*, p. 285.

3   *Ibid.*, p. 284.

4   *Ibid.*, pp. 285, 287.

5   Kenyon, *The Bible and Recent Archaeology*, p. 63.

19   THE PROMISED LAND

1   Osman, *Stranger in the Valley of the Kings* and *Moses: Pharaoh of Egypt*.

2   Osman, *Moses: Pharaoh of Egypt*.

3   *Ibid.* The reason why the names of Moses and the Israelites are not mentioned in the Karnak accounts is that Moses was the deposed Pharaoh Akhenaten and, after his fall from power, every effort was exerted to wipe his name out of Egyptian memory.

4   *Journal of Egyptian Archaeology*, vol. 50, 1964, p. 66.

5   *Ibid.*

6   *Ibid.*, p. 67.

7   *Ibid.*, p. 65.

8   *Ibid.*, p. 67.

20   THE TWO DAVIDS

1   In one of the many battles with the Philistines reported in the two Books of Samuel we find another reference to Goliath: '. . . Elhanan, the son of Jaareoregim, a Bethlehemite, slew the brother of Goliath, the Gittite, the staff of whose spear was like a weaver's beam' (II Samuel, 21:19). Insertion of 'the brother' in this text, taken from the King James Version of the Old Testament, is a piece of biblical editing resulting from the fact that we have already had an account of the slaying of Goliath by David in I Samuel. The text of *The Holy Bible Revised Standard Version*, translated from the original tongues, first published in 1611 and later revised on several occasions, reads simply 'Elhanan . . . slew Goliath the Gittite.' This agrees with the Masoretic text, a more 'sophisticated' version of early Hebrew texts. *The New English Bible*, published by Oxford and Cambridge University Presses jointly in 1970, also omits any mention of 'the brother' and confines itself to saying 'Elhanan . . . killed Goliath of Gath.' The confusion surrounding this matter may be explained by the belief of some scholars that Elhanan was David's original name (see also Appendix C).

21   JOURNEY TO HEAVEN

1   Redford, *History and Chronology of the Eighteenth Dynasty of Egypt*, p. 86.

2   Breasted, *Ancient Records of Egypt*, vol. 2, pp. 60–61.

3   Ibid., p. 61.
4   Osman, Moses: Pharaoh of Egypt.
5   Maspero, The Struggle of the
    Nations, p. 289.
6   Ibid.
7   Hayes, The Scepter of Egypt, part II,
    pp. 116–17.

22 ARMAGEDDON
1   Gardiner, Egypt of the Pharaohs,
    p. 190.
2   Stern, Encyclopaedia of Archaeological
    Excavations in the Holy Lands,
    vol. 3, p. 831.
3   Pritchard, Ancient Near Eastern
    Texts, pp. 236–7.
4   Ibid., p. 237.
5   Ibid., p. 238.
6   Gardiner, Egypt of the Pharaohs,
    p. 194.
7   Maspero, The Struggle of the
    Nations, p. 265.
8   Pritchard, Ancient Near Eastern
    Texts, p. 238.

23 A TALE OF TWO CITIES
1   Stern, Encyclopaedia of Archaeological
    Excavations in the Holy Lands,
    p. 845.
2   Ibid., p. 846.
3   Ibid., p. 850.
4   Ibid.
5   Ibid., p. 851.
6   Simons, Handbook for the Study of
    Egyptian Topographical Lists Relating
    to Western Asia, pp. 112, 118.

24 JERUSALEM, CITY OF DAVID
1   Pritchard, Ancient Near Eastern
    Texts, p. 236.

2   Osman, Moses: Pharaoh of Egypt.
3   Stern, Encyclopaedia of Archaeological
    Excavations in the Holy Lands,
    vol. 3, p. 590.
4   Pritchard, Ancient Near Eastern
    Texts, p. 236.
5   Thomas, Documents from Old
    Testament Times, pp. 39, 43.

25 JERUSALEM, CITY OF PEACE
1   Simons, Handbook for the Study
    of Egyptian Topographical Lists
    Relating to Western Asia,
    p. 34.
2   Finkelstein, The Archaeology of the
    Israelite Settlement, p. 18.

26 DAVID AND ABRAHAM
1   Wagner, Abraham and David,
    p. 127.
2   Ibid., pp. 138–9.
3   Ibid., p. 138.
4   Osman, Stranger in the Valley of
    the Kings.
5   Clements, Studies in Biblical
    Theology, second series, vol. 5,
    Abraham and David, p. 64.
6   Wagner, Studies on the Ancient
    Palestinian World, pp. 132–3.
7   Clements, Studies in Biblical
    Theology, p. 55.
8   Maspero, The Struggle of the
    Nations, pp. 267–8.
9   Osman, Stranger in the Valley of
    the Kings.
10 Clements, Studies in Biblical
    Theology, pp. 10–11.

27 DAVID AND BATHSHEBA
1   Gray, A History of Jerusalem, p. 67.

Book 3: Christ the King

28 THE LIVING IMAGE OF THE LORD

1 *Journal of British Archaeology*, 1928, vol. 14, p. 74.
2 Carter and Mace, *The Tomb of Tutankhamen*, vol. 2, 1927, p. 85.
3 Redford, *History and Chronology of the Eighteenth Dynasty of Egypt*, p. 156.
4 Osman, *Moses: Pharaoh of Egypt*.
5 Redford, *Akhenaten the Heretic King*, p. 201.
6 Morenz, *Egyptian Religion*, p. 36.
7 The custom of anointing with crocodile fat survives up to the present time in Upper Egypt where it is regarded as strengthening sexual prowess.
8 Gardiner, *Egyptian Grammar*, p. 475, and Faulkner, *A Concise Dictionary of Middle Egyptian*, p. 32.
9 Morenz, *Egyptian Religion*, p. 38.
10 *Ibid.*, p. 39.

29 THE VIRGIN BIRTH

1 Boslooper, *The Virgin Birth*, p. 28.
2 *Ibid.*, p. 28. The fact that Matthew (1:16) and Luke (1:27) relate Joseph, the spouse of Mary, to King David is nothing to do with the child, who was himself descended from King David, not from Joseph.
3 *Ibid.*, p. 30.
4 *Ibid.*, p. 46.
5 *Ibid.*, p. 49.
6 Pages, *The Gnostic Gospels*, p. 75.
7 Allegro, *The Dead Sea Scrolls*, p. 171.
8 *Journal of Egyptian Archaeology*, vol. 56, 1970, pp. 194–5.

30 THE HOLY FAMILY

1 Osman, *Moses: Pharaoh of Egypt*.
2 *A Brief Description of the Principal Monuments of the Egyptian Museums*, pp. 144ff.

3 *Journal of Egyptian Archaeology*, vol. 76, 1990, p. 97.
4 Carter and Mace, *The Tomb of Tutankhamen*, vol. 1, pp. x–xi.

31 THE HIDDEN ONE

1 Redford, *Akhenaten the Heretic King*, p. 205.
2 *Ibid.*, p. 208.
3 Carter and Mace, *The Tomb of Tutankhamen*, pp. 118–19.
4 Redford, *Akhenaten the Heretic King*, p. 210.
5 Bromiley, *The International Standard Bible Encyclopaedia*, vol. 2, p. 807.
6 Yahuda, *The Language of the Pentateuch in its Relation to Egyptian*, vol. 1, p. xxvi.
7 Leusden, *Biblica Hebraica*, p. 7.

32 EVIDENCE FROM THE TOMB

1 Leek, *Tutankhamun's Tomb Series*, vol. 5, p. 19.
2 Harrison and Abdalla, 'The Remains of Tutankhamen', *Antiquity*, vol. 46, 1972, p. 9.
3 *Ibid.*
4 *Ibid.*, p. 11.
5 *Ibid.*, p. 12.
6 *Ibid.*, p. 13.
7 *Ibid.*, p. 9.
8 Bennett, 'The Restoration Inscription of Tutankhamun', *Journal of Egyptian Archaeology*, vol. 25, 1939, p. 9.
9 Carter and Mace, *The Tomb of Tutankhamen*, vol. 3, pp. 123–6.
10 *Ibid.*, p. 126.
11 *Ibid.*, p. 132.
12 *Ibid.*, p. 134.
13 *Ibid.*, p. 203.
14 *Ibid.*, vol. 2, p. 228.
15 *Ibid.*, vol. 2, p. 196.

16 Maspero and Daressy, *The Tombs of Haramhabi and Toutankhamanou*, pp. 129–30.

33 THE LOST SHEEP
1 Brownless, *The Meaning of the Qumran Scrolls for the Bible*, p. 9.

Appendices

A TESTAMENTS OLD AND NEW
1 Listed in Wells, *The Early Christians*, pp. 109–11.

B THE DESTRUCTION OF HAZOR
1 Simons, *Handbook for the Study of Egyptian Topographical Lists Relating to Western Asia*, p. 177.
2 Yadin, *Hazor (1975)*, p. 145.
3 *Ibid.*
4 Yadin, *Hazor (1972)*, p. 37.
5 *Ibid.*, p. 87.
6 *Ibid.*, p. 92.
7 *Ibid.*, p. 36.
8 Furumark, *The Mycenean IIIC Pottery*, pp. 262–3.
9 Yadin, *Hazor (1972)*, pp. 129–30.

C DAVID AND GOLIATH
1 *Encyclopaedia Judaica*, vol. 7, p. 757.
2 *Ibid.*

D THE AUTOBIOGRAPHY OF SINUHE
1 The translation of *The Autobiography of Sinuhe* here is based on the work of Alan H. Gardiner, *Note on the Story of Sinuhe*, as well as *The Literature of Ancient Egypt* by William Kelly Simpson.
2 *The Times Atlas of the Bible*, p. 32.
3 Simpson, *The Literature of Ancient Egypt*, p. 64.

E THE VIRGIN FOUNTAIN
1 *Second Quarterly Report on the Excavation of the Eastern Hill of Jerusalem*, Palestine Exploration Fund, p. 63.
2 *Ibid.*, pp. 63–5.
3 Kenyon, *Jerusalem*, p. 23.
4 Stern, *Encyclopaedia of Archaeological Excavations in the Holy Lands*, vol. 2, p. 594.
5 *Ibid.*
6 Kenyon, *Palestine Exploration Quarterly*, Jan.–June 1963, pp. 12–13.
7 *Ibid.*, p. 13.

F KING OF PEACE
1 Redford, *Akhenaten the Heretic King*, p. 20.
2 *Ibid.*, p. 34.
3 *Ibid.*, p. 35.
4 Eissfeldt, *The Cambridge Ancient History*, vol. 2. p. 597.
5 Bright, *A History of Israel*, p. 205.

G REBELLION
1 Eissfeldt, *The Cambridge Ancient History*, vol. 2, pp. 588–9.
2 *Ibid.*, p. 589.
3 *Ibid.*, p. 590.
4 Bright, *A History of Israel*, p. 193.
5 Conder, *The Tell Amarna Tablets*, p. 140.
6 *Ibid.*, p. 145.
7 Giles, *Ikhnaton*, p. 174.
8 Conder, *The Tell Amarna Tablets*, pp. 11–12 (Letter No. 36 in the British Museum).
9 Bezold, *The Tell el-Amarna Tablets in the British Museum*, p. lxix.
10 Giles, *Ikhnaton*, p. 159.
11 *Ibid.*, p. 174.
12 Bezold, *The Tell el-Amarna Tablets in the British Museum*, p. lvii.
13 *Ibid.*, p. 101.
14 *Ibid.*, p. 103.
15 *Ibid.*
16 *Ibid.*, pp. 101–2.

H DISTRICT COMMISSIONERS
1 Noth, *The Old Testament World*, pp. 63–4.
2 *Ibid.*, p. 66.
3 Stern, *Encyclopaedia of Archaeological Excavations in the Holy Lands*, vol. 2, p. 485.
4 *Ibid.*

I THE QUEEN OF SHEBA AND
THE GLASS LAKE

1 Hayes, 'Inscriptions from the Palace
of Amenhotep III', *Journal of Near
Eastern Studies*, vol. 10, no. 1,
1951, p. 35.

2 *Ibid.*, pp. 35–6.

3 Badawy, *A History of Egyptian
Architecture*, p. 49.

4 Hayes, 'Inscriptions from the Palace
of Amenhotep III', p. 36.

5 *Ibid.*

6 Badawy, *A History of Egyptian
Architecture*, p. 50.

7 Ali (trans.), *The Meaning of the
Glorious Quran*, p. 539.

8 Badawy, *A History of Egyptian
Architecture*, p. 339.

9 Redford, *Akhenaten the Heretic
King*, p. 45.

10 Badawy, *Architecture in Ancient
Egypt and the Near East*, p. 166.

11 Eissfeldt, *The Cambridge Ancient
History*, vol. 2, p. 599.

12 Stern, *Encyclopaedia of Archaeological
Excavations in the Holy Lands*,
vol. 2, p. 480.

J THE WISDOM OF SOLOMON

1 Redford, *Studies on the Ancient
Palestine World*, pp. 154–6.

2 *Ibid.*, p. 141.

3 Bright, *A History of Israel*, p. 184.

4 Rowley, 'Zadok and Nebushtan',
Journal of Biblical Literature, 1939,
p. 113.

5 *Ibid.*

6 *Ibid.*, p. 123.

7 Eissfeldt, *The Cambridge Ancient
History*, vol. 2, p. 604.

8 Osman, *Stranger in the Valley of
the Kings*.

9 Osman, *Moses: Pharaoh of Egypt*.

10 Scott, 'Solomon and the Beginnings
of Wisdom in Israel', *Wisdom in
Israel and in the Ancient Near East*,
p. 265.

11 *Ibid.*

12 Bright, *A History of Israel*, p. 199.

BIBLIOGRAPHY

Ali, Abdullah Yusuf, trans., *The Meaning of the Glorious Quran*, London, 1976.

Allegro, John Marco, *The Sacred Mushroom and the Cross*, London, 1970.

The Dead Sea Scrolls, London, 1964.

Apuleius, *The Golden Ass*, London, 1956.

Badawy, Alexander, *A History of Egyptian Architecture*, Los Angeles, 1968.

Architecture in Ancient Egypt and the Near East, Cambridge, Massachusetts, and London, 1966.

Baigent, Michael, and Leigh, Richard, *The Dead Sea Scrolls Deception*, London, 1991.

Bennett, John, 'The Restoration Inscription of Tutankhamun', *Journal of Egyptian Archaeology*, 1939.

Bezold, C., *The Tell el-Amarna Tablets in the British Museum, London*, London, 1892.

Black, Matthew, *The Scrolls and Christian Origins*, London, 1961.

Boslooper, Thomas, *The Virgin Birth*, London, 1962.

Brandon, S. G. F., *Myth, Ritual and Kingship*, Oxford, 1958.

Breasted, James H., *Ancient Records of Egypt*, Chicago, 1906.

Bright, John, *A History of Israel*, London, 1960.

Bromiley, Geoffrey W., *The International Standard Bible Encyclopaedia*, Grand Rapids, Michigan, 1982.

Brownless, William Hugh, *The Meaning of the Qumran Scrolls for the Bible*, New York, 1964.

Bruce, F. F., *Jesus and Christian Origins Outside the New Testament*, London, 1974.

Burrows, Millar, *The Dead Sea Scrolls*, London, 1956.

Carter, Howard, and Mace, A. C., *The Tomb of Tutankhamen*, London, 1923.

Clements, Ronald E., *Studies in Biblical Theology*, second series, vol. 5, *Abraham and David*, London, 1967.

Conder, C. R., *The Tell Amarna Tablets*, London, 1893.

Couchod, Paul Louis, *The Enigma of Jesus*, London, 1924.

Dupont-Sommer, André, *The Jewish Sect of Qumran and the Essenes*, London, 1954.

The Essene Writings from Qumran, trans. G. Vermes, Oxford, 1961.

Eissfeldt, Otto, *The Cambridge Ancient History*, Cambridge, 1975.

Encyclopaedia Judaica, Jerusalem, 1971–2.

Faulkner, Raymond O., *A Concise Dictionary of Middle Egyptian*, Oxford, 1962.

Finkelstein, Israel, *The Archaeology of the Israelite Settlement*, Jerusalem, 1988.

Freud, Sigmund, *Moses and Monotheism*, London, 1951.

Furumark, Arne, *The Mycenean IIIC Pottery*, Skrifter Utgivna Av Svenska Institutet I Fom, Opuscula Archaeologica, vol. 3, Lund, Sweden, 1944.

Gardiner, Alan, *Egypt of the Pharaohs*, Oxford, 1961.

Egyptian Grammar, London, 1950.

Note on the Story of Sinuhe, Paris, 1916.

Giles, Frederick J., *Ikhnaton*, London, 1970.

Gray, John, *A History of Jerusalem*, London, 1969.

Hanson, Anthony Tyrrell, *Jesus in the Old Testament*, London, 1965.

Hanson, R. P. C., *Allegory and Event*, London, 1959.

Harrison, R. G., and Abdalla, A. B., 'The Remains of Tutankhamen', *Antiquity*, vol. 46, Gloucester, 1972.

Hayes, William C., *The Scepter of Egypt*, Cambridge, Massachusetts, 1959.
'Inscriptions from the Palace of Amenhotep III', *Journal of Near Eastern Studies*, vol. 10, no. 1, 1951.

Herford, R. Travers, *Christianity in Talmud and Midrash*, London, 1903.

Jewish Encyclopaedia, managing editor Isidore Singer, New York and London, 1904.

Journal of British Archaeology, 1928, vol. 14.

Journal of Egyptian Archaeology, vol. 14, 1928; vol. 25, 1939; vol. 50, 1964; vol. 56, 1970; vol. 76, 1990.

Journal of Jewish Studies II, no. 2, 1951.

Kenyon, Kathleen M., *The Bible and Recent Archaeology*, rev. ed. by P. R. S. Moorey, London, 1987.
Jerusalem, London, 1967.
Palestine Exploration Quarterly, Jan–June 1963.

Leek, F. Filce, *Tutankhamun's Tomb Series*, vol. 5, Oxford, 1972.

Leusden, Jan, *Biblica Hebraica*, ed. R. Kittel, Stuttgart, 1945.

Maspero, Gaston, *The Struggle of the Nations*, London, 1896.
(with George Daressy) *The Tombs of Haramhabi and Toutankhamanou*, London, 1912.

Migne, J. P., *Origenis Op. Omn., Selecta in Genesim, PG*, vol. 2, Paris, 1957.

Morenz, Siegfried, *Egyptian Religion*, London, 1973.

Mowry, Lucetta, *The Dead Sea Scrolls and the Early Church*, Chicago, 1962.

North, Christopher R., *The Suffering Servant in Deutero-Isaiah*, London, 1956.

Noth, Martin, *The Old Testament World*, London, 1966.

Osman, Ahmed, *Stranger in the Valley of the Kings*, London, 1987.

Moses: Pharaoh of Egypt, London, 1990.

Pages, Elaine, *The Gnostic Gospels*, London, 1982.

Polano, H., trans., *Selections from the Talmud*, London, 1894.

Pritchard, J. B., *Ancient Near Eastern Texts*, Princeton, 1955.

Redford, Donald B., *History and Chronology of the Eighteenth Dynasty of Egypt*, Toronto, 1967.
Akhenaten the Heretic King, Princeton, 1984.
Studies on the Ancient Palestine World, Toronto, 1972.

Robertson, J. M., *Jesus and Judas*, London, 1927.

Romer, John, *Testament*, London, 1988.

Rot, Cecil, and Wigoder, Geoffrey, *The New Standard Jewish Encyclopaedia*, London, 1970.

Rowley, Harold Henry, 'Zadok and Nebushtan', *Journal of Biblical Literature*, vol. 59, Philadelphia, 1939.

Scott, R. B. Y., 'Solomon and the Beginnings of Wisdom in Israel', *Wisdom in Israel and in the Ancient Near East*, Leiden, Netherlands, 1955.

Simons, J., *Handbook for the Study of Egyptian Topographical Lists Relating to Western Asia*, Leiden, Netherlands, 1937.

Simpson, William Kelly, *The Literature of Ancient Egypt*, Yale, 1972.

Smith, A. D. Howell, *Jesus Not a Myth*, London, 1942.

Stern, Avi-Yonah and Ephraim, *Encyclopaedia of Archaeological Excavations in the Holy Lands*, Oxford, 1977.

Thomas, D. Winton, *Documents from Old Testament Times*, London, 1958.

Wagner, N. E., *Abraham and David*, Toronto, 1972.
Studies on the Ancient Palestinian World, Toronto, 1972.

Wells, G. A., *Did Jesus Exist?*, London, 1975.
The Early Christians, London, 1971.

Whiston, William, trans., *The Works of Flavius Josephus*, London, 1842.

Yadin, Yigael, *Hazor*, London, 1975.
Hazor, The Schweich Lectures of the British Academy, Oxford, 1972.

Yahuda, A. S., *The Language of the Pentateuch in its Relation to Egyptian*. Oxford, 1933.

A Brief Description of the Principal Monuments of the Egyptian Museums, Cairo, 1964.

Second Quarterly Report on the Excavation of the Eastern Hill of Jerusalem, Palestine Exploration Fund, London, 1924.

The Times Atlas of the Bible, 1987.

INDEX